Prais

"This series provides a practic[illegible] today." – John V. Biernacki, Pa[illegible]

"*Inside the Minds* draws from the collective experience of the best professionals. The books are informative from an academic, and, more importantly, practical perspective. I highly recommend them." – Keith M. Aurzada, Partner, Bryan Cave LLP

"Aspatore's *Inside the Minds* series provides practical, cutting edge advice from those with insight into the real world challenges that confront businesses in the global economy." – Michael Bednarek, Partner, Shearman & Sterling LLP

"What to read when you want to be in the know—topical, current, practical, and useful information on areas of the law that everyone is talking about." – Erika L. Morabito, Partner, Patton Boggs LLP

"Some of the best insight around from sources in the know" – Donald R. Kirk, Shareholder, Fowler White Boggs PA

"The *Inside the Minds* series provides a unique window into the strategic thinking of key players in business and law." – John M. Sylvester, Partner, K&L Gates LLP

"Comprehensive analysis and strategies you won't find anywhere else." – Stephen C. Stapleton, Of Counsel, Dykema Gossett PLLC

"The *Inside the Minds* series is a real hands-on, practical resource for cutting edge issues." – Trey Monsour, Partner, Haynes and Boone LLP

"A tremendous resource, amalgamating commentary from leading professionals that is presented in a concise, easy to read format." – Alan H. Aronson, Shareholder, Akerman Senterfitt

"Unique and invaluable opportunity to gain insight into the minds of experienced professionals." – Jura C. Zibas, Partner, Lewis Brisbois Bisgaard & Smith LLP

"A refreshing collection of strategic insights, not dreary commonplaces, from some of the best of the profession." – Roger J. Magnuson, Partner, Dorsey & Whitney LLP

"Provides valuable insights by experienced practitioners into practical and theoretical developments in today's ever-changing legal world." – Elizabeth Gray, Partner, Willkie, Farr & Gallagher LLP

"This series provides invaluable insight into the practical experiences of lawyers in the trenches." – Thomas H. Christopher, Partner, Kilpatrick Stockton LLP

ASPATORE

Aspatore Books, a Thomson Reuters business, exclusively publishes C-Level executives and partners from the world's most respected companies and law firms. Each publication provides professionals of all levels with proven business and legal intelligence from industry insiders—direct and unfiltered insight from those who know it best. Aspatore Books is committed to publishing an innovative line of business and legal titles that lay forth principles and offer insights that can have a direct financial impact on the reader's business objectives.

Each chapter in the *Inside the Minds* series offers thought leadership and expert analysis on an industry, profession, or topic, providing a future-oriented perspective and proven strategies for success. Each author has been selected based on their experience and C-Level standing within the business and legal communities. *Inside the Minds* was conceived to give a first-hand look into the leading minds of top business executives and lawyers worldwide, presenting an unprecedented collection of views on various industries and professions.

INSIDE THE MINDS

Defending Medical Malpractice Claims

Leading Lawyers on Navigating Medical Malpractice Developments and Mounting a Successful Defense

ASPATORE

For additional copies or customer service inquiries, please e-mail west.customer.service@thomson.com.

ISBN 978-0-314-28467-9

Mat #41326840

CONTENTS

Mounting Effective Medical Malpractice Defenses in the Face of Unsatisfactory or Even Tragic Outcomes

William E. Galeota

Member

Steptoe & Johnson PLLC

ASPATORE

Introduction

One of the most daunting challenges in the defense of any malpractice case is usually in the nature and extent of the "bad outcome" that drives it. Without that, and the proposition that it may entitle the usually sympathetic patient or family member to a monetary recovery, there would literally be no case. The attorneys or firms who have to make contingent fee commitments and sizable expense investments in malpractice cases would not do so, but for the prospect of a large monetary award. Therefore, the most tragic and intrinsically sympathetic cases make their way into the civil justice system in the hands of the most experienced and accomplished plaintiffs' attorneys. Adopting a proven persuasive approach, then applying that from the beginning of the case through the entire process to a jury trial and verdict, is the most important element of a successful defense.

Legal Protections for Health Care Providers and the Tactical Countermeasures

The law in most states permitting patients to sue for injuries caused by substandard care was for many years the common law of negligence, shaped by case law, until statutes defined it more specifically. In West Virginia, for example, this occurred in 1986, 2001, and 2003, when the legislature set caps on some damages and prescribed the essential elements and requisite proof for a sustainable malpractice claim.[1] There remains an ongoing debate about whether the reforms are necessary and appropriate, but one thing is certain: as reforms have imposed restrictions and limitations on recoveries, patients and their lawyers have developed new theories and strategies to avoid them. Frequently, those strategies are based on making an individual doctor, nurse, or other caregiver appear "blameworthy." Those efforts can be doubly fruitful if they are based on legal theories that fall outside the scope of caps or other limits.[2]

---

[1] W. VA. CODE §§ 55-7B-1, *et seq.*

[2] *See, e.g., Boggs v. Camden-Clark Memorial Hospital Corporation,* 216 W. Va. 656, 609 S.E.2d 917 (2004) (The Medical Professional Liability Act of 2003 [MPLA] does not apply to other claims related or contemporaneous to alleged act of malpractice). *Compare Blankenship v. Etnicon Inc.*, 221 W. Va. 700, 656 S.E. 2d 451 (2007); *Gray v. Mena,* 218 W. Va. 564, 625 S.E. 2d 326 (2005).

The burden of proof is on the complaining patient seeking money; most caregivers can ably explain what they did in the circumstances and why; and "dueling experts" will often neutralize each other. Therefore, even with the most tragic consequences and sympathetic circumstances, a jury's resolution of close questions on the standard of care or causation may favor the health care provider. That fairly balanced presentation of the issues is completely skewed, however, and shifted heavily to the patient's favor if the individual caregiver can be made to appear generally incompetent, dishonest, or uncaring. Add to this the reality that most health care is provided in the context of a hospital or other facility operated by a corporate organization, much more easily cast as impersonal or greedy. Thus, we have seen the development of theories like negligent credentialing[3] (making the doctor's claim and suit history arguably relevant), spoliation of evidence (altering a health care record to conceal an error is particularly reprehensible),[4] and abandonment (a judgment not to intervene can be so characterized).

Juries are made up of good folks who are doing their best to follow their oath and determine the truth, often on conflicting accounts and disputed evidence. Experience has taught us that persuasion begins with giving the jury what it needs to tip the scale with the impressions made by the parties, and the most dramatic are those made by the accused health care professional. Therefore, the winning approach to defending a malpractice case starts with that individual.

Top Medical Malpractice Defense Strategies

Lawyers effectively representing health care providers must present their clients as the caring, compassionate caregivers they are, even in the face of vigorous attacks and harsh accusations. While it is difficult and even counter-intuitive, once clients understand and embrace this approach, they begin to feel more comfortable with the process and are better situated to explain to a jury, using simple terms, how a procedure is intended to help the patient and what went wrong. The defense must answer all essential questions, including what the health care provider did and why, and how a bad outcome alone does not prove negligence.

---

[3] *See, e.g., Darling v. Charleston Community Memorial Hospital,* 211 N.E. 2d 253 (Ill. 1965); *Roberts v. Stevens Clinic Hospital,* 176 W. Va. 492 (1986).

[4] *See, e.g., Hannah v. Heeter,* 213 W. Va. 704, 584 S.E.2d 560 (2003).

In my practice, we set up a sort of "lay clinic" using illustrations, videos, charts, diagrams, and, if a surgical procedure is involved in the case, the instruments associated with that procedure. We bring everything to the courtroom we can to acquaint the jury with the issues at hand. As defense attorneys, we do not want cases to be so complicated that it takes a panel of doctors to understand what happened; instead, we attempt to demystify medicine and surgery using a logical, thoughtful process to explain medical procedures in lay terms. We want to be able to open the case with a preview of all this demonstrative evidence and reassure the jury that they will learn all they need to decide the issues. In closing argument, we invoke the jury's common sense and life experience ("you do not have to be a doctor to understand what happened here") to a conclusion that the patient's dissatisfaction is misplaced; the bad outcome did not result from the care, but in spite of it.

This strategy includes demonstrating that the plaintiff did not suffer any injury as a result of the defendant's actions. Defense attorneys should begin by fully explaining all the pre-existing, predisposing, or later-developing conditions the client experienced as being the primary factors causing or contributing to the bad outcome. There are risks and complications inherent in any surgical procedure, and usually the plaintiff has signed a consent form showing the plaintiff was properly informed and assumed those risks and complications in asking the physician to perform the procedure. Otherwise, there would be liability for proceeding without permission.[5] While a full and legally sufficient informed consent form does not excuse negligence, it is important for a jury to understand complications may be associated with the procedure even in the absence of negligence, that medicine and surgery are imprecise and fallible, and that the patient knew that going in.

The defense attorney should also emphasize the standard of care by definition. Most states define it as what the ordinary or average physician or surgeon is expected to do in the same or similar circumstances. "Standard of care" does not include perfect or prophetic insight, or even using the ideal approach. It is simply reasonable and prudent care.[6] Of course, what a reasonable, prudent physician would be expected to do in the same or similar circumstances is for a jury to decide.

[5] *See, e.g.*, *Cross v. Trapp*, 170 W. Va. 549, 294 S.E.2d 445 (1982).
[6] *See, e.g.*, W. VA. CODE § 55-7B-3.

Developing an Effective Medical Malpractice Defense

There are some basic steps associated with putting a successful medical malpractice defense in place. The defense attorney should enlist the client's help early in identifying the best treating and independent experts. Treating experts are the caregivers who were involved and understand the issues in the case firsthand and may include prior or subsequent treaters. If inclined in the defendant's favor, they can be very helpful. The next step is to select the most highly qualified and presentably appealing independent experts available to defend the quality of care and causation issues. The most highly qualified experts are not always the best choice; the defense attorney may favor someone in the same kind of practice as the defendant or an academic with a teaching role. When choosing the person who will play best before a jury, the defense attorney must make an overall assessment instead of simply picking the expert with the most impressive *curriculum vitae.*

It is essential in the beginning to plan for and develop an appealing presentation of the case to a jury. This means disabusing the client, whether an individual or an institution, of the idea that it is beneficial to act righteously indignant about being sued. Acting offended and conveying that attitude to a jury will only result in the jury being less inclined to give the defendant any benefit of the doubt. This may be harder than it seems. It is a natural human reaction to feel offended and wronged by an accusation of wrongful conduct causing harm, and those feelings may be amplified if the plaintiff did not ask the doctor directly about the bad outcome when it happened.

The defense attorney must reassure the client that a lawsuit is simply the plaintiff's way of getting answers, and this is the defendant's opportunity to explain what happened and why the defendant's judgment was good at the time and consistent with the standard of care. Even though the burden of proof is on the plaintiff, the burden of persuasion is on the health care provider, so it is essential for the defendant to present a palatable explanation for the jury that shows the outcome was not a result of negligence or professional misdeed. Often, the explanation the plaintiff receives in the courtroom is the one the plaintiff could have had by simply talking directly to the doctor, and I have frequently used that observation in closing arguments.

Using Medical Experts to Build a Defense

Medical experts are essential to building an effective defense strategy. In nearly thirty years, I have tried only two cases without a malpractice standard of care expert. Both of those cases turned on disputed facts, so I did not need independent support for the quality of care defense. Even though I did not disclose and call an expert in those cases, I benefited from the client's expertise and guidance through the medicine, as well as confidential consults with trusted physicians and surgeons to help shape my defenses.

A good medical malpractice expert can help guide the defense attorney through the entire process. Even if the expert does not support the quality of the care provided, it is critical to know what the expert thinks—good, bad, or indifferent—as an impartial view. Experts are in a position to explain some things better than clients can. While the client may be able to explain the procedure involved and impress a jury with explanations, diagrams, or charts and demonstrations of tools and materials, experts are also great sources of information. Of course, it is possible to be redundant, and the attorney should avoid having an expert repeat or reiterate what the client just said.

Defense attorneys should not overlook their clients as experts, and it is important for the court to so recognize the defendant health care professional, who will usually qualify.[7] In the usual array, the defendant is the only expert in the case with firsthand knowledge of the circumstances in which the questioned judgment (his own) was exercised. The client is typically deposed early in a case, and the defense attorney can confidentially challenge the client on areas of vulnerability to prepare for that test. It is also important to ensure the client knows what to expect, so it is beneficial for the defense attorney to confront the client with the criticisms in the complaint, demonstrating the tactics and techniques the opposition is likely to use in the deposition. It is wise to send a transcript of the deposition to outside experts, both to see how it may affect their impressions and to give the defense expert a more complete basis for his opinions.

[7] *See, e.g.*, W. VA. R. EVID. 702; *Mayhorn v. Logan Medical Foundation,* 193 W. Va. 42, 454 S.E.2d 87 (1994).

Common Defense Challenges

One of the top challenges in defending against a medical malpractice claim is in thwarting aggressive opposing lawyers who effectively try the caregiver or the institution instead of the care itself. This includes finding ways to make the defendant look blameworthy or impersonal and making an institution appear bureaucratic and profit-focused. Because the relationship between a patient and a health care provider is tremendously personal, a large measure of professionalism, caring, and compassionate personification must be brought to the case through the defendants. Ultimately, the goal is to have the jury conclude that the defendant is a valuable asset to the community and that they would seek him or her out if they or their family member had the same problem or condition.

One of the most recent developments is the use of so-called "corporate responsibility theories" against hospitals and other institutions that credential physicians and surgeons. The tactic is to allege the institution negligently credentialed the health care provider, a tactic that is developing around the country, intended to move the plaintiff past the caps to substantial damages against an institution. It also may give the plaintiff the advantage of bringing up other disparaging information from the doctor's past—prior claims, medical board complaints, questionable training, or failed certification.[8] This makes it challenging for the attorneys defending the staff physician or surgeon or the credentialing institution. The use of bifurcation to minimize the prejudice of anything the court may determine to admit on the credentialing issues is also critical.[9]

Another challenge presents if multiple caregivers are named in a claim or suit. Because the suit is about a bad outcome, and litigation is all about fixing blame, there is a compelling, but usually misplaced, inference that someone must be at fault. Defendant caregivers—and all too often their inexperienced lawyers—will therefore decide their best defense may be in deflecting responsibility to others, giving the jury someone else to blame. Of course, this may be met with an equally misplaced counterattack, with the result that the patient's lawyer simply sits back and watches it play out inevitably in his

[8] This invokes the application of "other acts" analysis and objections or motions to exclude. *See, e.g.*, W. VA. R. EVID. 404(b).

[9] *See, e.g., Schelling v. Humphrey*, 916 N.E.2d 1029 (Ohio 2009). *Compare Purcell v. Zimbelman*, 500 P.2d 335 (Ariz. Ct. App. 1972) (within court's discretion to deny severance).

favor. This is counterproductive and toxic for all of the defendants. My personal rule is not to indict someone else to exonerate my client—which is toxic to the entire defense—but many defense attorneys do not subscribe to that rule. In a system that encourages involving everybody with any involvement in the situation in the case, I prefer to force the plaintiff to prove the case against my client alone, from the outset of the case to jury verdict, and I encourage other defendants and their lawyers to do the same.

Another challenge involved with defending a medical malpractice case is coping with the attendant sympathy early and palatably. As far as possible under the court's rules and practice, it should begin with jury selection, but certainly no later than opening statement. It is the defense attorney's duty to make sure the jury members are prepared to recognize and acknowledge the natural human reaction, and then set it aside, as the court will instruct them to do.

The persuasive power of retrospect almost always presents a challenge; everything looks clear in retrospect, and it is easy to argue that different decisions may have led to a different outcome. Retrospect has the effect of converting what the defendant *could have* or *might have* done into what the defendant *should have* done, and *might* have made a difference becomes *would* have made a difference. This dynamic also should be addressed early so that the jury is considering all the evidence with a clear understanding that the issues are all posed in the context of what the caregivers did in the circumstances at the time, and specifically *not* with the benefit of retrospect.

Nowhere is retrospect more compelling than on the causation element. Most states have moved away from strict, traditional principles of proximate cause, and adopted "lost chance" or "increased risk of harm" causation. This means the plaintiff does not need to prove the health care provider gave the wrong care, which in turn directly caused the outcome. Instead, the plaintiff need only prove that some deficiency in the care deprived the patient of a significant chance of a good outcome, or increased the risk of a bad outcome, and that lost chance or increased risk was a substantial factor in bringing about the injury or harm. Patients with significant pre-existing and presenting problems—e.g., traumatic injuries, cancer, heart disease—may sincerely wish and even believe that all they needed was good care, and their life-threatening condition would have been cured or healed. All their evidence and arguments will be based on that thoroughly speculative application of retrospect, and the jury must recognize that from their first exposure to the case if we expect them to resist its effect.

Conclusion

Although medical malpractice cases appear to be all about the medicine—science, objective facts, and technical details—they are not. The practice of medicine or surgery is as much art as it is science, and the persuasive presentation of a medical malpractice defense must be the same. Opinions, impressions, and judgment calls are the focus, from the care at issue to the conflicting opinions of trial experts. The facts are important, but only where and as they make impressions, and those impressions must be good ones for the defense. Adopting appealing and palatable positions from the beginning will set a foundation on which a successful defense can be built and presented and a jury will feel comfortable delivering a defense verdict.

Advice for New Medical Malpractice Defense Lawyers

New personal injury lawyers must realize that jurors will not decide malpractice cases based just on science or their resolution of disputed facts, but on the impressions created by the evidence and how the lawyers present it. While a physician may be able to describe what happened in technically perfect language, with an analysis impressive to a group of physicians, it is pointless if it does not impress a jury of lay persons. The fundamental trial advocacy rule is that persuasion and the burden of proof are two different things; persuading a jury, especially in a medical malpractice case, is much more important.

New lawyers must also learn to ignore first impressions and acquire impartial and qualified insight into the case. The client will provide one side of the case, but it is important to get the opinion of an independent and objective observer who can provide a confidential review. This is crucial in determining the strengths and vulnerabilities of any claim or case. Often, an outside expert is able to identify potential, but undeveloped or unasserted, criticisms, helping the defense lawyer avoid those landmines on the path of litigation.

Key Takeaways

- To develop an appealing presentation of the case to a jury, disabuse the client of the idea that it is beneficial to act righteously indignant about being sued. Acting offended and conveying that attitude to a jury will only result in the jury being less inclined to give the defendant the benefit of the doubt. Jurors want to see the health care professional act in the courtroom the same as he would act in the caregiving relationship with a patient, and make that connection.

- Do not indict others to exonerate your client. In cases with multiple caregivers involved, there is a tendency to deflect responsibility to each other. This is a counterproductive approach for a lawyer to take, and it is toxic to the entire defense.
- Create a "lay clinic" using illustrations, videos, charts, diagrams, and, if a surgical procedure is involved in the case, the instruments associated with that procedure. Bring everything to the courtroom to acquaint the jury with the issues at hand. This will help demystify medicine and surgery using a logical, thoughtful process to explain medical procedures to help juries understand what happened.
- If the patient signed a medical consent form, emphasize that the patient assumed all risks and complications by asking the physician to perform the procedure. While a full and legally sufficient informed consent form does not excuse negligence, it is important for a jury to understand complications may be associated with the procedure, even in the absence of negligence, and that medicine and surgery are imprecise and fallible.
- Do not overlook your clients as experts. Ask the court to recognize the defendant as an expert. In this manner, the client becomes the only expert in the case with firsthand knowledge of the situation in question and involvement with the patient.

William E. Galeota, member of Steptoe & Johnson PLLC, devotes his practice to personal injury and commercial litigation, particularly medical professional and hospital liability, as well as commercial disputes and fiduciary litigation. He has tried dozens of medical professional liability civil actions to jury verdicts in state and federal district courts over nearly three decades and has argued cases at both the state and federal appellate levels.

Mr. Galeota is a member of the American Board of Trial Advocates, AV-rated by Martindale-Hubbell, and recognized in The Best Lawyers in America, Chambers USA, America's Leading Lawyers for Business, *and* Super Lawyers. *He is a past president of the Defense Trial Counsel of West Virginia and currently serves on the Board of Governors for the West Virginia State Bar.*

Presenting an Effective Malpractice Defense before a Lay Jury

Charles L. Bach Jr.

Partner

Heidell Pittoni Murphy & Bach LLP

ASPATORE

Introduction

It is often said that medicine is an art, as well as a science. Certainly there is an art to the trial attorney's task of defending physicians, and this chapter will address fundamental precepts for preparing the defense to prevail at trial. As the director of a play must consider the impact staging will have on the audience, the trial attorney defending a physician must consider his audience and gear the defense to that audience.

Three Key Steps in Mounting an Effective Medical Malpractice Defense

Our firm's overall goal in mounting a medical malpractice defense is to demonstrate that the defendant physician's treatment of the plaintiff was eminently reasonable at the time it was rendered, and/or the patient's outcome was caused by an underlying medical problem or a complication of that condition. Of course, when we are defending a medical center, we have the same goal: to demonstrate that the treatment rendered at the time of the event met the standard of care.

The seminal case in New York setting forth the standards by which a physician is judged is *Pike v. Honsinger*, 155 N.Y.201, 209, 49 N.E. 760, 762 (1898). This case articulates the physician's duty to use "reasonable care and diligence" in his treatment of a patient. Another important case is *Nestorowich v. Ricotta*, 97 N.Y.2d 393 (2002), which holds that a medical caregiver may not be liable if he merely chooses between medically acceptable forms of treatment.

It is our goal to demonstrate that our client acted prudently and exercised sound judgment in weighing the risks and benefits of potential treatment plans. Indeed, if the patient's condition worsened or she did not survive, it was the underlying condition, complications of that condition, and complications of the treatment that are responsible for the poor outcome. Hence, the first step in mounting an effective defense is to thoroughly investigate the facts that were presented to the physician or health care professional at the time of the treatment at issue. This requires an exhaustive interview of the physician and close examination of his office records and hospital chart entries, including all laboratory tests, radiographic studies, and reports from consulting physicians. Once we have a complete understanding of the factual context in which the plaintiff or plaintiff's decedent consulted our client, we are able to identify the critical areas that must be addressed in mounting our client's defense.

At the initial stages of the investigation, we identify renowned experts in the particular medical specialty involved in the claim who are conversant with the standard of care at the time treatment was rendered. This second step will require some Internet research, review of medical literature, and close consultation with our client. Indeed, defense counsel must obtain a thorough understanding of the plaintiff's disease process, including any co-morbidities or risk factors plaintiff presented. This requires intense medical research using search engines such as Google's Scholar, Pub Med, and Uptodate. Many defense firms maintain medical libraries and databases with *curriculae vitae* of the leading experts in every specialty.

Once we have an understanding of the standard of care and recognize all of the accepted treatment alternatives and the downside risks of the treatment at issue, we are ready to proceed to step three: an exhaustive document discovery process during which we obtain all of the plaintiff's medical records, including health insurance records. We examine the records of each prior and subsequent treating physician or hospital and produce a timeline of the plaintiff's treatment. It is of critical importance that we understand the context in which our client made treatment decisions and ensure that the physician was thorough in his approach. We want to establish that when our client assessed this particular patient, he took a complete history, performed a thorough examination of the patient, ordered the tests that were indicated at the time, and came up with a reasonable assessment of the disease process—i.e., a reasonable differential diagnosis—before recommending a treatment plan for the condition diagnosed.

Presenting the Case: Key Arguments

At trial, the plaintiff's lawyer will try to convince a lay jury that her client was injured by a physician who "may be an excellent doctor, but was negligent on the day in question." During jury selection, opposing counsel will often give the analogy that a person can be an excellent driver 999 days out of 1,000, but the one day he rushes through a stop sign and injures a person, the good driver is negligent and must compensate the plaintiff for injuries. As defense counsel for physicians and medical centers, we need to demonstrate that this is a poor analogy because the patient who consults a physician has an underlying health problem. A physician's efforts to cure or improve the patient's condition involve complex matters of professional judgment and are not analogous to a driver who runs a stop sign and hits another driver's automobile.

We teach our attorneys that our clients do not "injure" their patients. The word "injury" is derived from the Latin *injuria,* which means "to harm." Barnhart, CHAMBERS DICTIONARY OF ETYMOLOGY, 529 (2003). Our clients follow the Hippocratic Oath of "First do no harm." If the patient has gotten sicker despite treatment, this was because of the underlying condition. We thus argue that the patient was not "injured."

It is our goal to defend our client by educating the jurors and the judge about the nuances of the plaintiff's disease and treatment options. Claims against physicians ought to be decided by thinking jurors who use their heads, rather than their hearts, in analyzing the facts of the given cases. During trial we use audio and visual equipment to explain the anatomy, the disease process, and our client's own thinking process at the time treatment was rendered. We retain certified medical illustrators to create trial exhibits that graphically portray the diseased anatomy in question and the surgery our client performed to address the disease. These visual aids enable our client and experts to communicate to jurors in a language they can understand.

Considerations in Creating a Successful Defense Strategy

If we are representing a physician who, for example, is sued for an alleged failure to diagnose cancer in a timely manner, our initial investigation requires interviewing the physician and some of her staff members and analyzing her office records. When the claim is against a medical center and it involves allegedly improper surgery or postoperative monitoring, the initial investigation may be far more time-consuming. In those cases, we interview all of the staff members who were involved in the care and treatment in the operating room, the recovery room, or the intensive care unit. We may also need to inspect a medical device if there is an allegation that the surgeon mishandled a device, and have the device tested to determine whether it was maintained and functioned properly. Other departments may have been involved in the patient's care. For example, we may need to obtain pathology slides or radiographic studies, such as CT scans and MRIs so that they can be reviewed by experts in those specialties.

Every step of the way, the success of a malpractice defense strategy is measured by the attorney's understanding of the medicine and the unique factual setting of the plaintiff physician's interaction with her patient. Ultimately, success is measured by the disposition of the case through a voluntary discontinuance, a favorable settlement, a dismissal on a summary judgment motion, or a defense verdict at trial. These results cannot be achieved unless the attorney masters the underlying medical facts.

Skills and Resources Needed to Successfully Defend Medical Malpractice Claims

The primary legal skill needed to defend physicians and medical centers is the ability to identify the material issues ("issue spotting") in the context of a complex medical situation. The attorney must have a sound working knowledge of the medicine involved; she must be willing to put in long hours to understand the significance of each chart entry; and she must be willing to become an expert in the plaintiff's disease and the particular medical procedure at issue in the malpractice claim. The defense attorney must then be able to communicate to laypeople the bases for the physician's judgment calls and demonstrate how each one was reasonable at the time it was made. This means the attorney must understand how to weigh the risks and benefits of each treatment decision her client made.

Frankly, trial attorneys who defend physicians and medical centers do more medical research than legal research. For example, if the case involves the performance of a colonoscopy on a patient with ulcerative colitis, an inflammatory bowel disease, who suffered a perforation of the colon resulting in a colectomy, the defense attorney must become an expert in ulcerative colitis. Defense counsel must understand the medications used to treat ulcerative colitis, the significant complications the disease presents to the patient suffering from it, and why a colonoscopy performed on an ulcerative colitis patient is far more complicated than a routine screening colonoscopy in a healthy adult. The defense attorney must understand why the gastroenterologist performs endoscopic surveillance on his patient's entire colon to determine how the patient's disease is responding to the prescribed treatment at the time of the colonoscopy. In addition, the gastroenterologist treating an ulcerative colitis patient must be concerned about the increased risk for colon cancer that his patient presents as an inflammatory bowel disease patient. Thus, a colonoscopy in an ulcerative colitis patient is generally performed on at least an annual basis to screen for dysplasia or other precancerous signs and to assess the response of the disease to prescribed medications. In an appropriate case, the defense may be able to argue that the ulcerative colitis patient who suffered a perforated colon necessitating a colectomy is better off without his diseased colon because the patient is cured of colitis and has avoided the risk of colon cancer.

Hopefully, your client will be a primary resource of medical knowledge during the course of litigation. The physician is part of the defense team, helping the trial partner understand the standard of care based on the medical literature, treatment guidelines, and advancements in treatment and whether there is any causal connection between the care and treatment and the plaintiff's outcome.

Malpractice Investigation Procedures: Preparing the Client to be Interviewed

Physicians may face investigations of their care and treatment of a former patient by a state disciplinary board, a hospital administrative board, or a plaintiff's attorney in the context of the lawsuit.

In New York, any complaint concerning a physician's treatment that is made to the New York State Department of Health is referred to its Office of Professional Medical Conduct (OPMC). OPMC has subpoena power over medical records, and New York's Public Health Law mandates that it investigate every complaint confidentially. *See* N.Y. PUB. HEALTH LAW § 230(11)(a); *Michaelis v. Graziano*, 5 N.Y.3d 317 (2005). Hence, the physician is not told who lodged the complaint.[1] It may have been brought by a patient, a patient's family member or legal counsel, or by a former medical colleague. The staff at the OPMC opens a file and assigns an investigator who obtains relevant medical records, including the office records of the target physician—the one whose care is the subject of the complaint. That physician is required to supply a copy of his office chart on request by the OPMC investigator. Working with a staff physician at the OPMC and the investigator, the agency decides how exhaustive the investigation should be.

[1] If a patient later testifies at a formal disciplinary hearing, his identity and any written complaint are subject to disclosure to allow the physician to fully cross-examine the patient. The proceedings remain confidential to the public. *See McBarnette v. Sobol*, 83 N.Y.2d 333 (1994).

After the complainant is interviewed and records are obtained, the physician may be called in for an interview, and he has the right to counsel at this interview. Defense attorneys need to prepare their clients for these interviews as if they were preparing for grueling depositions or trials. The physician must be ready to explain in detail his treatment of the patient and how he met the standard of care at the time of treatment. The role of the defense attorney remains behind the scenes during an OPMC investigation. Defense counsel identifies the critical issues, makes a checklist of what must be covered by the physician, and then quietly attends the meeting. Allow the physician client to answer all of the questions and concerns of the investigators.

At the OPMC interview, the defense attorney may make a brief statement to ensure that the investigators learn the important details of the plaintiff's care and treatment that may not be so apparent from the chart. At this interview, the goal is for the physician to convince the OPMC that the standard of care was met so that the investigation will be closed without any administrative charges. Unlike a trial, the issue of patient outcome is not dispositive: the focus is on whether the physician met the standard of care or is in need of further training. If charges arise, OPMC hearings are held before an administrative judge, an OPMC panel member representing the public at large, and a physician who should practice in the same specialty as your client. These hearings do not follow strict rules of evidence, and they can result in findings that adversely affect your client's medical license, including its revocation or the placing of the client on probation. To be sure, there is much at stake in representing physicians in disciplinary investigations and proceedings.

Hospital investigations may wind up in disciplinary proceedings by the OPMC. If there is a subsequent private lawsuit, the details extracted during hospital investigations are generally protected from discovery under a "quality assurance" privilege. *See* N.Y. EDUC. LAW § 6527(3); N.Y. PUB. HEALTH LAW § 2905-m. As in OPMC matters, the physician is expected to cooperate voluntarily and speak freely about her treatment, explaining the outcome without holding back. There is no public role for defense lawyers at, for example, a mortality and morbidity conference where a particular surgery is analyzed after an unanticipated outcome. The same is true of any typical hospital board investigation of the physician's treatment. The goal is always to establish that at the time of the events, the physician's judgment was sound, and the care was acceptable. A lawyer's involvement in a hospital investigation may arise if a sanction is about to be imposed, and a physician seeks a hearing under the hospital's bylaws.

In sharp contrast to these settings is the investigation that is pursued as part of medical malpractice litigation. Before suit is filed, the physician will be placed on notice that she may be sued when she receives a lawyer's letter requesting copies of her records. In New York, the Public Health Law gives patients the right of access to their treatment records and mandates that physicians release copies of their chart in a timely manner for no more than seventy-five cents per page to copy the records, and then send them to the former patient's attorney. *See* N.Y. PUB. HEALTH LAW § 18(2). Once in receipt of such a request, the physician ought to consult counsel to discuss the nature of her care so that efforts can be made early to identify potential medical and legal issues, important witnesses, documents, laboratory results, etc., that need to be obtained and analyzed.

Once the case is in suit, the physician is urged to cooperate with counsel and become part of the defense team. Together, the physician and lawyer must prepare for the battles that medical malpractice litigation entails.

Common Targets of Recent Medical Malpractice Lawsuits

One of the most common medical malpractice lawsuits involves a failure to diagnose cancer or some other life-threatening condition in a timely manner. The mantra "early detection offers a better chance of a cure" is so well known by the public that it puts the defendant physician who did not diagnose breast cancer, for example, in a difficult position when sitting at the defense table. The plaintiff may have died or suffered horrendous complications of the treatment for her cancer, so the physician must explain to a lay jury that he did not order particular tests because they were not clinically indicated. This can be a difficult argument to make in a courtroom because lay jurors tend to use 20/20 hindsight and assume that earlier tests would have pointed the physician to an earlier diagnosis, affording a "better chance for a cure."

But New York law with respect to causation is construed liberally. Proximate cause is established where the defendant's conduct was a "substantial factor" in bringing about the injury. *Stewart v. New York City Health & Hosps. Corp.*, 207 A.D.2d 703, 704, 616 N.Y.S.2d 499 (1st Dep't 1994), lv denied 85

N.Y.2d 809, 651 N.E.2d 920, 628 N.Y.S.2d 52 (1995). "[P]roximate cause is a legal concept which cannot be dissected and measured in terms of percentages," and it "has proven to be an elusive [concept], incapable of being precisely defined to cover all situations." *Mortensen v. Memorial Hosp.*, 105 A.D.2d 151, 157, 483 N.Y.S.2d 264 (1st Dep't 1984); *see also Goldberg v. Horowitz*, 73 A.D.3d 691, 694, 901 N.Y.S.2d 95 (2d Dep't 2010) ("proximate cause may be found legally sufficient even if (the plaintiff's) expert is unable to quantify the extent to which the defendant's act or omission decreased the plaintiff's chance of a better outcome or increased the injury").

Also common are claims against obstetricians on behalf of infants who later develop cerebral palsy. These cases involve tremendous monetary exposure to the physician and medical center and are, of course, extraordinarily sympathetic. Frequently, the claim is that the physician should have recognized signs of fetal distress and performed a Caesarean section, rather than allow labor to continue to a natural vaginal delivery. The obstetrician who allowed labor to continue is accused of carelessness resulting in hypoxic brain damage to the baby. By the time this case reaches trial, the infant plaintiff is often wheelchair-bound with significant cognitive deficits. The plaintiff's attorney argues that that the child would have been "normal" but for the negligent conduct of an obstetrician.

To overcome the challenges obstetrical cases present, we search for an alternative reason the infant is impaired. Often, analysis of the placenta by a skilled obstetrical pathologist will provide facts that indicate the fetus was damaged *in utero* before the events of labor and delivery. Another potential defense is that the infant's severe neurological deficits are attributable to his extreme prematurity, and the obstetrical team could not extend the pregnancy or avoid the delivery of such a premature baby. An analysis of cranial MRIs by a pediatric neuroradiologist may demonstrate that the child's brain lesion was not caused by hypoxia during labor and or delivery, but by other factors outside the control of the obstetrician. In a rare case, a geneticist may be able to identify a syndrome that is the cause of the child's neurological deficits, thereby providing a medical defense for the obstetrician and neonatologist.

Risks of Being Sued for Medical Malpractice

Physicians who perform high-risk procedures on patients with comorbidities or additional risk factors, such as diabetes, obesity, or high blood pressure, are at the highest risk for suit. Insurance premiums paid by a neurosurgeon are exponentially higher than those paid by an internist. A neurosurgeon who operates on the brains and spinal cords of his patients will have patients who suffer brain injuries or death or paralysis. That is the nature of the practice.

As noted, obstetricians/gynecologists are also at high risk for litigation, not only in neurologically impaired infant cases, but also in cases involving alleged failure to diagnose breast cancer, ovarian cancer, cervical cancer, or other types of gynecological cancer. The obstetrician/gynecologist is often the *de facto* primary care physician for a woman and is expected to field complaints—for example, for a breast lump, select the proper work-up—i.e., a mammogram or ultrasound—and then act accordingly, based on the result of the tests.

Cardiothoracic surgeons operate on the heart. When things go wrong, their patients may die or suffer many untoward complications. We have had cases where patients wound up with amputations of their legs after open-heart surgery because medical complications required the use of vasopressors, which constrict blood supply to the periphery to guarantee better blood supply to the brain, kidneys, and other major organs. This, in turn, leads to ischemia in the outer extremities (fingers, feet, and toes). As a result, these specialists are often sued based on complications of life-saving surgery.

Radiologists are also at risk for suit. In suits against radiologists, we often employ a "Where's Waldo?" analysis. Looking at a radiographic study cold, a radiologist may not interpret a particular finding as problematic. However, when shown a film by an attorney, the radiologist is looking for a finding to explain the lawyer's interest in the case. If, for example, a subsequent radiographic study demonstrates the mass that has now been determined to be malignant on biopsy, it is easy to see where "Waldo" was and how a particular shadow on an earlier film should have been identified as a mass that required an earlier work-up. This is classic "outcome bias," and the defense attorney must be prepared to overcome it.

Finally, a high-risk patient who has diabetes, hypertension, obesity, sleep apnea, or any combination of chronic diseases, is at increased risk for a poor outcome, and his physician is, in turn, at increased risk to be sued.

Demonstrating that the Client Acted Reasonably

My primary strategy in demonstrating that a malpractice suit client acted in a reasonable manner involves understanding the medical context in which my client physician rendered treatment. Any interaction of physician and patient is a consultation that can best be described in an organized "SOAP note." SOAP is an acronym taught in medical school where the "S" stands for the subjective information the patient communicated to the physician at the outset of the office visit. A patient's medical, surgical, and social history should be carefully taken by the physician, and the pertinent parts should be well documented.

In an office setting, I advise my clients to hand a questionnaire to their patients at the first visit so that each patient fills out in his own hand exactly why he is consulting this physician and writes down all of the information concerning his prior medical and surgical history; family history of cancer, etc.; his social history—whether he smokes, drinks, etc.; the medications he takes; and any allergies he may have. This questionnaire should be made part of the physician's chart and scanned in and electronically maintained, along with the other medical records, laboratory results, and consultant reports concerning the patient. A good deal of medical malpractice litigation revolves around the question of whether the patient was a poor historian or the physician a poor listener. Trial lawyers refer to this as "the swearing contest," and the physician who has well-organized, well-documented records will win that contest.

Defense counsel must also demonstrate that her client performed an appropriate "objective" examination of the patient. This is a hands-on examination that can be described by the physician in the "O" part of her SOAP note. An internist will likely have a note describing findings on examination of the patient's head, eyes, ears, nose, throat, cardiac system, pulmonary system, and extremities. A thorough head-to-toe, hands-on examination can easily be described on one sheet of paper. A spinal surgeon will perform a neurological evaluation and describe the strength of the patient's leg muscles in evaluating a patient who complains of back pain.

Next comes "A" for assessment: in other words, what are the possible explanations for this patient's complaints? Once there is a diagnosis, the physician articulates a plan of treatment, and that is documented in the "P" portion of the SOAP note. For example, a patient who came to the office of an orthopedic surgeon with a subjective complaint of lower back pain radiating down the left leg must supply a complete history before being examined. A physician presumes that the patient is feeling pain, but must perform an evaluation to see whether physical findings support a factual basis for that subjective complaint. The physician may then order radiographic studies (nowadays an MRI, as opposed to an x-ray or a myelogram in the old days) and rely on a neuroradiologist's report and his own review of the MRI images to make a diagnosis concerning the cause of the back pain. If it is a lumbar disc impinging on a nerve root, a laminectomy may become the "P," the plan of treatment.

In addition to defending the plaintiff's care and treatment, we like to know something about the plaintiff that may impact the merits of the plaintiff's claim or the plaintiff's credibility as a witness. Today, with social networking sites and blogs, we can sometimes discover that the plaintiff is a malingerer, an unreliable historian, or a litigious person if we have carefully searched the Internet.

At the time of trial, we scan in all of the material medical records so that we can project them onto a screen and highlight particularly important parts of the charts, rather than using blow-ups. Today's jurors are trained to understand things visually, rather than through mere audio presentations. They prefer to see exactly what the records made at the time of events demonstrate and view medical illustrations to understand what the surgery was all about, rather than merely listen to a lawyer's description of this data.

Choosing a Good Medical Expert and Proving the Physician Did Not Cause Plaintiff's Damages

The finest medical expert is one who has a great deal of experience in the particular procedure or disease at issue in the case and the ability to communicate in simple terms to a lay jury. Our experts tend to be at the top of their profession, and they know it. However, the best experts relate to a jury as humble individuals who have a particular gift. To obtain these experts, we first speak to our own clients to see who they have heard lecture at national meetings. We research peer-reviewed medical literature to identify authors of seminal articles on the disease. At the same time, defense counsel must retain an expert who does not have any professional or social ties to the client. The expert should not be retained if, for example, she has co-authored any articles along with your client.

The expert must be able to relate to jurors from all walks of life and teach them the relevant medicine so that the finders of fact understand the plaintiff's disease process, how the defendant weighed the risks and benefits of various treatment options, and why the defendant chose the option that is now the subject matter of litigation. Jurors can be turned off by physicians who do not make eye contact with them and come across as arrogant, impatient, or disorganized. By searching the medical literature, including PowerPoint presentations available on the Internet and medical center websites, it is not difficult to identify good experts, but it may be difficult to convince them to take the time required to review the documents that are in a case file and then be willing to come to court to testify at trial.

In New York, there are no depositions of experts except in rare circumstances. *See* N.Y. C.P.L.R. 3101(d). Rather, there is a document prepared by attorneys known as "expert disclosure" that does not identify the expert, but merely summarizes what the expert is likely to testify about at trial and provides some background information, including the date of medical school graduation, the date of internship and residency, and any fellowships and board certifications. Computer software allows both sides to identify the experts and then obtain their medical literature, prior testimony in other cases, and any other information that may be used to challenge their credibility or expertise during trial.

Once they are retained based on their assurance that they can defend the care and treatment at issue, experts are part of the defense team. Experts can point us to relevant peer-reviewed medical literature and specialty guidelines to show us the complication rates for various procedures and to explain the standard of care. For example, we like to call as witnesses medical experts who are members of a national board who give examinations that must be passed to obtain board certification, or experts who are chairs of departments at major medical institutions. These physicians are aware of the standard of care because they teach it daily to their residents.

We can then contrast the defense experts to a plaintiff's "expert," who in many cases merely has an office practice, no real publications, no significant teaching appointments, and is being paid an astronomical sum to testify even though he does not have any true expert credentials. We like to demonstrate that the plaintiff's expert has testified all over the country and offers his services on "find an expert.com." In addition, if the plaintiff's expert presents an opinion on causation that we consider to be "junk science," we challenge the expert by applying to the trial court for a *Frye/Daubert* hearing where the expert must establish that his hypothesis has a valid scientific basis. *See, e.g., Cumberbatch v. Blanchette*, 35 A.D.3d 341, 825 N.Y.S.2d 744 (2d Dep't 2006) (precluding plaintiff's expert testimony where expert could cite to no relevant scientific data or studies to support his causation theory that fetal distress resulting from the compression of the infant plaintiff's head due to labor contractions, augmented by Pitocin, resulted in ischemia, which, in turn, resulted in an infarction, and he could cite to no instance when this type of injury had previously occurred in that manner).

Typically, the plaintiff's attorney is looking for experts who can sound convincing to a lay jury when they testify in support of a plaintiff's theory of negligence. They often do not care about the contents of an expert's *curriculum vitae*. Rather, they want to be sure the expert will "toe the party line" and be an advocate for the plaintiff in front of a jury by refusing to make any concessions when cross-examined by the defense attorney. A common trick of a plaintiff's expert is to testify as to how he would have treated the plaintiff while couching his testimony in the usual language about the "standard of care." Such second-guessing is more convincing when there is a strong sympathy factor. However, by obtaining the expert's prior depositions and trial testimonies in cases pending around the country, the defense can often discredit the plaintiff's expert as a hired gun who has developed a cottage industry by reviewing cases and testifying against his fellow physicians, shaping his testimony about the standard of care to fit the needs of the case at hand.

Top Challenges of Defending against a Medical Malpractice Claim

The biggest hurdle for the defense is the plaintiff's medical outcome and the need to overcome "outcome bias." We ask jurors not to judge our clients using a "retrospectoscope." Rather, we establish the timeline of treatment and ask the jury to pretend they are watching a DVD as the case unfolds. The defense must prove that at the point in time the physician made his recommendations or performed his surgery, he acted reasonably. If the patient's outcome was poor, that fact is after-acquired knowledge that cannot be used to judge the physician's conduct. Once the facts are proved, the DVD is stopped at a particular "frame" or point in time, and the jury is asked to determine whether the physician's judgment was reasonable at that time, regardless of subsequent events. In this respect, the physician's contemporaneous records are of paramount importance, and we always point out that the records made at the time of the events are the best evidence of what occurred years before the trial. After all, memories fade, but a computer entry or a written note does not. Today, plaintiffs often want to obtain the metadata behind the computer entry to see when it was actually entered and by whom. This can present a problem in cases involving large medical centers using computer software systems that produce a trail of who knew what, where, and how.

Nevertheless, it can be difficult to overcome the sympathy factor, particularly in cases involving neurologically impaired infants or adults. We have had some success in making pretrial motions to bifurcate medical malpractice cases into two phases: the first liability, and the second damages. We argue that the first phase of the trial should focus on whether the standard of care was met before the jury hears any evidence about the plaintiff's current predicament, with the usual showing of a "day in the life" video and testimony about millions of dollars in past, present, and future damages, that might render a dispassionate deliberation on the liability issues impossible.

Avoiding Medical Malpractice Claims

To avoid medical malpractice claims, a physician ought to organize his treatment note so that it is legible and so that when it is subpoenaed to court and blown up to four feet by three feet, he would be proud to stand next to it and explain every entry. It does not have to be a lengthy dissertation, but it ought to be a well-organized SOAP note.

In addition to good documentation, it is critically important to have a good bedside manner and build a rapport with the patient and her family. Thus, it is extraordinarily important for the surgeon to see the patient after surgery, talk to the family after surgery, and stay in touch with the family as the patient remains in the hospital. The attending physician who relies on residents to do all of his post-operative work on patients is playing a dangerous game. The attending physician must take ownership of the case and build a rapport with his patient and the family.

In some hospitals, including the University of Michigan, The Mayo Clinic, and the Harvard Medical Centers, physicians and hospital administrators have been encouraged to hold meetings with family members when a patient experiences an untoward outcome. Patient apology programs have been successful when the family is receptive to hearing the physician describe what occurred in the operating room, what the hospital's investigation entailed, and when they are placed at ease as to why a particular complication occurred and what the medical center intends to do about it. We are cautiously optimistic that these meetings, when handled properly, will result in less litigation.

We caution our physician and medical center clients not to discuss their treatment with the patient or family members over the telephone. Telephone calls may be taped unbeknownst to the doctor or risk manager, and statements taken out of context may impair the defense that sound medical judgment was employed at the time of the treatment at issue in the litigation.

Conclusion

When defending a physician at trial, the lawyer must turn back the clock to the hour, day, month, and year treatment was rendered. Understand the nuances of plaintiff's disease and explain to a lay jury how eminently reasonable the physician's medical or surgical judgment was at the time treatment recommendations were made. Establish the concept of acceptable treatment alternatives, and demonstrate how your client met the standard of care by recommending one of those acceptable alternatives.

In an appropriate case, the defense must challenge plaintiff's causation theory by demonstrating that there is no peer-reviewed study or accepted medical evidence to link the physician's treatment to the patient's outcome. Interview or depose key subsequent treating physicians to expose the fallacy of plaintiff's theories of causation. Conduct the defense as though you have the burden of proof by being proactive at trial. You must convince the fact finders that objectivity requires they find facts that will exonerate your client. In that respect, justice will be done.

Key Takeaways

- Thoroughly investigate the facts that were presented to the physician or health care professional at the time of the treatment in issue. Interview the physician, and closely examine his office records, hospital chart entries, laboratory tests, radiographic studies, and reports from consulting physicians.

- Identify renowned experts in the particular medical specialty involved in the claim who are conversant with the standard of care at the time treatment was rendered and who can communicate well with a jury. Obtain a thorough understanding of the plaintiff's disease process, including any co-morbidities.
- Obtain all of the plaintiff's medical records, including health insurance records. Examine each prior and subsequent treating physician or hospital, and produce a timeline of the plaintiff's treatment to understand the context in which your client made treatment decisions and ensure he was thorough in his approach.
- Use audio and visual equipment to explain the plaintiff's anatomy, the disease process, and your client's thinking process at the time treatment was rendered. Be able to communicate to laypeople the bases for the physician's judgment calls and demonstrate how each one was reasonable at the time it was made.
- Advise physician clients who wish to avoid malpractice suits to maintain good documentation and a positive relationship with the patient and her family, during and after her hospital stay.

After serving four years as an assistant district attorney in The Bronx, Charles L. Bach Jr. started as an associate at Heidell Pittoni & Moran in June 1981. Since that time he has been defending physicians and staff members of university medical centers at trial, in professional disciplinary proceedings, and on appeal. In 1985, the name of his firm was changed to Heidell Pittoni Murphy & Bach LLP, and as a senior partner with more than thirty years of experience defending physicians, he has recognized the need to effectively communicate complex medical concepts to a lay audience.

Acknowledgment: *I would like to thank my appellate partner, Dan Ratner, for his help in preparing this chapter.*

New Strategies for Representing Doctors in Malpractice Litigation

Robert W. Frank

Vice President and Senior Shareholder

Neil Dymott Frank McFall and Trexler APC

ASPATORE

Introduction

Medical malpractice lawsuits likely are the most common of lawsuits filed against licensed professionals. The practice of medicine, as it is said, is an art, not a science. With art, they say, beauty is in the eye of the beholder. With the practice of medicine, malpractice often is in the eyes of a patient beholden to unrealistic expectations of perfection. Not always is there a clear, black-and-white line of what is and what is not malpractice. Lawsuits over undesired patient outcomes will continue.

This chapter addresses some of the tort reform legislation impacting medical malpractice claims, laws and strategies for evaluating and defending medical malpractice lawsuits, and some practice pointers for physician clients to minimize the risk of being sued. Keeping abreast of the trends, strategies, and tactics available in these areas is important. Medical malpractice has been and will be with us for many years; so, too, will lawsuits result from its occurrence.

Including Untraditional Causes of Actions and Claims against Health Insurance Plans in Malpractice Complaints

One trend I have noticed in the medical malpractice area over the past few years is that many plaintiffs' lawyers have been attempting to include causes of action in the complaints they file, such as battery, fraud, breach of contract, and intentional infliction of emotional distress. Many states have now instituted tort reform measures that include caps on the amount of damages that can be recovered in medical malpractice cases. For example, since 1975, California has had a $250,000 cap on general damages in malpractice cases, although there is no cap on economic losses.[1] Many other states have some type of cap system, even systems such as California, which also abrogates the traditional collateral source evidence rule barring the admission of evidence of health insurance payments for needed medical care, which the lawyers on the plaintiff's side of the case do not like.[2] These cap systems limit the amount of damages they can recover in malpractice litigation. Consequently, plaintiffs' lawyers often try to plead causes of action that are permissible outside the boundaries of tort reform legislation—i.e.,

---

[1] CAL. CIV. CODE § 3333.1.
[2] CAL. CIV. CODE § 3333.2.

most states do not have a cap on battery, fraud, breach of contract, or intentional infliction of emotional distress claims.

Plaintiffs' lawyers may also plead such causes of action to avoid a statute of limitations problem that might exist with respect to a negligence claim. In California, for instance, a negligence claim for malpractice generally has a one-year statute of limitations; whereas, a breach of contract or fraud claim has a longer statute of limitations, typically up to three years. Hence, when the plaintiff's attorney knows the traditional medical negligence claim may be barred by a one-year statute of limitations, he will disguise the malpractice claim by alleging these other causes of action, too.

Another recent trend in this area involves efforts by plaintiffs' lawyers to make claims for breach of the covenant of good faith and fair dealing—i.e., bad faith, in terms of arrangements with health insurance plans. Health plans, such as Kaiser, have hospitals and doctors who are a part of the Kaiser system; basically, those hospitals and doctors have a contract with Kaiser's health plan to perform medical services. Plaintiffs' lawyers are now trying to cut some new territory in this area by making claims asserting bad-faith administration of a particular health plan or fraud in entering into the health plan agreement. For instance, they may allege that there is an agreement in place among the health plan, its physicians, and its hospital to cut or minimize costs. If the plan/physician/hospital does not tell patients about such arrangements, and the doctors who are part of the plan receive bonuses because of the cost-cutting measures that have been employed throughout the year, plaintiffs may allege that the health plan and its doctors and hospitals are working together to deny patients important care, such as MRI testing, simply because of the high costs of such testing.

The plaintiffs' lawyers who are bringing these cases claim they do not involve medical negligence; rather, they are cases about bad-faith administration/application of a health plan involving a system to coerce doctors into cutting costs and denying care to patients, or fraud in entering into the health plan for failure to disclose to the patient such cost minimization systems. Consequently, no tort reform caps on damages apply to the claims; yet, in reality, they still all involve some underlying poor outcome with patient care, such as a delayed diagnosis of cancer.

Ultimately, I believe that tort reform legislation in various states will reduce the number of malpractice lawsuits because lawyers do not want to take such cases when there are caps in place on the amount of damages that can be recovered. Medical malpractice cases can be some of the most costly personal injury cases to pursue through trial or arbitration. Already, fewer questionable malpractice cases are being filed, and more legitimate cases are being filed by good lawyers who are doing a better job of screening the good cases from the poor cases.

Physicians at Risk for Malpractice Claims

I categorize malpractice litigation into two types of cases: the "doctor didn't do anything" or "doctor didn't do enough" type and the "doctor did something wrong" case—the "no action taken case" and the "poorly performed action" case. In either case, we are dealing with some type of bad patient outcome—i.e., some type of injury or harm from either want of care or poorly performed care. The "want of care" cases typically involve a delay in diagnosis of some condition; in other words, if a disease goes undiagnosed for too long, the patient ends up with a severe problem, such as an untreatable cancer. It may be that the doctor failed to do a certain study—for example, he failed to order a colonoscopy, follow up with more mammograms, or obtain a biopsy. As a result, the patient's cancer did not get diagnosed in a timely fashion, and now his or her life expectancy is reduced. Or certain tests were not obtained to diagnose an infection, which caused a patient to become septic and die.

Many of the "poor performance" cases stem from advancements in the use of new medical devices and imaging technology in the operating room, such as the robotic or laparoscopic surgical techniques that now are often used to perform minimally invasive surgical procedures, such as hysterectomies, hernia repair, and gallbladder and prostate gland removal. In some cases, there is a bad outcome with these surgeries because there is a learning curve for most physicians with respect to using these new devices and imaging techniques.

Simply put, physicians need to get used to using the equipment and become familiar with it before operating. All too often, however, we see injuries to organs adjacent to the ones intended to be operated on, simply because physicians are still learning how to use this equipment, which allows for less visualization than traditional open-cavity surgeries. Many more "senior" physicians, in particular, learn how to use this equipment during some type of weekend seminar or program; whereas, younger physicians who have been trained in the use of this equipment during their residencies and fellowship programs are less likely to have problems with it. The more senior physicians did not grow up playing videogames, which bestow unique hand-eye coordination skills at a young age.

Similarly, radiologists are now using equipment and technology that essentially allow them to do procedures that were traditionally done by vascular surgeons or cardiologists; whereas, in the past, their role primarily involved reading X-rays and MRI and CT scans. These days, radiologists are much more like surgeons, and the technology in this area is essentially eliminating the field of vascular surgery. Unfortunately, radiologists tend to be more prone to making errors when they are just starting to use this new surgical stenting and catheter equipment.

Obstetric and gynecologic (OB-GYN) physicians have always been at high risk for being sued for malpractice because nobody wants to have an imperfect child. A plaintiff who files such a case tends to be sympathetic to the jury, no matter what type of medical defense is involved.

I have worked in this practice area for more than thirty years, and the types of clients I deal with have not changed to any great extent. However, as noted, the types of claims against those clients have changed—again, because of growing advancements in new technology, medical devices, and medications. Essentially, family practice doctors and internists are still being sued for failing to follow up and diagnose cancer and other conditions; surgeons are sued for making mistakes in the operating room; radiologists are sued because they fail to see something on an X-ray or other imaging study; and pathologists are sued because they do not properly read a pathology slide; and, of course, obstetricians are still sued for failing to deliver by C-section before a baby allegedly suffers significant anoxic brain injury.

State and Federal Laws Involved in Malpractice Litigation

Anybody can go down to the courthouse, pay the price of filing a malpractice lawsuit, have the clerk stamp it and file it, and then have the complaint served on the doctor. Nobody can prevent these filings from happening; nobody at the courthouse screens a lawsuit to see whether it is good or bad before it is filed. Some states, however, such as Nevada, do require such suits to be approved by a panel of physicians before they can be filed, although these states are few. Most states have statutes that allow doctors to take action if they can prove that a lawsuit against them was filed with the intent of malicious prosecution. For example, let us say that a patient did not pay a bill, and the doctor sent it to a collection agency. The patient then sues the doctor, hoping that this will stop the bill collector from taking action against him or her. Most states allow a doctor to sue a patient for malicious prosecution under such circumstances, but only after the physician prevails in the malpractice case against him or her. Obviously, however, this does not stop the initial lawsuit from being filed.

Fortunately, many things can be done to eliminate a malpractice lawsuit before it goes to trial, especially if it can be proved that the lawsuit is frivolous. A motion for summary judgment can be filed to have the case dismissed for lack of evidence on the patient's side, or if the plaintiff does not have an expert witness to support the claims being made. If the doctor can produce evidence or a retained expert who says that the doctor met the required standard of care, the court will have to dismiss the case—unless the patient's expert makes a declaration that says the opposite. Unfortunately, although some states have statutes that allow the court to impose penalties for frivolous motions and filings of cases, such assertions are hard to prove, and, again, you cannot prevent the initial lawsuit from being filed.

All state and federal laws allow patients to sue for substandard care. For example, the basic negligence law has been around since the concept of tort recovery came into being, and it applies at both the state and the federal levels. Also, the Federal Tort Claims Act comes into play when a patient wants to sue a health care provider from the Veterans Administration or a federally funded facility. In such cases, the plaintiff is subject to the Federal Tort Claims Act limitations. Such limitations include no right to a jury trial, 20 percent recovery of attorney's fees if settled prior to filing and 25 percent after filing, a two-year statute of limitations requiring that a written claim first be presented to the appropriate government agency within those two years and that the lawsuit can only be filed and must be filed within six months of denial of the claim for recovery. Still the federal court is bound by the law of the state regarding medical negligence claims, including any applicable tort reform recovery limitations, such as damages caps.[3]

Laws that Provide Immunity for Physicians

Other laws exist in most states that provide immunity for physicians. For example, certain hospitals have a Code Blue response system in effect in the event of a medical emergency. Essentially, there is a designated Code Blue team who responds when someone has a heart attack or goes into cardiac arrest in a hospital. The people on the team will come to the scene to try to resuscitate the person; if that person does not survive or an injury occurs during the resuscitation attempt, the patient or the patient's family may later allege that someone made a mistake. However, a law in California says you cannot sue the physicians who are involved in a Code Blue response unless you can prove they did something in the course of the Code Blue teamwork that was not in good faith—simply saying that they failed to meet the standard of care or they were negligent is not enough[4]. Those doctors are immune from liability unless the patient or the family can prove that they acted in bad faith, and that means they have to prove that one or more of the doctors intentionally did something they knew was wrong. For example, if during the Code Blue response, a physician mistakenly stuck a chest tube into the patient's lung, causing a collapsed lung, the patient would have to prove that the physician knew he would be puncturing the lung when inserting the tube and did so anyway or with reckless abandon—i.e., disregarding an existing chest X-ray showing the chest cavity structures—intentionally inserting it into an area all doctors know would cause a collapsed lung. Still these "Good Samaritan" immunity statutes are difficult to overcome.

Many states also employ a concept called "litigation privilege," which may provide immunity for a physician against a lawsuit. In California, for instance, no communication a doctor disseminates in connection with a judicial or quasi-judicial proceeding can be the basis on which to file a claim against the doctor for negligent medical care.[5] For example, a neurologist has a duty to report to the Department of Motor Vehicles (DMV) of any state that a patient has a

---

[3] 28 U.S.C. § 2402; 28 U.S.C. § 2401(b); 28 U.S.C. § 2675(a); 28 U.S.C. § 2678; 28 U.S.C. § 1346(b); *Richards v. United States*, 369 U.S. 1 (1962). (*See* Appendix C)

[4] CAL. HEALTH & SAFETY CODE § 1317(f); *Lowry v. Henry Mayo Newhall Memorial Hospital*, 185 Cal. App.3d 188 (1986).

[5] CAL. CIV. CODE § 47.

neurological disorder, such as epilepsy, that makes the patient unfit to drive—in other words, the patient should not have a driver's license. Let us say that the neurologist, when asked about the patient's condition in connection with a DMV issue, does not report that the patient has epilepsy or some other disabling condition because the doctor failed to properly diagnose it, and the patient gets a license and then hurts someone while driving. Let us say that the doctor is asked to assess the patient in connection with the DMV license proceeding—i.e., "Do you think that this patient has a disorder that should prevent him from getting a license?" and the doctor says, "No." In either case, the person who got hurt in that automobile accident involving the patient with epilepsy cannot sue the physician on the basis that the physician submitted a report or statement to the DMV stating that the patient was fit to drive a car. Basically, the physician is immune from liability under the concept of litigation privilege because the courts have interpreted the phrase "judicial or quasi-judicial proceeding" to include any type of government agency interaction that is related to medical care. In other words, sending a report to the DMV that says the patient does or does not have a particular disorder is considered a communication with the government, and the litigation privilege clause in some states says that all of the care leading up to that determination by the doctor cannot be the basis for a medical malpractice lawsuit because that care was prefatory to the quasi-judicial proceeding—i.e., the communication with the government agency.

I am aware of one recent case where a plaintiff did try to sue a neurologist for submitting a report to the DMV that said that their patient could drive and did not have such a degree of epilepsy that the patient should be on medications. In that case, the court ruled that the plaintiff could not sue the doctor. In a recent case against Kaiser, the plaintiff tried to pursue the bad-faith theory of liability, alleging that the health plan was scheming with its doctors to cut costs, and, therefore, it was essentially acting in bad faith with respect to the plaintiff, who was covered by Kaiser's insurance plan. In this case, the state Supreme Court said that the plaintiff could bring such a claim and that it was not limited by the tort reform recovery statutes that have a cap on damages and that limit other types of recovery. Each case in this area has a different outcome.

Mounting an Effective Malpractice Defense

An attorney should utilize a standard formula to set up defense strategies in a medical malpractice case. First, you need to learn the facts of the case. Of course, you should listen to your client's version of what happened, but perhaps more important is that you also need to learn what the other side is contending—i.e., what its theories are and what it will claim—so that you can figure out how to best defend against those claims. Essentially, the more you know about your enemy, the better off you are. I always emphasize the importance of learning the other side of the case before you try to figure out your client's side of the case.

One strategy I use to make my client a valuable resource for information is to ask, "If you had to be critical of yourself in this situation, what areas would you scrutinize?" You should also enlist the services of an expert in the area of medicine you are dealing with and have the expert look at the records and information you have available to see whether your client has support for his or her case. Once you figure out the pros and cons of your client's position, you can then determine whether you have a case that is good enough to defend, or one that needs to be settled because you do not have enough support for your client's actions. In other words, you need to decide whether you will go down the settlement path or the defend-at-trial path.

Next, you need to assess whether your client is capable—emotionally and intellectually—of presenting himself or herself in a good light in front of a jury and has the ability to go through a trial. Litigation is a stressful, nerve-wracking, and difficult process for most physicians because most of them truly do care about their patients and try to do their best—and when they get sued, they often lose confidence in themselves. So you have to figure out whether your client can make a good presentation in front of a jury. If you feel your client cannot do so, but you know that you need to defend her because she did not do anything wrong, you can hire consultants who specialize in helping physicians become better witnesses. They can help your client be better able to stand up for herself, be stronger and more articulate, and come across better to a jury. I use such experts as needed, as I have found that they can help doctors present their side of the case more confidently and come across well in court.

Client Misconceptions about Malpractice Litigation

Among the many misconceptions my physician clients often have with respect to malpractice litigation is the belief that all they have to do is tell their side of the story and then the case will be over; the court will simply dismiss the plaintiff's charges. I have to tell them it does not work that way. The judge does not get to decide whether your expert or the plaintiff's expert is the most credible before the case gets heard by the jury—they get to decide only whether there is a legitimate dispute. A client might wonder how the testimony of an emergency medical technician (EMT) physician can match up against the testimony of a plastic surgeon in a rhinoplasty case, and I have to tell my client that under the law, the jury must weigh the credibility of the experts on both sides.

Also, in many initial meetings, some clients will be adamant in saying they did not do anything wrong, and therefore the case should not have been filed. Those are the clients whose cases truly need to be investigated, as you are likely to find that there is something wrong with the client's position. For example, you may find that one of the plaintiff's medical records has been altered or added to in some way—for example, as I have encountered before, on receiving a copy of your client's records from plaintiff's counsel, you may find that the exonerating note about a prescription, lab test, X-ray, or call to another physician or to the patient is not in your copy of your client's record because your client added it to the chart after the doctor received notice of the lawsuit and after the patient already had obtained a copy of his chart from the doctor's office. Under these circumstances, you can only hope you find out about such alteration before your client at deposition says under oath that his chart is accurate and unaltered.

On the other hand, those doctors who tell me, "I feel horrible about what happened, and I do not know if I did something wrong," have, in many cases, simply lost their confidence as a result of being sued. Quite often, after working on a case and hiring experts, you will find that the doctor did not do anything below the standard of care, and he is just being hard on himself. These clients often ultimately make the best witnesses.

Skills and Resources for Mounting a Malpractice Defense

One of the most important resources for defending a medical malpractice case is a good databank of experts who have testified in various specialty areas in the past on behalf of both plaintiffs and defendants. For example, when you find out who the expert on the other side will be, you can look to see whether she has provided testimony in similar cases and determine whether the testimony she is likely to provide in the present case will be inconsistent with that past testimony.

However, the most important resource in this area is your own experience and knowledge and that of your partners who have been through these types of cases before. It is always important to put sufficient time and effort into learning the medicine that is involved in the case and getting to know your client and people on the other side so that you are not surprised by or unprepared for anything that happens later. Ultimately, the more of these cases you try, the better your skills will be.

Defending Doctors versus Health Care Institutions

Defending doctors in malpractice litigation can be easier than defending a health care institution, because you are often better able to personalize the activity that is being questioned in the case. You can help the jury understand who the doctor is and why he has taken a certain position. You can put the doctor on the witness stand and let him talk about things that are unrelated to the specific malpractice claim at issue in the case so that he can establish some rapport with the jury. Have the radiologist talk about how an MRI machine works; show them how a stent and catheter are used; and use diagrams and models to educate the jury about medical concepts about which they know little. Teach them as if they are students in a high school or college class.

It is important to tell the doctor to look directly at the jury and tell his story in laymen's terms. Ultimately, you want the jury to feel as if they are dealing with a person; jurors are less prone to worry about what they might do to an institution in terms of a verdict than what they might do to an individual to whom they have become attached or for whom they have established some feelings of benevolence. Therefore, when defending a doctor, I typically personalize the presentation to the jury as much as possible. I go over the doctor's history—i.e., where he went to school, why he became a doctor, what charitable work he has done, if any, etc.

When defending medical institutions, you talk about what the hospital has done for the community, including any charitable efforts, so that the jurors will feel positively about that institution. You try to show the institution is made up of an array of different people just like the jury hearing the case. Have a designated hospital representative sit through the trial next to you so the jury can identify the institution with a person about which they can feel good.

Demonstrating that Your Client Acted Appropriately

To demonstrate to the jury that your client acted in a way that any reasonable doctor would, you have to get across the concept that medicine, like other professions, is fraught with potential complications and risks. In many cases, things are not going to turn out as you would have hoped, but the occurrence of a complication does not mean that someone was acting negligently or below the standard of care. Making a mistake does not always mean the person was at fault. Therefore, we might use the testimony of experts—or our own client, if she makes a good witness—to inform that jury that bowel perforations occur in relation to colonoscopies in a certain percentage of cases, and unfortunately, the plaintiff was just one of the 7 percent to 10 percent of patients who suffer that type of complication. Simply put, you want the jury to know that these complications can occur even if the plaintiff had the best medical care possible; the best doctors in the world have had patients with this complication, and that does not mean that the doctor did something wrong.

In those cases where the doctor failed to order an MRI or some other test or failed to diagnose the patient's cancer early enough, you might point out that other physicians who were not parties to the case but had treated the patient in the past did not think to do that type of testing either—and yet they are not on trial. In a case of failure to diagnose, you might present a list of all of the potential diagnoses a doctor might make with respect to certain symptoms and explain that medicine often involves a process of elimination. In other words, some diseases cannot be correctly diagnosed until the doctor is able to rule out common causes of other diseases. In most cases, when going to the emergency room or urgent care center for a bad headache, you do not immediately obtain an MRI to check for a brain tumor; you might not get an MRI that would show you have an early-stage brain tumor. Essentially, diagnosing a disease takes time, and some diseases or medical problems manifest themselves only after reasonable efforts are made to figure out what the problem is after first exploring the most common causes for the symptoms, not the zebras that lurk within the horse herd.

In some cases, you are looking to prove that the plaintiff was not injured by the doctor's actions. For example, if the plaintiff has cancer, you need to look into the medical literature and get expert testimony with respect to the question of causation—i.e., would an earlier diagnosis have made a difference in this case? Would the doctor have been able to operate and remove the patient's brain tumor without causing damage to the surrounding neurological structures? It may be that the tumor was already so big when the patient first came to the doctor that the outcome of the operation would have been the same. Essentially, you need to look for ways to say that the end result would not have been any different, even if the doctor had found the problem when the patient first came to see the doctor. That is best done by talking to experts in the field and looking for medical literature that supports that conclusion and that your experts can use when they testify.

Again, if you are dealing with a case where the doctor's actions during surgery led to a bad result, you need to demonstrate that the plaintiff did not suffer an injury due to your client's malpractice. This is best done by discussing the "informed consent" process the patient went through with the doctor before surgery. Typically, the doctor will explain that there are risks inherent in every procedure the doctor does, and there is a statistical outcome in relation to certain complications. Just as there is risk involved every time you drive a car, there is risk involved in every medical procedure. Similarly, you may need to explain to the jury that the patient's cancer had already spread and was metastatic by the time it was diagnosed; therefore, it cannot be proved that an earlier diagnosis would have given the patient a better chance of living for another twenty-five years.

New Issues in Obtaining Expert Testimony

Generally, we are seeing the same types of experts in medical malpractice cases as in past years. However, there is now more of an overlap between specialties in terms of expert testimony. For example, if you have a case that involves neurosurgery, you may ask a neurosurgeon and an orthopedist to testify in the case, as both types of specialists may be involved in the procedure. Both neurosurgeons and some orthopedists specialize in spine surgery, removal of herniated discs. Plastic surgeons and ophthalmologists both perform cosmetic eye procedures. Cardiologists, vascular surgeons, and radiologists perform procedures to eliminate occlusion of arteries, and podiatrists and some orthopedists perform foot and ankle surgeries.

Also, a growing number of experts are available for hire through various services and organizations that advertise on the Internet. I often get e-mails from companies that say, in effect, "We have doctors who are able to review your case and testify on your client's behalf." Currently, more experts are advertising their services to testify on the patient's side of these lawsuits because plaintiffs' lawyers typically do not have the same level of access to experts as we do through our own clients and relationships in the medical field.

In addition, we are now better able to obtain data on experts who have testified in the past in cases that may involve similar issues because there are more organizations that catalog and track expert depositions and trial testimony. Consequently, as noted, we can easily find out whether an expert on the other side said something in another case that is contrary to what the expert is saying in our case on the same subject.

Choosing the Right Experts

The process of choosing the right experts in a medical malpractice case needs to be tailored to the specific case. Key considerations include whether the expert is a well-established, published, and authoritative person in his or her field and whether the person will make a good impression as a witness. You do not want to pick an expert who is so good on the stand that he or she makes your client look bad. In some cases, your client might be your best expert.

A good expert is generally someone who can speak in lay terms—someone who can talk to a jury as if talking to a group of school children or other people who do not know anything about medicine. As noted, it is important for the expert to use lay terms and analogies to convey difficult medical concepts in a way that ordinary people can relate to. It is also helpful if the expert has an impressive pedigree—i.e., he or she has published texts or journal articles in a certain field of medicine, in addition to being a doctor.

On the other hand, I have had some highly effective witnesses who did not have impressive pedigrees—they were what we call in-the-trenches experts, as opposed to a university icon who teaches many people and publishes many articles. In fact, an in-the-trenches expert who has done a number of medical procedures, as opposed to writing about them, will often come across to the jury as the more experienced expert. However, if your case involves an esoteric area of medicine, or a specialized and rare complication or procedure, you need to find an expert who has a pedigree and is a published author in that area. You can then tell the jury, "This person really knows what he is talking about because he is one of the leading experts in the country in this area." Keep in mind that the expert still has to be able to communicate well with the jury to be the best witness for your side.

In my opinion, you should stay away from an expert who has a long track record of testifying in malpractice cases. If a doctor derives 20 percent of her income from testifying as an expert, it is likely the other side will allege she is being paid to say what she is saying. Also, it is a good idea to choose an expert who has had experience in testifying for both patients and the defense. Again, the best witness will always be someone who can communicate effectively and get points across in a way a jury can understand and believe in, and who makes them willing to consider your side of the case.

Top Challenges of Defending a Medical Malpractice Claim

One of the biggest challenges in this practice area is representing a client who makes a poor impression as a witness and cannot communicate well with the jury. Typically, the other side will try to keep that type of witness on the stand for hours in an effort to embarrass him and make him look bad in front of the jury. In such cases, as previously noted, you need to get a witness coach—someone who can help the client be a better witness.

Another major challenge in defending these cases is a patient who has suffered a traumatic, serious, catastrophic, or sympathetic type of injury. In many cases, that type of patient makes a good impression as a witness; his testimony is believable, and the jury will have compassion for him. Ultimately, the jury has probably absorbed only about 20 percent to 30 percent of the expert testimony in the case; therefore, their decision typically boils down to their impressions of the patient and the doctor in the case, and the feelings they have for one side or the other. Simply put, if they really like the plaintiff, they will rule in the plaintiff's favor, or if they like the defendant, they will rule for him or her. In fact, when I interview juries after a trial is over, they will often tell me that the experts on both sides cancelled each other out—so their primary focus was on what the plaintiff and the defendant had to say.

Consequently, during *voir dire* questioning of the prospective jurors at the beginning of the case, it is important to try to determine whether they are likely to feel sympathy for the plight of the plaintiff and, again, to let them know that complications do happen even if there is no malpractice in the case—i.e., even if an injury occurred, it was not your client's fault.

Finally, it is important to behave respectfully when you are cross-examining the other side unless you have some strong impeachment evidence. Even a sympathetic injury plaintiff can exaggerate damages or other issues. If you have clear, black-and-white evidence of inconsistency or contradiction, do not hesitate to forcefully impeach even the sympathetic witness, especially with inconsistent deposition testimony on key issues in the case. A plaintiff may claim he cannot do an activity about which you have videotaped evidence to the contrary. You can show it to him while he is on the witness stand and embarrass his credibility before the jury, hoping the impeachment influences the jury's decision on liability.

Discrediting Plaintiff's Experts and Maximizing Your Expert's Credibility

If you are looking to discredit the plaintiff's experts, it is important to keep in mind that most experts in a medical malpractice case will have a board certification specialty in a certain area, and many of the medical board specialty areas have published rules and ethical guidelines for providing expert testimony. For example, the American Board of Plastic and Reconstructive Surgery publishes ethical rules about being an expert in a malpractice case. In some instances, I have found that even though the experts on the other side are members of these boards, they do not follow their own boards' ethical rules and guidelines—and you can confront them about those inconsistencies during their depositions or trial. Establishing that type of inconsistency can have a devastating effect on an expert's credibility in a case. Therefore, it is important to check out the ethical rules and guidelines for providing expert testimony that many medical organizations have implemented over the last ten years and compare them to what the expert is doing.

Further, it is also important to check out the authoritative medical texts and literature on the topic at issue and use it to impeach the plaintiff's expert if his opinion or position is contrary to the medical literature. First, have the expert acknowledge that the literature you have is a recognized, authoritative, reliable source for medical information on the topic.

To position your expert as the most credible, it is often effective to recreate your client's real-life circumstances for the jury and show how your expert was in the defendant's position in the past. For example, let us say that you are representing a radiologist in a case that involves an undiagnosed fracture in a patient's leg. The patient continued to walk on that leg after it was X-rayed, and it became a displaced fracture that required surgery, plating, and therefore lasting disabling residual side effects. X-rays that were taken after the first scan or X-ray demonstrate that the fracture can be easily seen. In most cases, the plaintiff's lawyer will send all of the X-rays that were taken to their expert, who will examine all of them at the same time. However, that is not how a radiologist practices medicine. In defending the radiologist, I will let the jury see that we are presenting our case from the viewpoint of an expert who is standing in the shoes of the defendant, so he or she initially evaluated only the first X-ray, MRI, or CT scan that was taken. I do not want my expert to be prejudiced by having the advantage of looking at the end result—i.e., subsequent X-rays that show the fracture more clearly—because that is not how radiologists actually practice medicine and was not the situation my client was in at the time of the alleged malpractice.

Future Developments in Medical Malpractice Litigation

The conversion of the medical system to electronic medical recordkeeping will cause more errors and lead to more cases we would not ordinarily see. For example, the people who input data into electronic medical systems can make mistakes; "0.5 mg." might become "5.0 mg.," and as a result, the patient received too much medication. Those types of errors will lead to more lawsuits, and such errors will become more apparent as a result of the inevitable learning curve of adapting to electronic medical recordkeeping.

It is also likely that there will be more cases involving a failure to diagnose and treat a condition in time because the recordkeeping under an electronic medical record system is not, in most cases, set up to be as detailed or explanatory as it can be with written records. So when patients see multiple specialists, some information can be missed or omitted. Some systems are set up in the form of a template, where the doctor simply clicks in or checks the standard language in relation to a physical exam and does not have to add much, if anything, to what is pre-printed on the template. An example would be a template that has preprogrammed that the head, heart, ears, respiratory, musculoskeletal, and neurological systems are all normal on exam. Basically, it would be up to the doctor to add any details to the record, and there is a risk that she will not do so because of the time pressures of seeing and charting patient visits in compressed schedules of ten or fifteen minutes for each patient.

Looking ahead, it is also likely that we will see some instances of tort reform in the opposite direction. For example, in states such as California and others, the caps on damages may be increased or adjusted, largely because they will be found to be out-of-date with respect to inflation.

Avoiding Malpractice Claims

Doctors can take several important steps to avoid malpractice claims. Bad outcomes and mistakes will happen; therefore, physicians need to learn how to apologize to patients soon after they are aware of an adverse event, error, or mistake—but do so in a way that does not admit fault. The doctor should not say, "It's my fault; I made a mistake"; rather, he should be compassionate and empathetic and tell the patient he knows that what she is going through must be difficult. If he talks to his patient about what happened, the patient is more likely to trust him, and that will reduce the risk of litigation.

At the same time, the doctor should keep records of all communications and follow-up with the patient wherein these "apologies" without admitting fault are discussed with the patient. There always is the risk the patient will misunderstand or misinterpret. Sometimes a follow-up letter to the patient or family confirming the discussion is a good idea.

Essentially, a doctor needs to take the extra steps he would not otherwise take to show compassion to this patient; as a result, the patient may be less likely to file a lawsuit because she will come to realize that mistakes can happen in the medical field. Simply put, the doctor needs to be upfront and honest with the patient as soon as something goes wrong.

Such strategies work; we have been seeing fewer malpractice lawsuits in instances where doctors apologize in proper ways that do not wind up being admissions that can be used in court to show fault. In addition, it is important to document only those assumptions and presumptions concerning the problems that led to the mistake or error. For instance, if a surgical patient inadvertently was given epinephrine instead of ephedrine because none was available on the medication cart to the anesthesiologist at the time, and it had to be obtained from the hospital pharmacy, which sent the epinephrine instead of the ephedrine, and the circulating nurse did not check the label before administration, the charting should just include the simple facts: "patient inadvertently administered epinephrine instead of ephedrine"—not the whole story of how that mistake came about.

Conclusion

Although future regulations in the form of tort reform may diminish the number of future medical malpractice lawsuits, such claims will continue to be filed against physicians, hospitals, and other health care professionals. Much of our society seems to expect perfection of care, which cannot humanly be provided consistently. Handling the defense of these lawsuits can be as complex as the medicine involved in the patient's care. Yet, basic strategies and practice pointers can provide a simplified framework within which to evaluate and perhaps well defend the claims that should be defended at trial.

As the medical field continues to advance in the technology and equipment it employs, new types of claims will emerge. The challenge for defense lawyers will be to keep up with knowledge of the medical advancements and to adapt the basic framework for defense of the cases to the new types of errors and mistakes that cause poor patient outcomes. A good defense lawyer will know the laws that pertain to the medical malpractice field in general, but also the laws that pertain to those specialized areas of medical practice, including applicable state statutory immunities. A good defense lawyer will know the medicine involved in the case, as well as the strengths and weaknesses of his client's abilities in the litigations arena, and use experts and other resources to best evaluate and defend the cases. Knowing your opponent's case better than or at least as well as your defense will best prepare you and your client for battle should it need to be waged. The client often will be the source for the armor that will see you successfully through the battle, but know your client as well as you know the case.

Key Takeaways

- Learn the facts of the case. Listen to your client's version of what happened, and learn what the other side is contending so that you can figure out how to best defend against those claims.
- Enlist the services of an expert in the area of medicine you are dealing with and have the expert look at the records and information you have available to see whether your client has support for his case. Determine whether you have a case that is good enough to defend or one that needs to be settled because you do not have enough support for your client's actions.
- Assess whether your client is capable—emotionally and intellectually—of presenting herself in a good light in front of a jury and has the ability to go through a trial. If you feel she cannot do so, but you know you need to defend her because she did not do anything wrong, hire consultants who specialize in helping physicians become better witnesses.
- Choose an expert who can communicate effectively and get his points across in a way that a jury can understand and believe in. Key considerations include whether the expert is a well-established, published, and authoritative person in his field and whether he will make a good impression as a witness.
- Compile a good databank of experts who have testified in various specialty areas in the past for both plaintiffs and defendants. However, the most important resource in this area is your own experience and knowledge and that of your partners who have been through these types of cases before.

Related Resources

- *Can Wang v. Shristianne Heck MD* (2012) DJDAR 2131. (*See* Appendix F)
- *Kaiser Foundation Health Plan Inc. v. The Superior Court of Los Angeles County* (2012) DJDAR 2093. (*See* Appendix G)

Robert W. Frank, senior trial lawyer, joined Neil Dymott Frank McFall and Trexler APC in 1980. He has been a shareholder in the law firm since 1988. Mr. Frank specializes in civil litigation defense trial work and administrative licensing hearings for various types of health care professionals, with an emphasis on medical, dental, chiropractic, and nursing specialties. He also handles a variety of other general civil litigation matters and administrative licensing matters, as well as medical staff privilege issues.

Since joining Neil Dymott, Mr. Frank has tried more than sixty cases to jury verdict in state and federal courts and has handled more than 100 health care professional licensing matters, including numerous successful trials and appeals of those cases. He has served as a board member, president, and vice president of the San Diego Defense Lawyers from 1993 to 1997 and is an elected member of the American Board of Trial Advocates. Mr. Frank is a past director of the San Diego County Barristers Club and faculty member of the San Diego Inn of Court College of Trial Advocacy.

Mr. Frank was named one of San Diego's Top Attorneys in Insurance Law by the San Diego Daily Transcript *in 2006 and has been selected one of San Diego's Super Lawyers by the publishers of* Law and Politics Magazine *since 2007, and in 2008, one of San Diego's "Top 50" Super Lawyers. Since 2009, he has been named by his peers as one of San Diego's Top Lawyers in* San Diego Magazine *and since 2008 by his peers for a listing in* Best Lawyers of America for Professional Malpractice Law.

The San Diego Superior Court has appointed Mr. Frank an arbitrator in civil cases, and he has served as a private mediator and arbitrator in other civil cases. Aside from practicing law, he is an avid surfer and enjoys golf and spending time with his children and friends.

Mr. Frank earned his JD at the University of California Hastings College of Law. He graduated from San Diego State University, Phi Beta Kappa, with a BA in liberal studies.

Defending Health Care Providers in an Era of Changing Technology and E-Charting

Troy S. Bundy

Partner

Hart Wagner LLP

ASPATORE

Introduction

Technology has changed the face of medical care today. That change, like any other, has brought with it a vast array of both benefits and costs, which surface in litigation without exception. The experienced litigator must be both wary and aware of these developments, along with the implications they raise. What was once almost inconceivable is now commonplace. Physicians and lawyers alike must learn to anticipate and utilize technology to the best of their ability to stay ahead of the curve, communicate effectively, and build a solid foundation for the case.

Trends in the Medical Malpractice Arena

The primary trend in medical malpractice today points toward technology and errors in practices, such as e-charting. Technology has also increased the speed at which information is available, raising standards for providers. Since the mid-1990s, large institutional clients have traded in handwritten chart notes for forms that can be filled out with the click of a button. This removes the subjectivity, interaction, and thought from this process. In addition, some institutions use multiple e-chart programs that do not interface well with each other.

The e-traffic of information and how people actually record it has also evolved in recent years. This can cause problems, for example, for a primary care provider who orders a CT scan of a patient and no longer receives a hard copy of the report, but instead receives an e-mail after the report has been dictated and transcribed. If the provider does not get the e-mail, it can wreak havoc in the general practice. Patients today can e-mail their doctors, as well, and have certain expectations regarding how fast the doctor should respond. Doctors may find it easy to approve or change a prescription over e-mail without seeing the patient. Some may even diagnose a condition in this manner. Obviously, this leaves room for error and subsequent lawsuits.

As time goes on, cases are more likely to involve technological failure instead of traditional medical negligence. Nevertheless, an omission or lack of information in a medical chart points to a failure in the system and leads to the assumption the doctor did not take certain steps in the patient's care because the doctor did not chart it. Many recent lawsuits have not proved meritorious because the doctor explained the issue in a deposition or at trial, but these are always problems that the old, handwritten charts documented. Overall, people expect technology to improve medical care, but that technology comes at a cost.

Effects of Health Care Reform

In Oregon, tort reform has had little impact on medical malpractice. In 1987, ORS 31.710 (formerly ORS 18.560) declared a cap of $500,000 for non-economic damages. However, the Oregon Supreme Court found it unconstitutional, as per Oregon's Constitution, as it deprived citizens of the right to a trial with a jury of peers determining the damages amounts. *Lankin v Senco Products Inc.*, 329 Or. 62 (1999). Now, only statutorily created rights, like wrongful death claims, provide cap limitations for malpractice suits. Ultimately, health care reform has not been effective in limiting malpractice claims in the Pacific Northwest.

Other states, like California and Texas, have achieved far more with tort reform. They have utilized a combination of abbreviated statutory limitations periods and damages caps to curtail lawsuits. Hawaii's Claims Conciliation Panels and a noneconomic damages limit of $375,000, on the other hand, has not proved an effective deterrent, to my knowledge.

Evolving Types of Medical Malpractice Lawsuits

The more "common types" of medical malpractice lawsuits seem to evolve over the years. At one time, fetal injury cases involving shoulder dystocia were common, then colon cancer. Later, came a wave of cases involving uterine rupture in women who attempted vaginal births after cesarean sections. In the past few years, however, the emerging trend has been for malpractice cases to involve laparoscopic and other minimally invasive surgeries. Cholecystectomy (gallbladder removal) cases are increasing, likely because of the incorrectly perceived limitations of laparoscopic surgery.

Although people have certainly perfected the technique, the fact remains that to the layperson, the surgeon looks through a pinhole camera when performing the procedure. Plaintiffs' counsel inevitably argues this increases the potential for complications. Patients also have high expectations for laparoscopic procedures, and patients and insurance companies are both demanding less time in the hospital. Laparoscopic procedures generally enable people to be discharged earlier, with a small incision and less postoperative pain. While they help keep costs down, as laparoscopic procedures gain popularity, the incidence of complications seemingly rises. The most common complication involves peritonitis caused by a bowel, ductal, or liver injury.

Gynecological surgery is another common source of lawsuits. This can be, again, due to laparoscopic or minimally invasive surgeries. There are also gynecological products that are fairly new to the market, as far as "new" products go. There has been a rash of cases involving vaginal mesh for the treatment of bladder and vaginal prolapse. The benefit of the newest method utilized in vaginal mesh procedures is that it is minimally invasive. The downside is that the surgeon does not use a scope and cannot otherwise visualize the procedure. In the most basic terms, an instrument is passed through the patient's pelvis, inserting the mesh, and pulling it taut. Entry points are varied, but in most cases, palpation is utilized in locating and stationing the mesh product. This can be hazardous, through no fault of the surgeon.

The problem we see is that sometimes these minimally invasive surgeries turn out to be maximally invasive surgeries in the end. Complications arise, and the patient immediately turns to blame the surgeon, claiming that the procedure and its complications should have been better explained, researched, performed, etc. Traditionalists easily jump on the bandwagon as they near retirement and are quick to discredit the "new-fangled approach." In other words, there is no short supply of critics.

State and Federal Protections for Health Care Providers

Not many state and federal laws protect doctors from frivolous lawsuits, and there is no consensus on the few laws in place. Washington used to require someone filing a claim for medical malpractice to file also a "certificate of merit"—a signed statement asserting that a qualified medical professional reviewed the records and believed a standard of care violation caused injury and damage. RCW 7.70.150. The Washington Supreme Court, in *Putman v. Wenatchee Valley Medical Center*, 216 P.3d 374 (Wash. 2009) decided that this requirement was unconstitutional, leaving defense attorneys to challenge claims based on the limitations accorded under summary judgment procedures and established case law.

The procedural rules in Oregon also allow any party to file a motion for summary judgment, but there is no true remedy that absolutely prevents frivolous lawsuits from being filed. When we identify such a claim, we frequently file a summary judgment motion, challenging plaintiff's counsel to come forward and confirm they have qualified support for the allegations in the claim. By either filing an affidavit from my client that confirms he met the standard of care and did not cause damage or injury, or by simply challenging the issue on prima facie grounds, I force the plaintiff's attorney to provide an affidavit attesting to the fact that the plaintiff has retained an expert who disagrees and will support the claim against the health care provider. This creates a "question of fact" that can be decided only by a jury.

In reality, the barrier the plaintiff's attorney must pass in preparing the affidavit to combat the motion is low. It is arguably possible, for example, for the plaintiff to hire a nurse with no knowledge of neurosurgery to review the care of a neurosurgeon. As long as the nurse has the medical opinion that there might be evidence of malpractice, the lawsuit can be filed. We frequently, however, disagree about whether such an affidavit is sufficient to satisfy a summary judgment standard.

Hawaii's system in ferreting out meritless claims is purely perfunctory. However, a party must go through the process and have an appointed Medical Claims Conciliation Panel review the complaint, evidence, and allegations before the patient can officially file the lawsuit in state court. It is recommended that the advisory panel agree the claim is meritorious before the plaintiff files it, but in reality, the panel's opinion is advisory and is largely ignored. This means the defense counsel, viewing the process as a waste of time, has no incentive to present the defense case to the panel. HAW. REV. STAT. 671-12 and 671.16.5 (1995).

These are all merely examples of how differing states lack laws that protect doctors and other health care providers from frivolous lawsuits. Plaintiffs with ridiculous allegations put them into complaints and sue the provider, engaging in extended motion practice. Occasionally, these cases can be eliminated relatively quickly—in six months or less—but realistically, there is not much protection from frivolous lawsuits. Additionally, judges do not have the authority to decide which suits are "frivolous," per se, as our Constitution gives juries that sole discretion.

Recent Cases Affecting Medical Malpractice

In Oregon, *Klutschkowski v. Oregon Medical Group*, 263 P.3d 1130 (Or. App. 2011) was decided. This was a case my partner and I tried to a jury in Lane County, Oregon. The plaintiff prevailed; however, there were several issues of law in that case that went up on appeal. In the summer of 2011, the Oregon Court of Appeals decided the case in our favor, holding that birth injury claims are generally subject to Oregon's noneconomic damages tort cap of $500,000.

In that case, Oregon Medical Group and its affiliated obstetricians and gynecologists (OB/GYNs) provided prenatal and delivery care to Mrs. Klutschkowski and her child, who had allegedly experienced a shoulder dystocia during the birthing process. Shoulder dystocia, which is when the infant's shoulder gets stuck against the mother's pubic bone, has been associated with injury to the brachial plexus and can leave the child with lifelong nerve injury.

Oregon's $500,000 non-economic damages cap in all torts had at that point been lifted. As discussed earlier, the Oregon Supreme Court had decided that it could apply only to cases created by statute, not those that existed at common law, prior to the adoption of the state constitution in 1857. After receiving the verdict, we argued that children, at common law, did not have the right to sue their obstetricians for injuries that occurred during the birthing process. Therefore, given the state of Oregon's case law, non-economic damages must be limited to $500,000.

The trial court disagreed, but the court of appeals ruled that the cause of action did not exist at common law and imposed a cap of $500,000 for birth injury claims in Oregon. The implications of this are far-reaching; birth injury claims undoubtedly present the most significant exposure and have resulted in massive jury verdict awards. Non-economic damages can reach tens of millions of dollars. In fact, in another recent Michigan case, the jury awarded $130 million for shoulder dystocia birth injury. In New York, a similar $56 million jury verdict was obtained. Limiting birth injury cases to economic damages plus $500,000 will have a significant impact on the insurability of doctors. It remains to be seen if the Oregon Supreme Court will agree that there should be a cap in birth injury cases, and if it does, whether the state legislature will attempt to change the law so that the cap does not apply. But the landscape of birth injury cases has been significantly altered in Oregon, at least for now.

Texas and California have both implemented similar tort reform to a certain degree. Texas caps non-economic damages in torts at $250,000 and is a notoriously difficult state in which to sue a doctor for malpractice.

Effective Strategies for Mounting a Medical Malpractice Defense

The most important step in mounting an effective medical malpractice defense is to review the medical records and gain an understanding of the medicine involved. Plaintiffs' attorneys are usually at a significant disadvantage because of capital limitations—they simply cannot afford to learn the medicine as well as defense attorneys can. A defense lawyer representing the medical community has access to free information from the client and may also utilize experts to learn the medicine. The defense attorney has a personal tutor in the form of the client, someone with a medical degree who can sit down for hours and walk the attorney through each step of the medical procedure or analysis.

When I take on a case, I first rely on my client to help me understand the pertinent issues, and then seek out additional help from other specialists. For instance, I may meet with a pulmonologist, a cardiologist, an internist, a radiologist, an emergency medicine physician, a vascular surgeon, and a general surgeon to learn about pulmonary embolism and deep vein thrombosis, when and why they occur, and the associated symptoms. I have a significant advantage in the case, as the plaintiff's attorney has talked to one or perhaps two people, and they may not be good-quality experts. They also may not have all the facts or records they need to provide a reliable opinion.

Before even meeting with a client, it is beneficial to review any available medical literature on the pertinent topic. This allows the attorney to ask the client appropriate questions and direct the focus of the case and the interview. If the case involves shoulder dystocia, for example, it is helpful to pull out the leading articles on shoulder dystocia from the American College of Obstetricians and Gynecologists, hire the person or people who wrote the article, talk with them about the article and shoulder dystocia, and learn everything they can teach about the subject and the case.

Different people have different ways of interacting with clients. However, I think we all must understand that, on many occasions, clients are nervous, upset, frightened, and perhaps even angry about having been sued. On occasion, this anxiety will be encountered by a new lawyer speaking with a client for the first time.

It is important for the attorney to introduce himself, explain his role in the case, discuss the hierarchy of individuals working on the matter, and provide as much reassurance to the client as he can before discussing and jumping into the facts of the case. Many clients know the process and will simply want to jump into the facts before introductions are made. It is more helpful to slow down the process, take it step by step, and begin with a short introduction.

Additionally, the initial client meeting is just as much about the process as it is about what the client has to say to the lawyer. The key to constructive and friendly client interaction is to simply let the client know that she is well-represented, that we are there to take the stress and burdens of litigation off her shoulders as much as possible, and that everything will be all right. Most often, clients will leave the initial conference feeling much better than they did at the beginning. Often, they are relieved simply to know someone is taking care of things for them, and they do not have to worry about deadlines or future planning issues, scheduling vacations, etc.

Clients are often interested about their obligations during the course of the litigation. This is generally handled in the introduction, but can be handled later. It is often helpful to inform them that the attorney is working with a team of individuals whose goal it is to make the process as smooth and stress-free as possible. They may receive a telephone call from a paralegal, the lawyer, a partner, or a legal assistant in an effort to schedule meetings or obtain discovery. They should be informed that there is always a way for the attorney to be reached through one or more of the individuals who are working on the case, and that all are available to them any time and for any reason.

Finally, I provide the client with a business card. It may also be helpful to include the name of any involved legal assistant and/or paralegal on the back of the card, as well.

Depositions

Eventually, it will be necessary to take and defend depositions in the case. When taking a deposition, preparing a lengthy, detailed outline of all of the questions to be asked an opposing party or witness during a deposition presents many problems. Unless the attorney is highly organized, it is easy to lose one's place, and it encourages the defense lawyer to simply move on to the next question, rather than to listen to the answer given to the last question.

In my opinion, this creates a number of problems for the lawyer taking a deposition. First, a laundry list of questions interrupts the flow of a deposition. It is always my intention to get the witness comfortable and speaking *with* me, rather than *to* me. If I am reading a laundry list of questions, often, I will not listen to the answer in detail. By engaging a witness in conversation, you are more likely to get the most out of your deposition. I follow up on issues mentioned in passing by the deponent. I often let the deposition and/or topic go its own way. It can be useful to create a flow to the deposition. Write down key words or phrases, so you can go back to any issues you wish to cover in more detail.

On the other hand, depending on the deponent, it might also be helpful to achieve just the opposite. Jumping from topic to topic in a way that seemingly makes no sense can keep the witness on edge, creating additional opportunities where they might volunteer useful information. Nevertheless, this is equally achievable with a bare-bones outline of issues to be covered, rather than a detailed list of all your carefully drafted questions set out in a lengthy, typed document. When I see this happening, I immediately conclude I am dealing with an amateur.

Keep in mind, everything that occurs in a deposition should be part of the lawyer's strategy. What that strategy is will vary from time to time and from person to person. Most of the time, more information will be gleaned when the lawyer is courteous, kind, and respectful to the witness. There are some rare occasions where more information will be gleaned with a direct frontal attack. Those situations are generally few and far between, however.

Every young trial lawyer should begin his or her career reviewing and summarizing depositions. This is a helpful and effective way to learn how to take and/or defend depositions. While reviewing depositions, take advantage of the opportunity by evaluating the various attorneys' strategies. What worked? What did not work? Why were certain questions asked, and why were some obvious questions not asked? What questions would you have asked? All of these things come together in preparing a new lawyer to take depositions.

Many of you reading this may have already taken dozens of depositions. Even so, the *practice* of law is exactly that. The learning process, literally, never ends. You should have a strategy planned before walking into the deposition. What key information do you seek? Are there admissions to be revealed in an effort to support your statute of limitations motion? Is there more discovery to be uncovered? Who are the eyewitnesses who might testify against your client? All of these things and more should be considered when approaching your deposition.

The learning process is not limited to lawyers you work with, but also those you work against. If something seems effective, it does not matter where the idea came from—use it. Make it yours. But, beware: some techniques simply will not fit with your style, no matter how effective they were for someone else. It is essential that the new lawyer develop his or her own style and be completely comfortable with it when engaging in active advocacy.

Although what I say and how I prepare my clients for deposition are my own trade secret, what I will share is that I generally assume my strategy is my opponent's strategy. I assume their deposition would be just as good, if not better, than any deposition I would take. Good lawyers are, indeed, like sharks. We naturally feel driven to feed off information, dissecting each morsel until there is nothing left for us to eat. The longer the response to my last question, the more I will feed off the information contained in the last answer. In a nutshell, the client should be encouraged to be brief. Let the attorney defend the case later at trial; it is not the client's obligation to defend himself or herself at the deposition. Obviously, different states will have different discovery rules. The extent of information shared by the client at deposition should be discussed and agreed on beforehand.

The Differences Between Defending Institutions and Defending Doctors

Defense strategies differ for doctors as opposed to health care institutions or health industry companies in various ways. Claims against hospitals are usually agency claims in which a plaintiff attempts to sue a hospital for the conduct of its staff, such as nurses or technicians. I structure those cases in the same way as I do when defending a physician.

Hospital claims can also take the form of institutional claims, which relate to technology and system failures. These cases can be complex because everyone involved is still learning how the technology works, and as a result there are not many credible experts on the subject. Most of the institutional claims I have worked on have collapsed, as plaintiffs find them burdensome and difficult to prove. My largest institutional clients are generally considered the "standard of care," with few other corporations as integrated and tied into a computer database.

A plaintiff's claim that an institutional organization failed to meet the standard of care is difficult to prove. Not many institutional organizations exist; the few that do are setting the standards, and no one in those organizations will say they do things in the best or most reasonable way. I handle these claims differently, getting more involved with the technology aspect of the way the institution runs and the way the different departments and pharmacies communicate. I hire an engineer or a technician to teach me the engineering behind the technology. Institutional claims are generally prone to fail absent clear evidence that there was negligence of some kind.

Using Experts and Technology

I have finely developed my use of experts over the years. Obviously, experts are an indispensable part of any case. In fact, winning or losing a case depends largely on how good the expert is. As I came to realize this, I began putting more emphasis on my experts than I had in the past. Experts also assist in bringing more technological exhibits into evidence by walking the jury through a visual presentation of a procedure or situation. With the advent and availability of technology to create movies or three-dimensional animation, an attorney can provide the jury with something interesting to look at, and experts are a tremendous help in explaining these visual aids.

The idea is to captivate the jury with the visual aids, as even the best expert testimony can seem boring to jury members, causing them to lose their interest and their focus and forget everything the expert says. The focus should be on the music, and not the conductor.

Helping Doctors Avoid Claims

Before a case actually becomes a case, a lawyer must review the medical records and determine whether the patient has a meritorious claim. So proper charting is immensely important in helping medical providers avoid medical malpractice claims.

When I counsel doctors and nurses, charting is always a topic of conversation. Nurses are generally better at charting because they are in constant contact with patients, especially in a hospital setting. In the past, before e-charting, they were able to record what they saw and what the patient said, painting a beautiful picture of what was truly happening to the patient. Checking off a box to show the patient has dry skin makes the charts difficult to read and even more difficult to present to a jury.

Generally, the more detail a doctor can use when charting, the better off the doctor will be at trial. There are times the doctor may write too much or use the wrong word, but a well-documented claim is always easier to defend. Inevitably, lawsuits occur years after the alleged malpractice, when the doctor does not even remember the situation. What would you remember better: a computerized form involving pull-down options and checkboxes, or a key quote from the patient and a detailed description the doctor added to the record? The answer is obvious, and the doctor being able to remember the situation can potentially dissuade a plaintiff's lawyer from moving forward with the lawsuit.

Surgeons should also get into the habit of writing and dictating operative notes on the day they perform the surgery. I have handled numerous cases where the surgeon wrote the notes two or more weeks after the surgery, allowing the plaintiff to use the argument the notes are not reliable. Unfortunately, surgeons have a tendency to think routine surgeries are all largely similar, and while they may be sure they took certain steps and achieved certain results, without proper charting, a defense attorney cannot prove anything. We are left to argue that it probably did or did not occur based on standard practice and routine.

Doctors should also avoid "disappearing" in the face of a bad outcome. It is nearly impossible for a doctor to avoid a lawsuit if that doctor signs off on a patient who will likely have complications or a bad outcome, or if the doctor is unable to face the patient's family with bad news. People immediately assume that the doctor exhibits that behavior because of a mistake the doctor made, but frequently bad outcomes occur without any malpractice on the part of the doctor.

Likewise, care providers must avoid openly criticizing themselves and other health care providers. Insinuating to a patient that a surgeon is anything less than stellar may lead the patient to think that a lawsuit will be successful and that the patient has the criticizing doctors' support. Meanwhile, the criticizing doctor may not be aware of all the facts involved in the case. Unfortunately, several medical professionals frequently come up in the cases I defend who criticize other doctors, mainly because of their own egos. Many of the cases they helped spur on ended up being meritless and might have been avoided if they had given their colleagues the benefit of the doubt.

Finally, when health care providers do make mistakes, they should avoid the tendency to blame others in an attempt to defuse the situation. Implicating other doctors inevitably backfires horribly. When I represent a doctor who has been wrongfully accused by another doctor, I might end up filing a third-party complaint to involve that other doctor in the lawsuit. Essentially, these doctors do not escape punishment, but instead cause trouble where it does not need to exist.

Top Challenges in Defending against Medical Malpractice Claims

The top challenges in defending against medical malpractice claims often revolve around judging the client's weaknesses and strengths. When I evaluate a case, much of the defensibility pertains to how the client feels about the care in question, how interested the client is in the case, and how the client will present to a jury. There is nothing worse than an overly confident client who scoffs at the prosecution or creates drama during a trial. I advise my clients before trial to avoid wearing expensive watches and $3,000 suits, to be respectful of everyone's opinion, and not to show any significant emotion. Conversely, weak clients who do not speak up and are not sure of themselves are equally as bad for the defense, as the jury tends to distrust them.

Sympathetic plaintiffs are a similarly difficult challenge to overcome. Frequently, my clients will come to me feeling bad about what happened to an elderly patient or a child. A baby with severe cerebral palsy who will remain a child until contracting pneumonia and suffocating at the age of twenty-six will inevitably make a case harder to defend. Having a sympathetic plaintiff requires the defense attorney to engage the jury's focus on the medicine. It can be difficult to provide the perspective that even though the child is severely handicapped, the situation could have been much worse. It is difficult to maintain the balance between following the instinct as an advocate to protect and defend the client and pushing the argument far enough that the defense appears to be monsters attacking a sympathetic plaintiff.

More specifically, however, the most difficult case to win is a radiology case. These cases involve substantial challenges, since radiologists are the only people in the world who know what it is like to be a radiologist. They spend much of their time in the dark reading hundreds of films in black and white. I have represented multiple radiologists in cases where physicians directed their attention to a specific part of the patient's body, and the radiologists incidentally found a fracture or a tumor elsewhere. Additionally, in the case of missed diagnoses, the plaintiff's attorney will present a normal film and the one image out of one hundred that shows a tumor, and it is difficult for a lay person or the jury to understand that looking at two different pictures with the benefit of hindsight is far different from the radiologist's reality.

Radiologists have the difficult job of looking through numerous images, day after day and hour after hour. They cannot be expected to notice every detail in every image and report everything they see. Things are much easier to see in hindsight, and inevitably a radiologist will mistakenly admit to a violation of the standard of care because he can see what the plaintiff's attorney points out after the fact. I have defended many of these radiologists who I did not think violated the standard of care; yet the practical issues associated with defending such a case in front of a lay jury were too difficult to overcome. People want things to be simple. They do not want to look at reality. Sometimes, it is my job to force them in that direction.

Conclusion

E-charting and health care providers' implementation of technology are sure to be major issues in medical malpractice in the next year and likely for the next decade or two. As the technology continues to evolve, problems will continue to occur, and this will continue to spur challenging malpractice cases. From advancements in surgical techniques to developing minimally invasive approaches, only time can dictate which direction defending medical cases will lead.

Over the coming years, we can expect to see more advances. I would anticipate that e-tablets will eventually come into play as the industry recognizes that the "Computer will see you now" approach to charting is deficient and costly. More personal charting simply must come back into the fray somehow. Personal locators, trackers, and perhaps even video monitoring will become commonplace. E-communicators will take the place of pagers, and informed consent discussions will inevitably involve more active patient participation by way of computer programs or video interaction.

Each of these advances will open further discovery opportunities for both sides. As a result, litigation costs will probably increase as more personnel are identified as "involved providers." Already, computer record audit trail requests are standard. These records document who reviewed what part of a patient's chart, when they did it, and how long the page was displayed. Depositions are becoming more intensive, and memories are being pushed as these documents become exhibits at trial.

Cases involving "treatment by e-mail" will likely become more frequent as providers become inundated with "e-requests" from patients wanting "e-advice" to save a co-pay. Providers will begin spending less and less face-time with patients as they deal out advice without seeing the patient, and new standards of care will begin to take shape. Today's greatest and newest thing will become tomorrow's lawsuit as patients demand faster information and quicker responses from health care providers they would rather avoid seeing in person.

Inevitably, however, improvements in technology are more helpful than hurtful. As a defense attorney, I see my role as more detective than biased advocate. I am a far better advocate when I understand all the facts. Being able to re-create an event or chain of events as accurately as possible triggers memories and fortifies my theories. Technology helps me do this. When I know the truth and can prove it, I am a far more formidable opponent than the lawyer who chooses to avoid the tough questions and bury his head in the sand, hoping opposing counsel will not catch on.

It has been my experience that, most of the time, health care providers do their best. They exercise well-thought-out professional judgment, given the facts as they exist. There are mistakes made from time to time, but, more often than not, the care is defensible. More often than not, the better I am able to explain the case, the better the jury will understand it. Information gleaned through medical technology allows me to fill in even more of those missing puzzle pieces that seem to get lost in time until I can dig them out and dust them off. Frankly, I would much rather be aware of a bad fact and either settle the case or be able to explain it, than to have no knowledge of it or understanding of how it works into the "story" behind the litigation.

Key Takeaways

- When mounting an effective medical malpractice defense, review the medical records to learn the medicine involved better than the opponent does. Plaintiffs' attorneys are usually at a significant disadvantage because of capital limitations—they simply cannot afford to learn the medicine as well as defense attorneys can—so take advantage of that by obtaining a free education from the client.
- Handle institutional claims, which relate to technology and system failures, differently than you handle those involving doctors. Get more involved with the technology aspect of the way the institution runs and the way the different departments and pharmacies communicate. Hire an engineer or a technician to teach you the engineering behind the technology. Most institutional claims will collapse, as plaintiffs find them burdensome, of low economic value, and difficult to prove.
- Use experts to assist in bringing more technological exhibits into evidence by walking the jury through a visual presentation of a procedure. Provide the jury with something interesting to look at, and let the expert explain the visual aids.

- When counseling doctors and nurses, emphasize the importance of proper charting. In the past, before e-charting, they were better able to record what they saw and what the patient said, painting a beautiful picture of what was truly happening to the patient. Checking off a box to document a patient's status makes the charts difficult to read and more difficult to present to a jury. It is also easier to dissuade a plaintiff's lawyer from moving forward with the lawsuit if the situation is well documented.
- Advise health care providers of the harm involved with disappearing in the face of a bad outcome. It is nearly impossible for a provider to avoid a lawsuit if that doctor signs off on a patient who will likely have complications or a bad outcome, or if the doctor is unable to face the patient's family with bad news. Likewise, providers must avoid openly criticizing themselves and other health care providers and, when they make mistakes, should avoid the tendency to blame others in an attempt to defuse the situation.

Related Resources

State Court Cases

- *Lankin v. Senco Products Inc.*, 329 Or 62 (1999)
- *Putman v. Wenatchee Valley Medical Center*, 216 P3d 374 (WA 2009)
- *Klutschkowski v. Oregon Medical Group*, Oregon Court of Appeals, 160615518 A138722 (Sept. 2011)

Oregon Revised Statutes

- ORS 18.560 (1987) renumbered ORS 31.710
- Haw.Rev.Stat. 663-8.7 (1995)
- Haw.Rev.Stat. 671-12 (1995)
- Haw.Rev.Stat. 671.16.5 (1995)
- RCW 7.70.150

Troy S. Bundy has been defending hospitals, doctors, nurses, and other health professionals since he joined Hart Wagner LLP in 1996. From complex obstetric and neonatal matters to more routine primary care issues, he has litigated and tried a wide variety of professional liability cases involving nearly every conceivable medical specialty over the course of his career, including the landmark case, Klutschkowski v. OMG, in which the Oregon Court of Appeals enforced the statutory damage cap against birth injury claims.

A frequent speaker at professional liability seminars hosted by the Oregon Medical Association, Oregon Health Sciences University, and other professional organizations, Mr. Bundy was given the honor of being selected by his peers as one of the "Top Oregon Lawyers" since 2006 and one of the "Best Lawyers in America" for the last two years.

For many years, Mr. Bundy has also served on the Multnomah County Arbitration Panel and has presided over a wide variety of matters, including personal injury claims, debtor/creditor issues, and domestic relations disputes.

Mr. Bundy earned his JD at the Lewis and Clark College Northwestern School of Law and his BA at the University of Colorado.

Dedication: *To my partner in law, John E. Hart. I learned from the best. And, to my wife for always understanding what it means to be married to a trial lawyer.*

Understanding the Field of Medical Malpractice Defense

Frederick W. Bode III,

Richard J. Kabbert, and Kristen Hock Prex

Shareholders

Dickie McCamey & Chilcote PC

ASPATORE

Introduction

The landscape of a medical malpractice case continues to evolve, from the advances in medicine and technology to the changes in the law, all causing medical malpractice cases to become that much more complex. Computerized and electronic medical records play an ever increasing role and is an area that both the attorney and the health care provider must be aware exists, as well as the role such electronic data plays in litigation. This data can provide a window in time to the care being rendered and can be used as either a sword or a shield for the educated practitioner. In addition, the changes in the law now require expert review prior to commencing a malpractice suit, virtually eliminating thc frivolous suit and requiring immediate attention by an expert. Such changes require the practitioner to utilize all available resources in defending such a claim.

Discovery Trends in Medical Malpractice Cases

One recent trend in medical malpractice cases has been in discovery—specifically, continued requests to hospitals for the audit trails pertaining to a patient's chart. The plaintiffs' bar has made pursuing these audit trails a priority, regardless of whether the issue of missing, altered, or destroyed records is an issue in the case. Hospitals are required to maintain records of who accessed the medical records of a patient. Pursuant to 45 C.F.R. § 164, *et seq.*, any disclosures must be provided to the patient on the patient's request. However, disclosures not required to be provided include those regarding treatment, billing, or other purposes related to health care operations.[1] In other words, only unauthorized disclosures must be produced. However, the position of the plaintiffs' bar is that this regulation entitles it access to all disclosures, including those necessary for treatment or other purposes related to health care operations.

In addition, the plaintiffs' bar relies on 45 C.F.R. § 164.312 in support of its assertion that they are entitled to "an audit trail." The audit trail enables counsel for the patient to determine who accessed the chart, what they reviewed, and when. It thus provides a window into specific care being rendered at a focused time. This assertion is again without merit. There is

---

[1] 45 C.F.R. § 164.528.

nothing in this provision that provides that a patient is entitled to a copy of an "audit trail." The purposes of this regulation are clear: to "guard against unauthorized access," to "verify that a person or entity seeking access … is the one claimed," and to generally ensure that only those who are entitled to access the records are the ones who access them.[2]

Another argument by the plaintiffs' bar is that, pursuant to 42 U.S.C. § 17935(e), a health care provider or entity is required to provide "all electronic/computer information" regarding that patient. This argument is false and without merit. As an initial matter, subsection (e) of the statute specifically involves "electronic health records."[3] The term "electronic health record" is defined as "an electronic record of health-related information on an individual that is created, gathered, managed, and consulted by authorized health care clinicians and staff."[4] Accordingly, the statute relates solely to "health-related information" created by "health care clinicians and staff" and has nothing to do with audit trails, accountings, etc., as these other forms of documents relate solely to access and disclosure of a patient's chart and do not involve "electronic health records."

Based on the foregoing, any assertion that this statute somehow broadly grants discovery of all "electronic/computer information" is misplaced. Second, 42 U.S.C. § 17935(c)(1) makes clear, "[i]f the same protected health information that is the subject of a request for access is maintained in more than one designated record set or at more than one location, the covered entity need only produce the protected health information once in response to a request for access." If a defendant has already produced the medical records of a patient, then there would be no requirement to produce any audit trail, as any request for such information is duplicative, and the statute makes clear that a hospital need not provide additional access for this information.[5]

In addition to the above, because of the statutes mandating that plaintiff's counsel secure experts prior to commencing lawsuits,[6] and because of the cost associated with bringing a lawsuit, the number of medical malpractice

---

[2] 45 C.F.R. § 164.312.
[3] 42 U.S.C. § 17935(e).
[4] 42 U.S.C. § 17921(5).
[5] 42 U.S.C. § 17935(c)(1).
[6] 42 PA. CONS. STAT. ANN. § 1042.1, *et seq*.

filings has decreased, but the value and types of cases have increased. In general, the number of meritless lawsuits has significantly decreased.

Accordingly, in the year to come, we will advise our clients that while the number of malpractice cases will be expected to decrease because of the requirements mandated by these reforms, the cases that are filed will likely be more difficult from a liability and damage standpoint insofar as only cases with true merit will survive this statute-imposed gauntlet. Indeed, while the new rules have in fact limited the frivolous lawsuit, we have seen a rise in cases that are more difficult to defend because there have already been expert review and comment from the plaintiff's side, thus increasing the relative merit of cases being filed.

Types and Target of Recent Medical Malpractice Lawsuits

Among the most frequent types of medical malpractice lawsuits we have seen over the past few years are cerebral palsy baby cases; Fleet enema cases, where physicians are joined to keep the product defendants out of multi-district litigation; cauda equina syndrome cases; and misdiagnosis of cancer cases. The underlying theme of these cases is large damages and significant jury sympathy generated therefrom. The sympathy flows from the human condition, which acknowledges that children saddled with medical issues have a difficult journey through life. The result is large jury awards to attempt in part to soften the blow caused by the medical condition.

The types of doctors generally sued are obstetricians; gynecologists; surgeons, including breast cancer and vascular surgeons; and anesthesiologists. These physicians perform high-risk/high-reward procedures with no guarantees of success or outcome, so generally, when there are complications, the complications are such that counsel for the patient is able to obtain a favorable review (one critical of the physician) to file a lawsuit.

State and Federal Laws Protecting Doctors from Frivolous Lawsuits

The most significant Pennsylvania state law that protects health care providers from frivolous lawsuits is the rule requiring that a Certificate of Merit be filed within sixty days of the filing of the complaint.[7] According to

[7] 42 PA. CONS. STAT. ANN. § 1042.3.

this rule, in any action that alleges a licensed professional deviated from an acceptable professional standard, the party causing such a filing must, within sixty days of filing the complaint, provide a certificate that an "appropriate licensed professional has supplied a written statement that there exists a reasonable probability that the care, skill or knowledge exercised … fell outside the acceptable professional standards and that such conduct was a cause in bringing about the harm."[8] In the alternative, a certificate can be filed that avers that "other licensed professionals for which this defendant is responsible deviated from an acceptable professional standard" or that expert testimony is unnecessary for the claims made.[9] This rule went into effect in January 2003. Since that time, the number of medical malpractice case filings has been reduced by more than 40 percent.[10]

In addition to the above, Pennsylvania enjoys a statute titled the Dragonetti Act.[11] Specifically, if a physician is sued and prevails, he can countersue the plaintiff for bringing a spurious lawsuit. Generally, these suits have not been widely employed and do not tend to limit the number of malpractice cases. This occurs because the facts needed to prevail against the lawyer who represented the plaintiff in the underlying suit are difficult to establish and require more time and energy from the physician than he or she is usually willing to provide. Moreover, the defendant lawyer now has the fallback position that he or she secured the opinion of a physician before the lawsuit was commenced against the doctor or hospital.

In addition to the above, physicians can also bring an action against experts who provide bogus testimony against them. While this will not assist in the case in which the doctor has been sued, it nevertheless limits the expert's ability to testify in future matters.

Mounting an Effective Medical Malpractice Defense: Key Steps

The first step in mounting an effective medical malpractice defense is to know the medicine that is involved in the case. This can be done by relying on your staff, and if the firm has them, either physicians or legal nurse

---

[8] 42 PA. CONS. STAT. ANN. § 1042.3(a)(1).
[9] 42 PA. CONS. STAT. ANN. § 1042.3(a)(2)(3).
[10] Data compiled by the Administrative Office of Pennsylvania Courts reflecting case filings through 2010.
[11] 42 PA. CONS. STAT. ANN. § 8351, *et seq*.

consultants. The key to any defense is to be prepared—i.e., know all of the medical and legal issues that could arise.

The utilization of experts is critical to this approach and leads to another step in the process—retain an expert(s) early in the case, not only to evaluate the claim, but also to assist in the defense. Make sure you work with someone who not only is a qualified expert, but also will make himself or herself available whenever an issue comes up that requires his or her perspective.

The next step is to know your opposition. This entails doing research on the opposing counsel and the plaintiff(s), including Internet research, criminal/civil docket checks, etc. Surprisingly, many people post pictures of themselves or tell stories on their various social media accounts that can be used later to impeach their credibility. One example is a recent case wherein the plaintiff claimed that she was permanently disabled and could not go out in public or enjoy normal activities of daily living. We were able to find pictures of her on the Internet at a celebration for the local town dancing and celebrating—all things she claimed she could no longer do after the alleged negligence.

Key questions include: In what county or court is the case filed? What is the make-up of the jury pool? Is your client likeable? Is your client an institution? These factors must be considered in determining how to approach and defend a case.

Once all of this is accomplished, the next step is to gather the information you have collected, digest it, and then put it together into a coherent defense that you will be able to present to a jury.

Also, do not try to go it alone. Utilize your firm's resources. This includes paralegals, medical resources, etc. Medical malpractice cases are becoming more complex, and the value of the cases merits that every detail be taken into account—you owe it to your client to ensure the best possible defense.

Finally, know your witnesses. Have all of the witnesses been deposed? What types of witnesses are you dealing with? Are your witnesses prepared? If necessary, have your witnesses participate in a mock trial; or at a minimum, engage in a mock question-and-answer session so that the witnesses are prepared. Take them to the courtroom before trial; let them sit in the witness chair; and let your client sit at the defendant's table, so that everyone is familiar and comfortable with the surroundings.

Critical Legal Skills and Resources When Defending Individuals or Institutions

There is no substitute for experience in the courtroom, whether it involves routine motions or a jury trial. Once you have sufficient experience, you will have the level of comfort necessary to proceed with a medical malpractice case. You need to know the Rules of Evidence, as well as the relevant and current law on the issues in your client's case. Your associates, law clerks, and other staff can assist in this learning process, as well as in trial preparation. Having a nurse consultant and paralegal familiar with the case and the medicine and issues it entails will be a great benefit during trial.

Keep in mind that you have to adjust your strategies when defending an institution as opposed to an individual practitioner, as you need to account for the public perception of that specific institution at the time. Often, large companies or hospital systems, despite all of the good they do, are viewed negatively in the community. This must be addressed somehow, either during your case or during jury *voir dire*. If your client is an institution, who will be at the defendant's table? Is it an officer, the nurse whose care is at issue, or some other individual? Regardless, having someone in that chair adds a human element that will impact the jury's decision. A jury may easily assign blame to a faceless corporation, believing that a corporation was wrong and therefore owes money to an individual who was injured. If, however, you can get the jury to understand that there are people behind the corporation, and it is those people to whom the jury is assigning blame, the jury may be more sympathetic to the corporate defendant and not so willing to find fault.

Locating a Good Medical Expert

A good expert is one who is a clinician first and an expert second. In addition, if you can find an expert who does not take on many cases or who also has a solid record of testifying for plaintiffs as well as defendants, this can be beneficial, as it will eliminate any perceived bias.

A key component in choosing an expert is his *curriculum vitae*. What is his exact specialty? Has he written any articles or presented on the topic being litigated, or one related to the issues at hand? If so, do his conclusions in those articles support your defense? If you are not familiar with the expert, talk to him, preferably in person, before he is retained. Does he make a good appearance, and will he hold up under cross-examination?

Finally, what are you looking for from the expert? Ideally, you need an expert who will support the case, but who is also smart enough to know when certain points need to be conceded. Not every claim or fact in a medical malpractice case is defensible. If the medicine is clearly against you, have your expert concede that point, and then explain why the claim still does not give rise to a breach in the standard of care or why there is no causal link. Medicine is not exact. It is not a recipe where you can plug in the ingredients and press "bake." It is always evolving, and your expert needs to appreciate and accept the human nature factor, as well as the medicine in a malpractice case.

It is important that the expert be available to discuss the case throughout the litigation process and to provide insight along every step of the way. An expert who can support his or her conclusions with literature or other documentation is beneficial to any defense. Another important role for the expert is to take the plaintiff's position and to attack the defense from the plaintiff's point of view so that you are aware of all of the weaknesses in your case well in advance.

Addressing Key Issues in a Malpractice Claim

Issues to address in any malpractice case include the economy, the reputation of your physician or institution client, the appearance of your witnesses, and the sympathetic nature of the plaintiff(s).

If your client is an institution, this issue needs to be addressed, as previously noted, by introducing the people behind the institution. For example, have the nurse(s) whose care is at issue be present for the opening statements and during the case, so that the jury can see whose actions they are evaluating. Make it a case about people, not a brick-and-mortar institution. In addition, if your physician client comes across as arrogant or impersonal, then additional work needs to be done to "humanize" your client. As a trial attorney, you want the jury to identify with the defendant health care provider/physician, to understand that the defendant health care provider/physician has only the plaintiff's best interest in mind and that he or she did everything possible to ensure a positive result. It is important to provide an explanation to the jury as to why the conduct of the defendant health care provider was not negligent.

Conclusion

Electronic medical records, as discussed above, will be at the forefront of medical malpractice cases in the future. Lawyers need to understand the entire system, as well as the capabilities of the behind-the-scenes electronic medical record systems of their clients. It will be the role of the attorney to educate the doctors and nurses in the case regarding their electronic blueprint. Many of those in the medical profession do not understand that everything they access or record in the medical record leaves an electronic trail that is not part of the chart typically viewed by the practitioner. This trail allows the viewer to see when a practitioner accessed the chart and typically what measures were done in the treatment of a specific patient.

Advice to other lawyers in this practice area is to address every situation and every opponent with reasonableness and professionalism. There has been a dramatic change in our profession in terms of moving away from respect and civility; however, one must be careful to remain honest and professional. To protect both yourself and your client, document all communications with opposing counsel.

Key Takeaways

- Know the medicine that is involved in a malpractice case. Consult with your staff, including any physicians or legal nurse consultants. Be prepared in terms of knowing all of the medical and legal issues that could arise.
- Utilize and retain experts early in the case, not only to evaluate the claim, but also to assist in the defense. Make sure you work with someone who is a qualified expert and who will make himself or

herself available whenever an issue comes up that requires his or her perspective.

- Know your opposition. Do research on the opposing counsel and the plaintiff(s). Also know your witnesses and make sure they are prepared for trial.
- Understand the behind-the-scenes electronic medical record systems of your clients. Educate the doctors and nurses in your case regarding their electronic blueprint.
- Address every situation and every opponent with reasonableness and professionalism. Document all communications with opposing counsel.

***Frederick W. Bode III** is a shareholder of Dickie McCamey & Chilcote PC. He concentrates his practice in the areas of commercial litigation, product liability, health care litigation, and technology matters. Over the years he has counseled clients on issues such as product development, appropriate language to include in product user manuals, and manufacturing process safety, as well as advising clients on options to consider before moving forward with litigation to meet the company's goals and objectives and work within its given legal department budget.*

Besides being a member of the Academy of Trial Lawyers of Allegheny County, Pennsylvania, Mr. Bode is active in the Product Liability Advisory Council (PLAC), the Defense Research Institute (Products Liability Sub-Committee), and the Pennsylvania Defense Institute (PDI). In addition, he has been a frequent lecturer on commercial law and health care topics for more than ten years and has authored a chapter in the Allegheny County Court of Common Pleas Civil Practice Manual.

Mr. Bode has been named in The Best Lawyers in America *in the fields of commercial litigation, product liability law, and medical malpractice law. In addition, he was named to the 2005, 2009, 2010, and 2011* Pennsylvania Super Lawyers *in the area of business litigation. For the past ten years he has maintained an AV Preeminent peer review rating from Martindale-Hubbell.*

In 1977, Mr. Bode graduated with honors from Grove City College with a BA in economics and history. He received his JD from the University of Akron (member of Bracton's Inn) in 1980.

Richard J. Kabbert *is a shareholder of Dickie McCamey & Chilcote PC. He concentrates his practice in the areas of general liability, premises liability, and professional liability. The majority of his practice focuses on health care law, with a particular emphasis in medical malpractice.*

Mr. Kabbert has been a lecturer on medical malpractice and health care issues. He has also served as an instructor and has taught students on various aspects of civil litigation.

Memberships of Mr. Kabbert include the Allegheny County Bar, Pennsylvania Bar, and West Virginia Bar Associations, and he is admitted to practice before the Supreme Court of Pennsylvania, the Supreme Court of Appeals of West Virginia, the United States District Court for the Southern District of West Virginia and the United States District Court for the Western District of Pennsylvania.

Mr. Kabbert was selected for inclusion in Pennsylvania Super Lawyers *Rising Stars 2010.*

After receiving his BA in political science from the University of Pittsburgh in 1992, cum laude, Mr. Kabbert graduated in 2002 with his JD from the Duquesne University School of Law, where he was a member of Law Review.

Kristen Hock Prex *is a shareholder of Dickie McCamey & Chilcote PC. She concentrates her practice in the areas of product liability, health care law, medical malpractice, and commercial litigation.*

Ms. Prex is admitted to practice before the Supreme Court of Pennsylvania, United States Court of Appeals for the Third Circuit, and United States District Court for the Eastern, Middle, and Western Districts of Pennsylvania. She is also a member of the Allegheny County, Pennsylvania, and American Bar Associations. In addition, Ms. Prex is a co-author of a chapter in the Allegheny County Court of Common Pleas Civil Practice Manual.

Mrs. Prex was selected for inclusion in Pennsylvania Super Lawyers *Rising Stars in 2008 and 2010.*

After receiving her BS degree in neuroscience from the University of Pittsburgh in 1996, Ms. Prex graduated from the Duquesne University School of Law in 2000 with her JD.

Medical Malpractice Liability Trends and Defense Strategies

Rodger A. Hagen

Partner and Group Head,

Health Care Professional Liability Practice Group

Meagher & Geer PLLP

ASPATORE

Introduction

Changes in the law are made far more slowly than changes in medicine, but changes do nonetheless occur. Unlike medical advances, changes in medical malpractice law are not uniform from state to state and are never truly evidence-based.

This chapter is an effort to identify—and in some cases to predict—new liability theories that attorneys who defend health care providers might expect to see in years to come. It discusses which physicians, by medical specialty, face the highest risk of being sued, explores some factors likely contributing to that, and provides some practical tips on how to plan and execute a sound defense strategy.

Current Medical Malpractice Developments

The most significant recent trends in medical malpractice are variations on a theme that is as old as the contingent fee. Plaintiffs' lawyers are always looking for ways to cast a wider net to capture more claims and access deeper pockets. One such trend finds lawyers advocating for later and later accrual dates for various causes of action, thereby increasing the amount of time in which they can bring certain claims. This is a trend seen in many states, even in those that have adopted the "discovery rule," whereby a malpractice cause of action is considered to accrue when the patient knew or should have known of the existence of a claim.

Judicial receptiveness to arguments for delayed accrual dates sacrifices fairness to the defendant providers in order to expand remedies available to patients. Cases that can be difficult to defend in the best of circumstances become more so as the years pass. Witnesses retire; they move to different employers, cities, and careers. Facts and details are forgotten. Sometimes witnesses pass away. Regardless, trying to reconstruct what the standard of care was at the time of the treatment that is the subject of the claim or suit becomes exponentially more difficult as the years pass.

Another trend finds traditional concepts of causation being challenged. Where tort theory once uniformly required proof of a *probability* that the malpractice alleged caused the harm complained of, that is no longer the standard in many jurisdictions. Now, the loss of chance theory is finding increasing acceptance. In simplest terms, loss of chance theory holds that, to be entitled to compensation, a plaintiff has to show only that the defendant's negligence decreased the plaintiff's chances of achieving a desired treatment outcome. For example, if a delay in diagnosing some disease process resulted in the chance of successful treatment decreasing from 40 percent to 30 percent, that loss of chance would be regarded as a compensable injury. With all that is now known about cure rates and long-term outcomes of various diseases, expect this to be a heavily litigated theory in the future. Cases alleging delayed diagnosis or negligent treatment of cancer provide the most fertile ground for litigating loss of chance theory.

Arguing that a joint enterprise exists—in even the most traditional of relationships, such as one between private practice physicians and hospitals—is yet another trend that seems calculated to expand liability. Plaintiffs' attorneys are motivated by a desire to create exposure among more persons and entities and to overcome the obstacles to recovery that damage caps and limits of insurance coverage create.

Health Care Reform's Impact on Medical Malpractice Claims

The Patient Protection and Affordable Care Act (PPACA) enacted in 2010 is a significant piece of federal health care reform that could have a substantial, but unintended, impact on medical malpractice litigation. PPACA, among its many provisions, calls for the creation of entities called Accountable Care Organizations (ACOs). ACOs are alliances of private practice physicians and health care institutions, such as hospitals, that will share in outcome-based financial incentives in the current legislative plan. ACOs, depending on how they are structured, may meet the legal definition of a "joint enterprise." The determinative factor in deciding whether participants in an ACO are engaged in a joint enterprise will be whether each entity truly has control and a voice regarding the organization's direction.

Tort reform is a highly fluid concept. What changes there may be in the wings are anyone's guess. But it seems that the recurring theme of medical malpractice tort reform is legislative efforts to level the playing field. Sometimes those efforts are ill advised; often they are ill conceived; and frequently they are ill founded. But the more success the defense bar has in advocating for health care providers in malpractice suits, the more it can expect legislative bodies, and probably some courts, to "handicap" the competition a bit. Similarly, legislative action is a predictable response if the balance tips too far in favor of plaintiffs.

"Loser pays" is a tort reform concept that has been discussed, but that perhaps would represent an over-reaction and, depending on circumstances, could even be vulnerable to constitutional challenge. Proposals to limit fees of plaintiffs' attorneys have also been talked about, but have yet to find much political support.

What approach do medical malpractice defendants and their attorneys need to take in response to the ever-changing landscape? The answer is simple and should come naturally: health care providers should continue to provide patient care without letting anxiety over possible malpractice exposure dictate their actions, and defense attorneys should continue to be advocates who vigorously, but ethically, protect the interests of these health care providers.

Risk of Malpractice Suit by Medical Specialty

According to a NEW ENGLAND JOURNAL OF MEDICINE article published in August 2011, physicians engaged in the practice of various surgical specialties are at the highest risk of being sued. Anupam B. Jena, M.D., Ph.D., Seth Seabury, Ph.D., Darius Lakdawalla, Ph.D., and Amitabh Chandra, Ph.D., *Malpractice Risk According to Physician Specialty*, 365 (7) New Eng. J. Med. 629 (2011). The authors analyzed data from 1991 to 2005 and tracked both total claims and claims that resulted in an indemnity payment. Shockingly, the data demonstrated that neurosurgeons face a 19.1 percent chance of being the subject of a medical malpractice claim or suit. Cardiovascular and thoracic surgeons trail by a narrow margin, with claims or suits brought against them at an annual rate of 18.9 percent. Next, in order of claim frequency, are general surgeons, orthopedic surgeons, and plastic surgeons.

If my own practice is any indication, however, claims and suits against plastic and reconstructive surgeons seem to be on the decline. The state of the US economy may play a big role in that decline, as fewer people are in a position to pay for the elective and cosmetic procedures that made up the clear majority of plastic surgery malpractice claims in the past. With economic recovery, I think we can expect plastic surgery claims to increase again. Patients who undergo elective plastic surgery procedures purely because of their own vanity are often people who have unreasonable expectations in terms of outcome. When they have the disposable income, they will be back and with them will come more lawsuits.

After plastic surgeons, gastroenterologists—who may not be surgeons, but certainly are proceduralists—are the practitioners most frequently sued for medical malpractice, according to the study by *Jena et al.* Following gastroenterologists are obstetricians/gynecologists (OB/GYNs) and urologists. Again, both are practices in which a significant component of patient care is provided in the operating room.

By broad category, the next highest incidence of claims the article found to have occurred during the period between 1991 and 2005 was in internal medicine and its subspecialties. Specifically, in order of frequency, the specialties included pulmonology, oncology, cardiology, and general internal medicine. Whereas the surgical specialties show a claim frequency well into double-digits, pulmonologists, oncologists, cardiologists, and internists have less than a 10 percent chance of having a malpractice claim asserted against them in any given year.

What is the reasoning behind the numbers? Surgeons are probably sued more often because the essential causation component usually *appears* easier for patients' attorneys to prove in surgery cases than in other medical malpractice cases. Regardless of whether it is a consequence of negligence, most undesired surgical outcomes are readily apparent. They may involve something as obvious as a retained sponge or other foreign body, or the doctor performing the procedure on the wrong limb or an otherwise incorrect surgical site. They may involve procedures that result in a patient's death. They may also involve unintended injury to an organ or organ system during the course of a procedure. The distinguishing factor in all these examples is that the result is clearly and palpably different than the surgeon intended and almost certainly (the procurement of a patient's informed consent notwithstanding) something other than the patient anticipated.

In a failure-to-diagnose claim or a negligent medical (non-surgical) treatment claim, the alleged unsatisfactory results can be more subtle. The causal connection is usually going to be less obvious, especially in situations not resulting in death or severe disability. It is easy to argue that if a patient enters the operating room one way and exits in a way that is appreciably and undesirably different, the surgery (and therefore, the surgeon) caused the untoward outcome. Outcomes following a failure to treat or resulting from ineffective medical treatment will generally be less obvious and take longer to manifest. The more subtle the adverse treatment outcome, the harder it will usually be for jurors to find the causal connection that is a prerequisite to recovery.

Risks for Neurosurgeons

Neurosurgeons, whose risk is statistically the highest among all medical specialties, are being sued more today than ever before, according to my personal observation. The reasons are many, and none of them relates to the neurosurgeons' lack of skill. Neurosurgery is a specialty in which advances in procedures and technology occur at a rapid rate. Neurosurgeons today operate on people who, until recently, never even would have made it into an operating room.

Perhaps the balance a neurosurgeon must strike between offering optimism to those in seemingly hopeless positions and trying to realistically manage patient expectations is what leads to more claims. Damage potential is undoubtedly another factor that drives the frequency of claims against neurosurgeons. When a surgical specialty's accepted risks for "routine" procedures include brain injury, blindness, hearing loss, paraplegia, quadriplegia, and even death, the chance of a big payday will entice some people to pursue cases even when proving liability is difficult.

Risks for Doctors Using Laparoscopic and Other Minimally Invasive Surgical Techniques

One explanation of why the incidence of malpractice claims against surgeons is steadily increasing is that they are now operating on people for whom surgery previously would not have been a viable option. Additionally, surgeons are now performing many routine surgical procedures in decreasingly invasive ways or with the help of new technologies.

As the risk-benefit analysis tips in favor of attempting surgical correction of conditions previously regarded as inoperable, there will inevitably be more suboptimal outcomes. It follows that more claims will ensue. This has become evident in the large number of laparoscopic surgical procedures resulting in unintended injury. The complication rate for laparoscopic cholecystectomy, for example, is about 3 percent. Slanetz PJ, Boland GW, Mueller PR., *Imaging and Interventional Radiology in Laparoscopic Injuries to the Gallbladder and Biliary System*, 201 Radiology 595–603 (1996). Surgeons are aware of this risk, and, despite the later disavowals of many patients are routinely informed of it, as well. Regardless, when the statistical possibility of a complication becomes a reality, the patient outcome undeniably is substantially different from what the surgeon and patient expected. It is easy for many, then, to make the logical leap from the patient believing there was a 97 percent chance of a complication-free surgery to the patient claiming the surgeon was negligent because he or she perforated the common bile duct and the patient almost died.

Robotic surgical techniques have become increasingly popular. There is not enough information at this point to indicate what type of impact they will have on malpractice claims. The precision the da Vinci® surgical system offers has, in some studies, been shown to optimize outcomes in a variety of ways. Speedier recoveries are a widely accepted benefit. Some centers have published results indicating that surgeries done with the da Vinci system minimize some of the undesired, but accepted, consequences of procedures such as prostatectomy. But the question of whether there will be negative implications as this technology comes into wider use looms. Will a surgical maloccurence be magnified in the eyes of jurors if a robot, rather than a human, ultimately commits it? It seems almost certain that patients and their attorneys will find expert witnesses to readily attack surgeons who literally do not lay a hand on a patient in the operating room, and, while such criticism may be completely unjustified, it might hold a certain appeal to some jurors.

Decreasingly invasive surgical techniques come at a cost. Procedures such as laparoscopic surgeries and those conducted through smaller incisions promote faster recoveries and shorter hospital stays. However, having less exposure to the anatomic surgical objective and operating without the benefit of direct vision create challenges for surgeons. The risk of causing unintended injury to a blood vessel, bowel, or other organ is higher, and, more significant, the challenge of addressing an unintended injury is much greater. For example, a surgeon who can easily manage a "bleeder" through a laparotomy incision will likely find it much more challenging to repair one while operating laparoscopically. All of these present issues the malpractice defense attorney must be prepared to address by focusing the jury on the fact that surgical options are offered and patient decisions are made *prospectively* and not with the benefit of hindsight.

The Enhanced Risk Presented by Chronically Unhealthy Patients

The prevalence of obesity and the high rates of diabetes, hypertension, and coronary artery disease arc other factors that contribute to the frequency with which surgeons find themselves the target of lawsuits. It is generally accepted that obese patients and patients with diabetes do not heal as well as others. Additionally, surgeons tell us that obese patients generally are, as a direct consequence of their body habitus, technically more difficult to operate on. Managing general anesthesia in patients with a history of poorly regulated hypertension is complicated and perilous. Patients whose circulatory systems have become accustomed to running at abnormally high blood pressure can experience catastrophic episodes of ischemia or hypoxia if blood pressure is allowed to drop for a prolonged period of time. Among the claims this can spawn are claims involving paralysis, brain injury, and death.

Surgery that has weight loss itself as the primary objective has become a major target for medical malpractice cases. Bariatric surgery has existed in various forms for more than fifty years, although it has become far more common in recent years, with many advances in techniques during the last fifteen years. Nevertheless, bariatric surgery involves a patient population already at high risk for complications. Because demand for these ostensibly miraculous procedures is high, surgeons sometimes perform them despite a lack of experience or appropriate staffing. The potential for adverse outcomes and resulting malpractice claims is readily apparent.

An important way for surgeons to protect themselves when operating on patients who have problems like weight, blood pressure, and diabetes—probably the most important way—is to engage in a thorough explanation of a procedure's risks and potential complications and how those are enhanced by that particular patient's overall state of health. After having that conversation with the patient, the surgeon would do well to thoroughly document that it happened. How should that be documented? Probably not by attempting to create a verbatim record of the conversation. The better practice will usually be to simply document the same as one would with a healthy patient, but then add some statement in the vein of "patient's morbid obesity and the added risk associated with it were discussed at length. Patient understands and appreciates this and wishes to proceed with surgery."

No matter what the surgeon does or how well she documents informed consent discussions, there will be patients who deny those conversations occurred and more who honestly do not remember. Tempting as it may sometimes seem, I still do not believe we have come to a point where an audio or video recording of informed consent discussions will be a good idea. The fact is that many surgeries are preceded by a series of discussions, and simply recording the last of those discussions will not provide a full picture of what the patient was told.

Effective Strategies for Mounting a Successful Medical Malpractice Defense

The basic steps for mounting an effective medical malpractice defense are rudimentary. First, the attorney must acquire the necessary medical records, including any relevant imaging studies or other information not necessarily contained in the client's chart. After reviewing those records, and armed with knowledge of the claim the plaintiff is making, the attorney must supplement his or her understanding of the issue by researching the specific condition, procedure, or disease process at issue and discussing it with the client.

With that as a backdrop, the next step is to find truly objective and knowledgeable experts to review the case. At least one reviewing expert should practice the same medical specialty as the defendant, but many other factors also enter into the attorney's selection of the reviewing expert(s). My preference is to retain an expert whose practice is in close geographic proximity to the venue in which the case would be tried. This frequently creates a beneficial contrast to the opposing expert, who often is from a distant locale. However, this cannot be done without carefully considering the opposing expert's qualifications. If the opposing expert is the most widely published authority on the subject matter of the case, it will not be beneficial to settle for someone with lesser credentials just because of geographic proximity.

In selecting a reviewing expert, it is beneficial to consult the client, other practitioners in the medical community, and medical literature to identify someone whose *curriculum vitae* will rival or surpass that of the expert the opposition hires. Occasionally, it will be wise to hire both a local expert and one who enjoys national stature. Why favor the local expert when all else is equal? The jury may be influenced by an unfamiliar accent, mannerisms, or use of idioms, impacting how the jury perceives that expert's credibility. Certainly the days of a "community standard" are all but extinct, so "local knowledge" is not important from that standpoint. Human nature comes into play, though, and in the case of many jurors, it will come naturally to them to feel as though they are in competition with or superior to people who come from somewhere else. There is also some value for the defense to be able to create the inference that the opposition's expert, coming from somewhere across the country, is a hired gun whose opinions are bought and given without fear of repercussion.

One useful way of having a case reviewed by whatever expert you select is to have it reviewed "blindly." Doing so will work better in some circumstances than in others. However, in the failure to diagnose case, for example, it can be highly effective. The notion of hindsight bias has been studied extensively, particularly in the context of X-ray interpretation by radiologists. *See, e.g.* Renfrew DL, Franken EA Jr, Berbaum KS, Weigelt FH, Abu-Yousef MM, *Error in Radiology: Classification and Lessons in 182 Cases Presented at a Problem Case Conference*, 183 Radiology 145 (1992). The concept of hindsight bias means that the reviewing physician has been somehow alerted that what they're looking at is abnormal or non-routine. In the malpractice context, hindsight bias mean that a reviewing physician has the benefit of knowing what a patient's ultimate diagnosis is and, thus, finds it easy to "predict" that on the basis of looking back at information acquired before the diagnosis was made. Medical malpractice defense attorneys will see this time and time again, where a plaintiff expert will go back to an early imaging study, lab result, or clinical observation and say that it was a clear bellwether of what ultimately was diagnosed. But, in virtually every one of those cases, that reviewing expert will have known the ultimate patient outcome before having reviewed a single medical record or imaging study.

To combat that, and to illustrate this hindsight bias, it can be beneficial to retain a defense expert and advise only that you would like the records or imaging studies reviewed. Usually, this will require that records only up to a certain point in time be provided, as subsequent records would reveal the diagnosis. After the reviewer has had a chance to go over the records you provide, arrange for a meeting to discuss the reviewer's differential diagnosis and discuss what your reviewer believes happened later in the patient's course. You may be surprised at just how often the ultimate diagnoses or outcome either did not make the list of possible diagnoses or was so low on that list as to make it not even a serious consideration.

In the case of interpretation of imaging studies, it may be useful to have the plaintiff's X-rays put into a pile with X-rays from several other patients, so that the reviewer does not infer that there must be some abnormal finding on a particular study. You will probably need to provide some basic clinical information, just as the radiologist would have when interpreting a study in the normal course of his practice. Again, after the images have been reviewed, meet with the reviewer to see whether he has made the elusive finding that caused your client to get sued. This most closely simulates the position your client was in at the time at issue.

If you have had an expert perform a "blind" review, lay that out for the jury as you begin to lay the foundation in preparation for eliciting her opinions. By this time, you will most likely have been able to establish that the opposing expert had prior knowledge of the diagnosis when the case was received for review, and you can drive home to the jury that this is an unfair and unrealistic way to review someone's care. The way your expert has conducted the review is the way your client encountered the information—without the benefit of hindsight. This can be a highly effective tactic, if executed well.

Conclusion

Medical malpractice defense attorneys find themselves having to react to an ever-changing medico-legal landscape and having to craft defenses to an array of novel liability theories. Our best allies in doing so are our clients themselves. While they rely on us for the necessary legal expertise, it is only when that is blended with a sound understanding of the underlying medical issues that an effective defense can be mounted. It's imperative that we rely on our clients and our experts to help us respond to these challenges.

Fortunately, the nature of our business is that we have the benefit of representing bright, intellectually engaged clients whose conduct is invariably motivated by a desire to help their patients. As medical advances continue to result in new cures and people living longer while enjoying better quality of life, we can continue to expect that the progress will be accompanied by the occasional untoward outcome and that some of those are going to turn into lawsuits. Physicians will continue to do their best for their patients and malpractice defense attorneys owe them the same commitment to do our best. Being able to work alongside these people and help them through what can be a devastating experience makes what we do truly fulfilling.

Key Takeaways

- When mounting a medical malpractice defense, acquire the necessary medical records. Be complete in your search, and include any relevant imaging studies or other information not necessarily contained in the client's chart. After reviewing those records, and armed with knowledge of the claim the plaintiff is making, supplement your understanding of the issue by researching the specific condition, procedure, or disease process at issue and discussing it with your client.
- Find a truly objective and knowledgeable expert to review the case. If practical, try to retain an expert whose practice is in close geographic proximity to the venue in which the case has been or will be filed. This creates an advantage for the defense, as the jury may be influenced by the opposing expert's unfamiliar accent, mannerisms, or use of idioms, and question the expert's credibility. Considering hiring two experts if necessary: one who is located locally and one who enjoys national stature.
- If the opposition's expert is not located locally, use this to your advantage by creating the inference that the opposition's expert, coming from somewhere across the country, is a hired gun whose opinions are bought and given without fear of repercussion.

Rodger A. Hagen is a 1984 graduate of the University of Minnesota Law School. After serving as a judicial law clerk in the Minnesota state court system, he joined the firm of Meagher & Geer PLLP, where he is a partner and has practiced for more than twenty-five years as a trial lawyer.

Mr. Hagen focuses his practice on the defense of physicians, hospitals, clinics, and other health care providers in professional liability matters. He was recently nominated to be inducted as a Fellow of the American College of Trial Lawyers and has earned both Best Lawyers in America *and* Super Lawyer *recognition in the area of medical malpractice defense. He heads the Health Care Professional Liability practice group at Meagher & Geer, which defends and tries more medical malpractice cases than any other law firm in Minnesota and is ranked in the top tier of medical malpractice defense firms by* US News & World Report *and* Best Lawyers.

APPENDICES

APPENDIX A

TREATISE ON PHYSICIAN AND HOSPITAL LIABILITY

DANIEL S. RATNER
MANAGING PARTNER
HEIDELL PITTONI MURPHY & BACH LLP

I. THEORIES OF PHYSICIAN LIABILITY

A. Elements

A plaintiff alleging medical malpractice must prove both a departure from good and accepted practice and that the departure was a proximate cause of the plaintiff's damages. Mendez v. City of N.Y., 295 A.D.2d 487, 744 N.Y.S.2d 847 (2d Dep't 2002); Mollo v. Rothman, 284 A.D.2d 299, 725 N.Y.S.2d 560 (2d Dep't 2001); Lo Presti v. Hosp. for Joint Diseases, 275 A.D.2d 201, 712 N.Y.S.2d 110 (1st Dep't 2000); Amsler v. Verrili, 119 A.D.2d 786, 501 N.Y.S.2d 411 (2d Dep't 1986); Monahan v. Weichert, 82 A.D.2d 102, 442 N.Y.S.2d 295 (4th Dep't 1981).

1. Departure from Good and Accepted Practice

From Pike v. Honsinger, 155 N.Y. 201, 209, 49 N.E. 760, 762 (1898):

> The law relating to malpractice is simple and well settled, although not always easy of application. A physician and surgeon, by taking charge of a case, impliedly represents that he possesses, and the law places upon him the duty of possessing, that reasonable degree of learning and skill that is ordinarily possessed by physicians and surgeons in the locality where he practices, and which is ordinarily regarded by those conversant with the employment as necessary to qualify him to engage in the business of practicing medicine and surgery. Upon consenting to treat a patient, it becomes his duty to use reasonable care and diligence in the exercise of his skill and the application of his learning to accomplish the purpose for which he was

> employed. He is under the further obligation to use his best judgment in exercising his skill and applying his knowledge. The law holds him liable for an injury to his patient resulting from want of the requisite knowledge and skill, or the omission to exercise reasonable care, or the failure to use his best judgment.

The mere happening of an injury is not proof of a departure from accepted medical practice. See Nabozny v. Cappelletti, 267 A.D.2d 623, 628, 699 N.Y.S.2d 589, 594 (3d Dep't 1999); Saliaris v. D'Emilia, 143 A.D.2d 996, 533 N.Y.S.2d 607 (2d Dep't 1988); Henry v. Bronx Lebanon Med. Center, 53 A.D.2d 476, 385 N.Y.S.2d 772 (1st Dep't 1976). Further, a disagreement as to the method of treatment chosen by the defendant does not, in and of itself, establish a departure from accepted medical standards. Seibert v. Fink, 280 A.D.2d 661, 720 N.Y.S.2d 564 (2d Dep't 2001); see also Holton v. Sprain Brook Manor Nursing Home, 253 A.D.2d 852, 678 N.Y.S.2d 503 (2d Dep't 1998). "Where alternative procedures are available to a physician, any one of which is medically acceptable and proper under the circumstances, a physician cannot be held liable for malpractice when he uses one of two acceptable techniques." Henry, 53 A.D.2d at 480, 385 N.Y.S.2d at 775, quoting Schreiber v. Cestari, 40 A.D.2d 1025, 338 N.Y.S.2d 972 (2d Dep't 1972); see Goldstein v. Hauptman, 131 A.D.2d 724, 516 N.Y.S.2d 783 (2d Dep't 1987) (directing judgment as a matter of law in favor of defendants in case involving failure to properly monitor IV where there was overwhelming proof that regular monitoring by palpating IV area and checking color and temperature conformed to accepted medical practice even though plaintiffs' expert testified that actual viewing of IV site was the "best method").

A doctor is not liable for a mere error in judgment if the doctor does what he or she deems best after carefully balancing the risks and alternatives. Topel v. Long Island Jewish Med. Ctr., 55 N.Y.2d 682, 431 N.E.2d 293, 446 N.Y.S.2d 932 (1981); Johnson v. Yeshiva Univ., 42 N.Y.2d 818, 364 N.E.2d 1340, 396 N.Y.S. 647 (1977). This is often referred to as the "error in judgment" rule. This rule applies only in cases where the parties present evidence of a choice between or among medically acceptable alternatives or diagnoses. Absent such a showing, the error in judgment charge will not be given to the jury. Nestorowich v. Ricotta, 97 N.Y.2d 393, 399, 767 N.E.2d

125, 129, 740 N.Y.S.2d 668, 672 (2002); see also Grasso v. Capella, 260 A.D.2d 600, 688 N.Y.S.2d 666 (2d Dep't 1999).

2. Proximate Cause

A plaintiff must also establish that the alleged breach was a substantial factor in bringing about the injury. Mortenson v. Mem'l Hosp., 105 A.D.2d 151, 483 N.Y.S.2d 264 (1st Dep't 1984); Monahan v. Weichert, 82 A.D.2d 102, 442 N.Y.S.2d 295 (4th Dep't 1981); White v. Southside Hosp., 5 A.D.3d 677, 773 N.Y.S.2d 565, (2d Dep't 2004). Although proximate cause normally is a jury question, if it is irrefutable that an injury could not have been avoided regardless of the alleged departure from accepted medical practice, proximate cause will not be established as a matter of law. See Raymundo v. Westchester Cty. Med. Ctr., 292 A.D.2d 437, 738 N.Y.S.2d 875 (2d Dep't 2002) (awarding summary judgment to defendant where defense expert affidavits established that, irrespective of the delay in surgery, the severed portion of the injured plaintiff's finger could not be reattached because of severe vascular damage caused by the initial trauma, and where plaintiff's medical expert did not opine that reattachment would have been successful absent a delay); Rampe by Rampe v. Cmty. Gen. Hosp., 241 A.D.2d 817, 660 N.Y.S.2d 206 (3d Dep't 1997) (awarding judgment as a matter of law to defendant hospital where there was no proof that an additional telephone call by hospital staff to attending physician would have prompted physician to order a cesarean section before 7 p.m., such that brain-damaged infant would have been born sooner); Bartha v. Lombardo & Associates, 212 A.D.2d 494, 622 N.Y.S.2d 527 (2d Dep't 1995) (awarding judgment to defendants where there was no evidence that defendants' consultation with another ophthalmologist would have resulted in a different treatment plan or that the failure to consult was a proximate cause of the injury).[1]

[1] See also, Calandrillo v. East Nassau Med. Group, 186 A.D.2d 703, 588 N.Y.S.2d 661 (2d Dep't 1992) (physician entitled to judgment where his failure to do more extensive testing of plaintiff's bladder responsiveness was not causally related to injury in light of jury's finding that subsequent prostatectomy was performed properly); Storniolo v. Bauer, 176 A.D.2d 550, 574 N.Y.S.2d 731 (1st Dep't 1991) (affirming directed verdict in favor of defendants where plaintiffs' expert failed to establish that post-surgical fistula was caused by negligence as opposed to underlying disease process or infection); Kenigsberg v. Cohn, 117 A.D.2d 652, 498 N.Y.S.2d 390 (2d Dep't 1986) (awarding judgment as a matter of law to defendant where defendant physician's alleged obstruction

To establish proximate cause, "plaintiff need not eliminate entirely all possibility that defendant's conduct was not a cause, but only offer sufficient evidence from which reasonable persons may conclude that it is more probable that the injury was caused by defendant than that it was not." Lo Presti, 275 A.D.2d at 203, 712 N.Y.S.2d at 112, quoting Monahan, 82 A.D.2d at 108, 442 N.Y.S.2d at 299. In Calvin v. New York Medical Group, 286 A.D.2d 469, 730 N.Y.S.2d 337 (2d Dep't 2001), the plaintiff's decedent went to the defendant physician complaining of a dry, hacking cough. Defendant did not take a complete history or a chest x-ray of the patient during this visit or during a follow-up visit that occurred four days later. Nine days after the follow up visit, another physician who did perform a chest x-ray detected a high-grade non-Hodgkin's lymphoma. The decedent died several days later from lymphoma complications. Denying summary judgment, the court found that the plaintiff's expert witness established that Dr. Witt's departures from good and accepted standards of medical care were a substantial factor in causing the decedent's death. "It was not necessary for the plaintiff to eliminate every other possible cause of the decedent's death." Calvin, 286 A.D.2d at 470, 730 N.Y.S.2d at 338.

3. The Expert Testimony Requirement

To establish the requisite standard of care and proximate cause, a plaintiff must produce qualified expert testimony. Petrillo v. Leather, 247 A.D.2d 368, 668 N.Y.S.2d 637 (2d Dep't 1998) (communication of patient's physiology from one physician to another is a part of a physician's medical judgment and therefore requires expert testimony to prove a deviation.); Evangelista v. Zolan, 247 A.D.2d 508, 669 N.Y.S.2d 325 (2d Dep't 1998); Milano v. Freed, 64 F.3d 91 (2d Cir. 1995); Coursen v. N.Y. Hosp.-Cornell Med. Ctr., 114 A.D.2d 254, 499 N.Y.S.2d 52 (1st Dep't 1986).

i) Qualifications

The testifying expert must possess the requisite skill, training, education, knowledge and experience from which it can be assumed that the opinion

of plaintiff's transfer to specialized burn-care facility where there was no evidence that skin graft procedure would have been done differently at specialized facility); Gayle v. Neyman, 91 A.D.2d 75, 457 N.Y.S.2d 499 (1st Dep't 1983) (affirming directed verdict in favor of defendants where the failure to conduct pelvic examination did not delay discovery of endometriosis requiring hysterectomy).

rendered is reliable. Matott v. Ward, 48 N.Y.2d 455, 423 N.Y.S.2d 645 (1979); Enu v. Sobol, 208 A.D.2d 1123, 617 N.Y.S.2d 960 (3d Dep't 1994). A physician need not be a specialist in a particular field of medicine in order to offer opinion testimony, so long as the trial court is satisfied that the witness is sufficiently familiar with the standard of care at issue. See Bodensiek v. Schwartz, 292 A.D.2d 411, 739 N.Y.S.2d 405 (2d Dep't 2002) (court erred in precluding the testimony of a medical oncologist regarding the quality of a gynecological surgeon's care; expert would have testified based on his past experience in diagnosing and treating gynecological cancers, and the necessity of performing a complete hysterectomy as opposed to a more conservative approach); Erbstein v. Savasatit, 274 A.D.2d 445, 711 N.Y.S.2d 458 (2d Dep't 2000) (pathologist qualified to testify regarding the standard of care for a general surgeon based on his familiarity with the subject. Any purported shortcomings went merely to the weight the jury would give his opinion.); Humphrey v. Jewish Hosp. and Medical Ctr. of Brooklyn, 172 A.D.2d 494, 567 N.Y.S.2d 737 (2d Dep't 1991) (general surgeon qualified to give an opinion in specialty of obstetrics and gynecology).

Nevertheless, a foundation must be laid to establish that the expert is knowledgeable or experienced with the specific procedure or condition at issue. In Behar v. Coren, 21 A.D.3d 1045, 803 N.Y.S.2d 629 (2d Dep't 2005), it was held that plaintiffs failed to raise a triable issue of fact in opposition to a summary judgment motion because their expert's affidavit did not mention whether the expert, a long-retired pathologist, had any specific training or expertise in surgery, gastroenterology, or pediatrics. Moreover, the affidavit did not indicate that he had familiarized himself with the relevant literature or otherwise set forth how he was, or became, familiar with the applicable standards of care in those areas. The court thus held:

> "While it is true that a medical expert need not be a specialist in a particular field in order to testify regarding accepted practices in that field . . . the witness nonetheless should be possessed of the requisite skill, training, education, knowledge or experience from which it can be assumed that the opinion rendered is reliable" (Postlethwaite v United Health Servs. Hosps., 5 A.D.3d 892, 895 (2004) (internal quotation omitted); see LaMarque v. North Shore Univ. Hosp., 227 A.D.2d 594, 594, 643

> N.Y.S.2d 221 ("An expert witness must possess the requisite skill, training, knowledge, or experience to ensure that an opinion rendered is reliable."). Thus, where a physician opines outside his or her area of specialization, a foundation must be laid tending to support the reliability of the opinion rendered (see Romano v. Stanley, 90 N.Y.2d 444, 451-452 (1997); Nangano v Mount Sinai Hosp., 305 A.D.2d 473 (2003)). In the circumstances of this case, as the plaintiffs' expert failed to lay the requisite foundation for his asserted familiarity with the applicable standards of care, his affidavit was of no probative value.

Behar, 21 A.D.3d at 1046-47; see also Stanski v. Ezersky, 228 A.D.2d 311, 644 N.Y.S.2d 220 (1st Dep't 1996) (awarding judgment in favor of defendants where plaintiffs' expert, who opined that an overdose of the anesthetic Tetracaine caused plaintiff to suffer abdominal myoclonus, could not cite a single reported case where this condition was linked to the administration of Tetracaine and conceded that the condition could occur spontaneously, without any drugs, trauma or evidence of disease); Bernard v. Block, 176 A.D.2d 843, 575 N.Y.S.2d 506 (2d Dep't 1991) (in setting aside verdict in medical malpractice action involving myelograms, court noted that plaintiff's expert failed to base his opinion on medical data or case studies and had not performed a myelogram in the eight years preceding trial); Hunter v. Szabo, 117 A.D.2d 778, 499 N.Y.S.2d 426 (2d Dep't 1986) (accord; expert was an internist who had never performed a myelogram); Jones v. U.S., 720 F. Supp. 355, 368 (S.D.N.Y. 1989) (applying New York law; setting aside verdict in favor of plaintiff in part because plaintiffs' expert, a podiatrist, lacked knowledge and experience in performing the orthopedic procedure in question).

ii) Testimony Must Be Based on Facts in the Record or Personally Known to the Expert

The expert's opinion must be based on the facts in the record or personally known to the witness. See Glorioso v. Schnabel, 253 A.D.2d 787, 677 N.Y.S.2d 604 (2d Dep't 1998); Clarke v. Helene Curtis Inc., 293 A.D.2d 701, 742 N.Y.S.2d 325 (2d Dep't 2002). "Where the expert states his conclusion unencumbered by any trace of facts or data, the testimony should be given no probative force whatsoever." Romano v. Stanley, 90 N.Y.2d 444, 451, 661 N.Y.S.2d 589, 592, 684 N.E.2d 19, 22, quoting Amatulli v Delhi Constr. Corp., 77 N.Y.2d 525, 533-534, n.2 (1997); Clarke, 293 A.D.2d at 702, 742 N.Y.S.2d at 327.

An expert may state his or her opinion and reasons without first specifying the data upon which they are based. CPLR 4515. Upon cross-examination, however, the witness may be required to specify the data and other criteria supporting the opinion. As a practical matter, therefore, an expert will be permitted to testify without first demonstrating his or her familiarity with the facts. But if it turns out the facts upon which this opinion is based were not introduced in evidence or that such evidence is deemed inadmissible, the expert's opinion testimony will be stricken. Hambsch v. N.Y. City Transit Auth., 63 N.Y.2d 723, 480 N.Y.S.2d 195, 469 N.E.2d 516 (1984); Pascuzzi v. CCI Companies, 292 A.D.2d 685, 739 N.Y.S.2d 209 (3d Dep't 2002).

iii) Professional Reliability Exception

While it is settled law that opinion evidence must be based on facts in the record or personally known to the witness, New York courts have recognized two exceptions to this rule and have held that an expert may rely on out-of-court material if "it is of a kind accepted in the profession as reliable in forming a professional opinion" or if it "comes from a witness subject to full cross-examination" at trial. People v. Sugden, 35 N.Y.2d 453, 460-61, 323 N.E.2d 169, 173 (1974). The first exception is commonly known as the "professional reliability" exception. Hambsch, 63 N.Y.2d at 726, 469 N.E.2d at 518, 480 N.Y.S.2d at 197.

Currently, there is a division amongst the appellate divisions regarding exactly what type of testimony is properly admissible under the professional reliability exception. For instance, in People v. Yates, 290 A.D.2d 888, 736 N.Y.S.2d 798 (3d Dep't 2002), an expert witness, a hospital physician, testified as to hospital test results for tests he had not personally conducted. Although the test results were never placed in evidence, the court nevertheless held that, "As these tests were administered to assist Walsh in treating his patient, they have inherent reliability and we find the omission of the actual test results from this record to be of little moment . . . we conclude that Walsh's opinions were properly admitted into evidence . . . ."

Yates, 290 A.D.2d at 889, 736 N.Y.S.2d at 800. In Fleiss v. South Buffalo Railway Company, 291 A.D.2d 848, 737 N.Y.S.2d 723 (4th Dep't 2002), the court reached a similar result, finding that defendant's examining physician was properly permitted to testify regarding the reports and findings of non-testifying treating physicians and to the results of a functional capacity examination because "those of out-of-court materials are of the kind generally accepted as reliable by experts in the medical profession." Fleiss, 291 A.D.2d at 849, 737 N.Y.S.2d at 724.

The Second Department recently adopted a markedly different position on this issue. In Wagman v. Bradshaw, 292 A.D.2d 84, 739 N.Y.S.2d 421 (2d Dep't 2002), the Second Department held that a chiropractor should not have been permitted to testify as to the contents of an inadmissible written report interpreting magnetic resonance imaging (MRI) films prepared by another healthcare professional who did not testify. The MRI's were not in evidence and there was no proof that, as out-of-court material, the written MRI report was reliable. Noting that recent case law had liberalized the rule regarding admissibility of opinion testimony based on out-of-court material, the court used the occasion to restate the evidentiary rules for admission of expert testimony and to caution against "intrusions into time-tested concepts limiting the use of secondary evidence." Wagman, 292 A.D.2d at 91, 739 N.Y.S.2d at 426. It held that the expert's opinion, "based on unreliable secondary evidence, is nothing more than conjecture if the only factual foundation . . . is another healthcare provider's interpretation of what an unproduced MRI film purports to exhibit." Id. at 87, 739 N.Y.S.2d at 424.

Plaintiff had sued for damages arising from an automobile accident. During plaintiff's direct case, counsel asked plaintiff's subsequent treating physician, Dr. Zelin, a chiropractor, to testify about the results of an MRI that Dr. Zelin had ordered but never reviewed. Relying on the MRI report prepared by the outside professional, over objection Dr. Zelin testified that the MRI revealed herniations at L4-L5 and L5-S1, and that the accident was the proximate cause of the injuries.

The Second Department ordered a new trial based on the error in allowing Dr. Zelin to testify in this manner. The opinion focused on the rule that an expert may testify based on materials not in evidence provided the out-of-court material is of the kind accepted in the profession as a basis in forming an opinion and the out-of-court material is accompanied by evidence establishing its reliability. Id at 85-86, 739 N.Y.S.2d at 423-24. It refused to apply the "professional reliability" exception because there was no evidence that the MRI report contained reliable data, and because the expert was equivocal as to whether he relied upon it to form his diagnosis or merely to confirm an already established diagnosis. Wagman, 292 A.D.2d at 89-90, 739 N.Y.S.2d at 425-26.

iv) The Expert's Opinion Must be Expressed With "A Reasonable Degree of Medical Certainty" Or In A Manner Equivalent.

To be admissible in court, the expert's testimony must also be expressed with "a reasonable degree of medical certainty" or, if not in those precise terms, according to "any formulation from which it can be said that the witness' whole opinion reflects an acceptable level of certainty." Matott v. Ward, 48 N.Y.2d 455, 460, 399 N.E.2d 532, 534, 423 N.Y.S.2d 645, 647 (1979) (internal citations omitted); see Giberson, 286 A.D.2d at 218, 729 N.Y.S.2d at 30 (rejecting "nebulous and conclusory" expert opinion).

v) Under Frye, The Expert's Theory Must Be General Accepted in the Medical Community

In Frye v United States, the court considered whether to admit evidence derived from a lie detector test. It held as follows:

> [j]ust when a scientific principle or discovery crosses the line between the experimental and demonstrable stages is difficult to define. Somewhere in this twilight zone the evidential force of the principle must be recognized, and while courts will go a long way in admitting expert testimony deduced from a well recognized scientific principle or discovery, the thing from which the deduction is made must be sufficiently established to have gained general acceptance in the particular field in which it belongs. Frye, 54 U.S. App. D.C. 46, 293 F. 1013, 1014 (D.C. Cir. 1923).

"The Frye test emphasizes counting scientists' votes, rather than on verifying the soundness of a scientific conclusion." People v. Wesley, 83 N.Y.2d 417, 439, 633 N.E.2d 451, 611 N.Y.S.2d 97 (1994)(Kaye, Ch. J., concurring). The court must determine "whether, theoretically, the accepted techniques, when performed as they should be, generate results generally accepted as reliable within the scientific community." Id.

Even where a court finds that the "thing from which the deduction is made is sufficiently established to have gained general acceptance in the particular field to which it belongs," id, the court also must undertake a separate foundational inquiry as to the specific reliability of the procedures followed to generate the evidence proffered, as the Court of Appeals emphasized in Parker v. Mobil Oil Corp., 7 N.Y.3d 434, 824 N.E.2d 1114, 857 N.Y.S.2d 584 (2006)(experts failed to lay an adequate foundation for their theory that plaintiff's exposure to benzene in gasoline caused him to develop acute myelogenous leukemia). The Court of Appeals has noted the "danger in allowing unreliable or speculative information (or 'junk science') to go before the jury with the weight of an impressively credentialed expert behind it." Parker, 7 N.Y.3d at 739.

The nature of this separate inquiry was explained in Marsh v. Smyth, 12 A.D.3d 307, 785 N.Y.S.2d 440 (1st Dep't 2004). In a concurring opinion, Justice Saxe observed that the court should:

> mak[e] sure that within the scientific field in question, there is a substantive, demonstrable, objective basis for the expert's conclusion. The appropriate question for the court at such a hearing is the somewhat limited question of whether the proffered expert opinion properly relates existing data, studies or literature to the plaintiff's situation, or whether, instead, it is "connected to existing data only by the ipse dixit of the expert" (see General Electric v Joiner, 522 U.S. 136, 146, 139 L. Ed. 2d 508, 118 S. Ct. 512 [1997]).

Marsh, 12 A.D.3d at 310 (Saxe concurring).

Increasingly, New York courts are applying Frye in medical malpractice cases. In Lara v. New York City Health and Hosp. Corp., 305 A.D.2d 106,

757 N.Y.S.2d 740 (1st Dep't 2003), the Appellate Division upheld the dismissal of a medical malpractice case involving a brain damaged infant because the plaintiff's expert could not demonstrate that his causation opinion was generally accepted in the medical community. In that case, the plaintiff's expert opined that a "slow bleed" in the fetal brain during a rapid second stage of labor caused the infant's cerebral palsy. The trial court set aside the jury verdict in its entirety because it determined that the expert had "cobbled the theory together using bits and pieces from one article along with paragraphs and sentences from another ..." and that the plaintiffs had failed to show that the "slow bleed" causation theory was generally accepted or "based on any scientifically valid methodology." Lara, 2000 N.Y. Misc. LEXIS 650, *8, 2003 NY Slip Op 50887U (Sup. Ct. New York Cty., Sept. 25, 2000). The Appellate Division agreed, noting that the malpractice claim "relied solely on a theory, which is neither recognized nor accepted." Lara, 305 A.D.2d at 107. See also, Stanski v. Ezersky, 228 A.D.2d 311, 644 N.Y.S.2d 220 (1st Dep't 1996) (in legal malpractice action based on handling of underlying medical malpractice suit, court holds that plaintiffs' experts did not establish an accepted causal link between the anesthetic Tetracaine and abdominal myoclonus).

In Saulpaugh v. Krafte, 5 A.D.3d 934, 774 N.Y.S.2d 194 (3d Dep't 2004), a medical malpractice action, all parties agreed that the plaintiff suffered brain damage. Plaintiff sought to introduce expert testimony by a pediatric neurologist that plaintiff's disabilities resulted from protracted fetal head compression due to labor contractions, which allegedly squeezed the blood out of plaintiff's head thereby depriving his brain cells of oxygen. The expert asserted that circulation to the head was interrupted and blood was shunted away from the middle cranial cavity of the brain during protracted uterine contractions. He opined that because of this mechanism, none of the usual symptoms of oxygen deprivation (such as hypoxic ischemic encephalopathy) would be present. Affirming the preclusion of this proposed testimony, the Appellate Division, Third Department ruled as follows:

> Defendants opposed Charash's testimony by proffering the affidavit of a pediatrician specializing in neonatology, who averred that Charash's theory was not generally accepted in the medical field or supported by medical literature. Plaintiffs responded by supplying three expert affidavits.

> Charash's own affidavit relied upon his experience and mentioned a textbook, lectures and conferences which discussed and supported his theory, but he failed to specify any such conferences and did not cite any specific portion of the textbook. The other two expert affidavits attest to general acceptance of Charash's theory regarding brain damage due to head compression and lack of oxygen, but do not expressly mention the core of his theory that uterine contractions can squeeze blood out of the fetal head and lead to the type of brain damage from which plaintiff suffers. They failed to explain how plaintiff's cerebral cortical cells could have been deprived of oxygen during birth with no clinical manifestations during his newborn period. These experts also generally mention having attended lectures, seminars and conferences that addressed this theory, yet failed to identify any specific conference. Charash did not refer to, nor did he mention that, he relied upon any controlled studies or accumulated clinical data. None of the affidavits refer to any scientific studies or reported medical cases which support Charash's theory. Saulpaugh, 5 A.D.3d at 935.

The court observed that "[b]road statements of general scientific acceptance, without accompanying support, are insufficient to meet the burden of establishing such acceptance. Absent any controlled studies, clinical data, medical literature, peer review or supportive proof indicating that Charash's theory was generally accepted by the relevant medical community, Supreme Court properly excluded testimony regarding that theory." Id.

Similarly, in Del Maestro v. Grecco, 16 A.D.3d 364, 791 N.Y.S.2d 139 (2d Dep't 2005), the infant plaintiff was born via caesarian section, preceded by 5½ hours of second-stage labor which was augmented by Pitocin. The gestational age of the infant plaintiff was 41 weeks. A cesarean section was performed due to cephalo-pelvic disproportion. The child had perfect Apgar scores of 9 at 1 minute and 10 at 5 minutes at birth. On the second day, the child experienced episodes of apnea or seizures and was transferred to intensive care. Tests performed in the days following revealed that the child suffered a left middle cerebral artery infarct, leaving him with cerebral palsy (right-sided).

The plaintiffs' expert theorized that the infant plaintiff's injuries were caused by birth trauma resulting from the compression of the child's head during prolonged second-stage labor and the mother's contractions, which were augmented by Pitocin. This, in turn, resulted in ischemia and later an infarction. The defendants contended that the infarction resulted from a clot and was unrelated to obstetrical care, and moved to preclude this testimony on the ground that it lacked general acceptance in the medical community, or for a hearing pursuant to Frye.

The Appellate Division held that the lower court properly ruled that the plaintiffs failed to meet their burden of proof of establishing that their expert's theory of causation was generally accepted in the medical community because plaintiffs' expert could not support his theory with references to medical literature on point. DelMaestro, 16 A.D.3d at 366; see also, Cumberbatch v. Blanchette, 35 A.D.3d 341, 825 N.Y.S.2d 744 (2d Dep't 2006)(accord).

Finally, the Appellate Division has limited the use of "differential diagnosis" to establish the element of proximate causation in tort litigation. Differential diagnosis is a process-of-elimination technique employed by physicians to determine which one of two or more diseases or conditions a patient is suffering from by systematically comparing and contrasting clinical findings. In the courtroom, expert witnesses often fall back on this methodology when they cannot pinpoint the exact cause of a plaintiff's injury.

In Marso v. Novak, 2007 NY Slip Op 6170, 2007 N.Y. App. Div. LEXIS 8626 (1st Dep't July 19, 2007), the Appellate Division held that expert testimony on this basis was not admissible because the expert did not establish that his ultimate conclusion about the cause of the plaintiff's stroke had gained general acceptance in the medical community. In so holding, the court made clear that an accepted "methodology" leading to a novel "conclusion" is not a proper basis upon which to introduce such testimony and to seek to hold a defendant liable.

In Marso, the plaintiff suffered a bilateral stroke at the age of 43. Her treating physicians became convinced that bradycardia (a low heart rate) was the only possible cause of the stroke, which could have been prevented had the defendant inserted a pacemaker. At trial, plaintiff's expert witness testified that all other possibilities for causation of the stroke were excluded by testing. He admitted, however, that it is not generally accepted in the scientific community that bradycardia is a risk factor for the type of embolic stroke suffered by plaintiff. After holding that this causation theory was not generally accepted in the scientific community as required by the Frye doctrine, the trial court directed a verdict in favor of the defendant.

On appeal, plaintiff argued the testimony was admissible because differential diagnosis is a generally accepted methodology, which when properly performed leads to admissible expert conclusions. Rejecting this argument, the Appellate Division held that an opinion based on this technique has no probative value "when there is a generally or widely held view in the scientific community rejecting such conclusions outright." The court added that "[t]o accept plaintiff's 'methodology-only, ignore-the-conclusion' approach would circumvent the rationale for the Frye doctrine. As defendants correctly contend on the basis of this Court's precedent, it is plaintiff's burden to show that his or her expert's theory is generally accepted in the relevant community."

II. THEORIES OF HOSPITAL LIABILITY

A. Direct Liability

1. Negligent Hiring or Credentialing

A hospital owes an independent duty to a patient being treated by a private attending physician if the hospital failed to properly review the physician's credentials before according him unrestricted use of a hospital's facilities. See Garcia v. Montefiore Med. Ctr., 293 A.D.2d 264, 740 N.Y.S.2d 307 (1st Dep't 2002) (requiring that the action at issue be foreseeable by the hospital); Sledziewski v. Cioffi, 137 A.D.2d 186, 528 N.Y.S.2d 913 (3d Dep't 1988). To sustain a claim based on this theory, a plaintiff must prove the hospital failed to develop and adhere to reasonable procedures for reviewing a physician's qualifications. Raschel v. Rish, 110 A.D.2d 1067, 488 N.Y.S.2d 923 (4th Dep't 1985), aff'd on other grounds, 69 N.Y.2d 694, 504 N.E.2d 389, 512 N.Y.S.2d 22 (1986). A necessary element of a cause of action for negligent hiring is that the employer knew or should have known of the employee's propensity for the conduct which caused the injury.

Kenneth R. v. Roman Catholic Diocese, 229 A.D.2d 159, 654 N.Y.S.2d 791 (2d Dep't 1997). In order to show that the employer should have known of the employee's propensity, the plaintiff must offer proof that a more thorough background check would have uncovered this knowledge. Id.

In Nelson v. Good Samaritan Hospital, 264 A.D.2d 412, 694 N.Y.S.2d 420 (2d Dep't 1999), the plaintiffs alleged that because defendant hospital was aware of prior malpractice actions against a physician, it should have restricted or revoked the physician's staff privileges. In support of its summary judgment motion, the hospital produced an affidavit demonstrating that the hospital implemented adequate procedures to review its physicians' staff privileges, including the consideration of any and all malpractice actions, and that these procedures were properly adhered to with respect to the physician in question. Despite plaintiffs' recitation of prior malpractice claims against Dr. Rella, only one of which resulted in a judgment, the court determined that Good Samaritan Hospital sufficiently established its entitlement to summary judgment.

In contrast, in Bush v. St. Clare's Hospital, 192 A.D.2d 772, 596 N.Y.S.2d 203 (3d Dep't 1993), rev'd, 82 N.Y.2d 738, 621 N.E.2d 691, 602 N.Y.S.2d 324 (1993), the hospital's executive committee had actual knowledge of a physician's drinking problem and placed the physician on preceptorship, which involves the close monitoring or observation of the activities of a physician. Bush, 192 A.D.2d at 773, 596 N.Y.S.2d at 204. The plaintiff was injured during surgery and claimed the hospital was negligent in its oversight of the physician. Reversing an award of summary judgment, the Court of Appeals identified a question of fact as to whether the physician was actually placed on preceptorship as directed. Bush, 82 N.Y.2d at 739, 621 N.E.2d at 692, 602 N.Y.S.2d at 325. Plaintiff thus stated a viable claim based on evidence that the hospital had actual notice of a physician's incompetence and may have failed to adhere to its own recommendations concerning a physician's status.

In Megrelishvili v. Our Lady of Mercy Medical Center, 291 A.D.2d 18, 739 N.Y.S.2d 2 (1st Dep't 2002), the plaintiff alleged that the hospital was liable for her injuries because it did not investigate prior complaints of malpractice against the attending physician. In addition, the plaintiff further alleged that the hospital allowed the doctor to retain staff privileges even though the doctor was practicing without medical malpractice insurance.

The First Department found that the plaintiff could sufficiently state a cause of action against the hospital for its failure to restrict the physician's privileges after the physician was no longer covered by malpractice insurance. The court held that a hospital's failure to develop and adhere to reasonable procedures for reviewing a physician's qualifications creates a foreseeable risk of harm, creating an independent duty to the injured patient.

Plaintiffs who assert negligent hiring/credentialing claims face an uphill battle in light of Logue v. Velez, 92 N.Y.2d 13, 699 N.E.2d 365, 677 N.Y.S.2d 6 (1998). In Logue, the plaintiff alleged she was injured during surgery by a physician who was inadequately trained to perform the procedure. She brought suit against the hospital claiming that the hospital negligently granted the physician privileges to conduct this specific type of surgery. Logue, 92 N.Y.2d at 16, 699 N.E.2d at 366, 677 N.Y.S.2d at 7. During discovery, the plaintiff issued a disclosure request seeking copies of the physician's initial and renewal applications for privileges, as well as supporting documentation.

The Court of Appeals held that these documents fell squarely within the materials exempted from disclosure pursuant to Education Law §6527(3),[2] as well as the parallel provisions of Public Health Law §2805-m, which confers complete confidentiality on all materials compiled by hospitals pursuant to Public Health Law §2805-j and §2805-k. Id. at 16-17, 699 N.E.2d at 366-67, 677 N.Y.S.2d at 7-8 . The Court acknowledged the policies underlying § 2805-j and §2805-k to reduce malpractice "by requiring more peer self-policing and by improving the investigation of, and methods of disciplining, physician misconduct." Id. at 17, 699 N.E.2d at 367, 677 N.Y.S.2d at 8. The Court further recognized that documents relating to the quality assurance function of a hospital are guaranteed confidentiality "to assure that medical review committees 'may frankly and objectively analyze the quality of health services rendered.'" Id. at 17, 699 N.E.2d at 366-67, 677 N.Y.S.2d at 7-8 (citations omitted).

[2] Education Law §6527(3) provides that "[n]either the proceedings nor the records relating to performance of a medical or a quality assurance review function" are subject to discovery under Article 31 of the CPLR. Public Health Law §2805-j requires every hospital to "maintain a coordinated program for the identification and prevention of medical . . . malpractice", including the periodic review of a physician's credentials and competence. Public Health Law §2805-k requires a hospital to obtain specific, detailed information from a physician, including incidences of misconduct, before granting or renewing professional privileges.

Notably, the Court rejected plaintiffs' assertion that these materials were discoverable under the statutory exception for "statements given at an otherwise privileged peer review meeting by a party to a lawsuit which involves the same underlying conduct that is the topic of discussion at the meeting." Id. at 18, 699 N.E.2d at 368, 677 N.Y.S.2d at 9. The Court refused to allow the plaintiffs to circumvent the confidentiality provisions[3] of the Public Health Law and Education Law "by the simple device of asserting a claim against the hospital for negligent credentialing." Id. at 19, 699 N.E.2d at 368, 677 N.Y.S.2d at 9.

2. Patient Security

A hospital has a duty to safeguard the welfare of its patients, even from harm inflicted by third persons, measured by the capacity of the patient to provide for his or her own safety. N.X. v. Cabrini Med. Ctr., 97 N.Y.2d 247, 765 N.E.2d 844, 739 N.Y.S.2d 348 (2002); Killeen v. State of N.Y., 66 N.Y.2d 850, 489 N.E.2d 245, 498 N.Y.S.2d 358 (1985); Morris v. Lenox Hill Hosp., 232 A.D.2d 184, 647 N.Y.S.2d 753 (1st Dep't 1996), aff'd 90 N.Y.2d 953, 688 N.E.2d 255, 665 N.Y.S.2d 399 (1997); Clinton v. City of N.Y., 140 A.D.2d 404, 528 N.Y.S.2d 108 (2d Dep't 1988). This does not, however, render a hospital an insurer or require it to keep each patient under constant surveillance. Killeen, 66 N.Y.2d at 851-52, 489 N.E.2d at 246, 498 N.Y.S.2d at 359, citing Hirsh v. State of N.Y., 8 N.Y.2d 125, 168 N.E.2d 372, 202 N.Y.S.2d 296 (1960).

Indeed, the courts regularly dismiss claims against hospitals arising from sexual abuse of patients by employees in the absence of evidence that the employer was or should have been aware of employee's propensity for sexual misconduct. See Judith M. v. Sisters of Charity Hosp., 249 A.D.2d 890, 671 N.Y.S.2d 400 (4th Dep't 1998), aff'd, 93 N.Y.2d 932, 715 N.E.2d 95, 693 N.Y.S.2d 67 (1999); Cornell v. State of N.Y., 60 A.D.2d 714, 401 N.Y.S.2d 107 (3d Dep't 1977), aff'd, 46 N.Y.2d 1032, 389 N.E.2d 1064, 416 N.Y.S.2d 542 (1979); Mataxas v. North Shore Univ. Hosp., 211 A.D.2d 762, 621 N.Y.S.2d 683 (2d Dep't 1995); Kirkman v. Astoria Gen. Hosp., 204 A.D.2d 401, 611 N.Y.S.2d 615 (2d Dep't 1994); Whidbee v. State of N.Y., 176 A.D.2d 798, 575 N.Y.S.2d 127 (2d Dep't 1991).

---

[3] It is the hospital's burden to prove that any statements sought to be disclosed fall under the ambit of these statutes. See Mong v. Children's Hosp., 259 A.D.2d 1038, 688 N.Y.S.2d 353 (4th Dep't 1999).

In N.X., the plaintiff was sexually abused by a surgical resident while she was still under the effects of anesthesia after undergoing vaginal surgery. The resident had no history of this type of conduct and he arrived in the recovery roomed identified and dressed as a hospital resident. Nevertheless, he assaulted the patient in close proximity to three recovery room nurses, who denied witnessing the event. The Court of Appeals thus held that there was a question of fact as to whether the nurses actually observed or unreasonably ignored events immediately preceding the misconduct which indicated a risk of imminent harm to plaintiff, triggering the need for protective action. N.X., 97 N.Y.2d at 252, 765 N.E.2d at 848, 739 N.Y.S.2d at 352. The Court was careful to emphasize the fact-specific nature of its ruling, and that it was not imposing a "gatekeeping" function upon nurses to stop and question physicians, ascertain reasons for their presence, or to stand guard and monitor their interactions with patients. Id. at 255, 765 N.E.2d at 849-50, 739 N.Y.S.2d at 353-54.

B. Vicarious Liability

1. For Negligence of Private Attending Physician

It is well established that a hospital will not be held vicariously liable for the acts of a private attending physician. Raschel v. Rish, 69 N.Y.2d 694, 696, 504 N.E.2d 389, 512 N.Y.S.2d 22 (1986); Culhane v. Schorr, 259 A.D.2d 511, 686 N.Y.S.2d 105 (2d Dep't 1999); Steiner v. Brookdale Hosp. Med. Ctr., 241 A.D.2d 516, 663 N.Y.S.2d 981 (2d Dep't 1997); Cirella v. Cent. Gen. Hosp., 217 A.D.2d 680, 630 N.Y.S.2d 93 (2d Dep't 1995). A hospital is not required to intervene in the relationship between a patient and a private attending physician unless the doctor's orders are "'so clearly contraindicated by normal practice that ordinary prudence requires inquiry into [their] correctness.'" Mertsaris v. 73rd Corp., 105 A.D.2d 67, 79, 482 N.Y.S.2d 792, 800 (2d Dep't 1984) (citations omitted); see also Nevarez v. N.Y. City Health and Hospitals Corp., 248 A.D.2d 307, 670 N.Y.S.2d 48 (1st Dep't 1998).

2. For Negligence of Staff

Nevertheless, a hospital may be held concurrently liable with a private practitioner for the independent negligence of the hospital's medical staff. See Pearce v. Klein, 293 A.D.2d 593, 741 N.Y.S.2d 89 (2d Dep't 2002); Barnes v.

Sheehan, 275 A.D.2d 1028, 714 N.Y.S.2d 917 (4th Dep't 2000); Gerner v. Long Island Jewish Hillside Med. Ctr., 203 A.D.2d 60, 609 N.Y.S.2d 898 (1st Dep't 1994) (identifying questions of fact as to whether hospital staff was negligent during post-natal monitoring of infant-plaintiff, including while plaintiff was technically under care of a private attending physician).

C. Apparent Agency

The other theory under which a hospital will be liable for the actions of a private, attending physician is that of "ostensible" or "apparent" agency. In Mduba v. Benedictine Hospital, 52 A.D.2d 450, 384 N.Y.S.2d 527 (3d Dep't 1976), the court held that a hospital may be held vicariously liable for a physician's malpractice when the patient sought medical care from the hospital rather than from a particular physician, even where the allegedly negligent physician was an independent contractor rather than an employee of the hospital. Although Mduba dealt only with a physician/independent contractor assigned to the hospital emergency room, subsequent cases suggest that Mduba extends beyond the geographic boundaries of the ER.

The decedent in Mduba was treated in the defendant-hospital's emergency room by the emergency room supervisor, whose contract deemed him an independent contractor rather than an employee of the hospital. Id. at 452, 384 N.Y.S.2d at 528. The trial court found, based on the contract language, that the hospital could not be held vicariously liable. In reversing, the Third Department offered two alternate theories in favor of vicarious liability.

First, the court observed that, in determining the nature of an employment relationship, contract language is not dispositive. Id. at 453, 384 N.Y.S.2d at 529. Rather, a right of control test respecting the manner in which the work is to be done governs. Id. Observing that the doctor was bound by hospital rules and regulations, the court concluded, as a matter of law, that the physician was actually an employee of the hospital since the hospital controlled the manner in which the doctor operated the emergency room. Id. at 452-453, 384 N.Y.S.2d at 529.

Second, the court stated that the hospital would be liable even if the doctor was an independent contractor. Here, the court distinguished between patients who engage a particular doctor at a defendant-hospital and patients who enter a defendant-hospital for hospital treatment. In the latter case, the defendant-hospital—having undertaken to treat the patient—has a duty to do so effectively. Id. at 453, 384 N.Y.S.2d at 529. Moreover, the court stated, "patients entering the hospital through the emergency room could properly assume that treating doctors and staff were acting on behalf of the hospital." Id. Based on apparent agency principles, therefore, "such patients are not bound by secret limitations as are contained in a private contract between the hospital and the doctor." Id.

While the Mduba court spoke of "patients entering through the emergency room door," later cases appear not to limit Mduba to its facts. In Riviera v. Bronx-Lebanon Hospital Center, 70 A.D.2d 794, 417 N.Y.S.2d 79 (1st Dep't 1979), the court found that where the decedent entered the hospital through the emergency room, but was later admitted to the hospital for surgical and medical treatment by an independent attending physician, the trial court erred in holding that the hospital was not liable for the doctor's acts. The court relied on Mduba and found that the degree of control exercised by the hospital would determine its liability, and that this was a jury question. Id. at 796, 417 N.Y.S.2d at 82. The court further noted that the decedent never retained the attending physician to act as such, but rather the hospital assigned the physician.[4] Id.

In a slightly different context, the Second Department has distinguished, not between "emergency room" patients and "private" patients, but rather between "service" patients and "private" patients. See Rodrigo v. Brookdale Hosp., 194 A.D.2d 774, 599 N.Y.S.2d 626 (2d Dep't 1993). In Rodrigo, the court defined "service" patients as patients of the hospital and its employee doctors, as opposed to "private" patients, which are considered patients of the attending physician who is affiliated with the hospital. Id. at 775, 599

[4] In McDonald v. Ambassador Construction Company, 273 A.D.2d 108, 709 N.Y.S.2d 177 (1st Dep't 2000), a patient's belief that a doctor was acting as an agent of the hospital, if reasonable, was sufficient to hold the hospital vicariously liable for the doctor's alleged malpractice. The court so held despite the fact that the doctor was actually an independent contractor. In Syracuse v. Diao, 272 A.D.2d 881, 707 N.Y.S.2d 570 (4th Dep't 2000), the court also held that there was a genuine issue of material fact was to whether the hospital was vicariously liable, where the plaintiff called the hospital, did not ask for a specific doctor, and the hospital worker referred the plaintiff to defendant-doctor, an independent contractor. See also Lockhart v. Grace, 189 A.D.2d 656, 592 N.Y.S.2d 328 (1st Dep't 1993); Harrington v. Neurological Inst. of Columbia Presbyterian Med. Ctr., 254 A.D.2d 129, 679 N.Y.S.2d 17 (1st Dep't 1998).

N.Y.S.2d at 627. Although the attending physician treated the decedent in Rodrigo for approximately seven years—from 1979 to 1986—the hospital was relieved for purposes of the "continuous treatment" doctrine in 1983, when the decedent re-entered the hospital as a "private" patient. Id. It was only at that point, the court reasoned, that the hospital no longer controlled the decedent's course of treatment. Id.

The Appellate Division, Third Department has adopted a more restrictive view of the Mduba doctrine. In Thurman v. United Health Services Hospitals, Inc., 39 A.D.3d 934, 833 N.Y.S.2d 702 (3d Dep't 2007), defendant hospital was sued on the basis of an independent radiologist's alleged misreading of a CAT scan. The radiologist was the "on call" radiologist at that time and he was not known to plaintiff's decedent or his treating physician. The radiologist was not employed by defendant but, rather, by an independent group of radiologists that had an exclusive contract to provide such services at defendant's hospital.

In dismissing the claim of vicarious liability, the Appellate Division held as follows:

> Plaintiff's reliance on the fact that decedent was never informed that Ralston was not a hospital employee is inadequate, as defendant was not "obligated to affirmatively disclaim [Ralston] as an employee in order to avoid the creation of ostensible agency" (King v Mitchell, supra at 960). Neither are Ralston's affiliation with defendant, his presence at defendant's facility or his assumption of the role of reading and interpreting decedent's CAT scan sufficient to impute his negligence to defendant (see Hill v St. Clare's Hosp., supra at 79; King v Mitchell, supra at 960; Nagengast v Samaritan Hosp., 211 A.D.2d 878, 879, 621 N.Y.S.2d 217 [1995]). Further, Ralston's use for the CAT scan report of defendant's stationery containing its logo "without more, is insufficient to satisfy the holding out portion of the test" (King v Mitchell, supra at 960; Nagengast v Samaritan Hosp., supra at 879), and plaintiff's reference to the content of defendant's Web site is unavailing in the absence of even an allegation that plaintiff or decedent accessed it or relied upon it (see King v Mitchell,

supra at 959-960; see also N.X. v Cabrini Med. Ctr., supra at 252 n 3). The record is bereft of any evidence showing that defendant made representations or engaged in any misleading conduct that Ralston was its employee or agent and that decedent submitted himself to Ralston's care by reason of such representations or conduct (see Nagengast v Samaritan Hosp., supra at 880).

Likewise inapposite are cases recognizing that hospitals may be held vicariously liable for the acts of independent physicians where the patient entered the hospital through an emergency room and sought treatment from the hospital and not a particular physician (see Salvatore v Winthrop Univ. Med. Ctr., 36 A.D.3d 887, 888, 829 N.Y.S.2d 183 [2007]; Monostori v Murphy, 34 A.D.3d 882, 883-884, 823 N.Y.S.2d 783 [2006]; Johnson v Jamaica Hosp. Med. Ctr., 21 A.D.3d 881, 883, 800 N.Y.S.2d 609 [2005]; Torns v Samaritan Hosp., supra at 967; Citron v Northern Dutchess Hosp., 198 A.D.2d 618, 620, 603 N.Y.S.2d 639 [1993], lv denied 83 N.Y.2d 753, 634 N.E.2d 603, 612 N.Y.S.2d 107 [1994]; see also McDonald v Ambassador Constr. Co., 273 A.D.2d 108, 109, 709 N.Y.S.2d 177 [2000]; Abraham v Dulit, 255 A.D.2d 345, 679 N.Y.S.2d 707 [1998]; Ryan v New York City Health & Hosps. Corp., 220 A.D.2d 734, 736, 633 N.Y.S.2d 500 [1995]). Here, while decedent presented to the emergency room, his care was almost immediately assumed by Marhaba, his treating gastroenterologist, who admitted him into the intensive care unit and either performed or ordered numerous diagnostic tests during decedent's admission over the next week. Indeed, plaintiff's affidavit reflects that decedent either requested or consented to Marhaba being called in to oversee his care. Under these circumstances, decedent could not have reasonably believed that he was receiving medical care from the hospital in general rather than from a particular physician (see Christopherson v Queens-Long Is. Med. Group, 17 A.D.3d 393, 394, 792 N.Y.S.2d 608 [2005]; Ventura v Beth Israel Med. Ctr., 297 A.D.2d 801, 802-803, 747 N.Y.S.2d 595 [2002], lv denied 99 N.Y.2d 510, 790 N.E.2d 275, 760

> N.Y.S.2d 101 [2003]). That is, defendant did not, through its operation of its emergency room, maintain control over the manner and means of Marhaba's treatment of decedent during which he ordered the CAT scan, and Ralston's interpretation and reporting on it did not occur in the emergency room setting or as part of the hospital's care (see Payant v Imobersteg, 256 A.D.2d 702, 704, 681 N.Y.S.2d 135 [1998]; Nagengast v Samaritan Hosp., supra at 879). Thus, since decedent obtained treatment in the emergency room and while admitted from his independent treating physician, during which Ralston's alleged negligence occurred, the emergency room setting line of cases in which patients seek and receive treatment from the hospital is inapplicable (see King v Mitchell, 31 A.D.3d 958, 960-961 [2006], supra; Christopherson v Queens-Long Is. Med. Group, supra at 394; Ventura v Beth Israel Med. Ctr., supra at 802-803; Nagengast v Samaritan Hosp., supra at 879-880).

Thurman, 39 A.D.3d at 936-37 (footnotes omitted).

Finally, the Mduba rule presupposes that the patient has a viable claim against the treating physicians. In Magriz v. St. Barnabas Hospital, 2007 NY Slip Op 6444, 2007 N.Y. App. Div. LEXIS 9177 (1st Dep't Aug. 16, 2007), plaintiff's Mduba claim against the defendant hospital was dismissed because her claims against the individual defendants were dismissed as untimely.

III. INFORMED CONSENT (PHL 2805-D/CPLR §4401-A)

Public Health Law §2805-d provides as follows:

> 1. Lack of informed consent means the failure of the person providing professional treatment or diagnosis to disclose to the patient such alternatives thereto and the reasonably foreseeable risks and benefits involved as a reasonable medical, dental or podiatric practitioner under similar circumstances would have disclosed, in a manner permitting the patient to make a knowledgeable evaluation.

2. The right of action to recover for medical, dental or podiatric malpractice based on a lack of informed consent is limited to those cases involving either (a) non-emergency treatment, procedure or surgery, or (b) a diagnostic procedure which involved invasion or disruption of the integrity of the body.
3. For a cause of action therefore it must also be established that a reasonably prudent person in the patient's position would not have undergone the treatment or diagnosis if he had been fully informed and that the lack of informed consent is a proximate cause of the injury or condition for which recovery is sought.
4. It shall be a defense to any action for medical, dental or podiatric malpractice based upon an alleged failure to obtain such an informed consent that:

   (a) the risk not disclosed is too commonly known to warrant disclosure; or
   (b) the patient assured the medical, dental or podiatric practitioner he would undergo the treatment, procedure or diagnosis regardless of the risk involved, or the patient assured the medical, dental or podiatric practitioner that he did not want to be informed of the matters to which he would be entitled to be informed; or
   (c) consent by or on behalf of the patient was not reasonably possible; or
   (d) the medical, dental or podiatric practitioner, after considering all of the attendant facts and circumstances, used reasonable discretion as to the manner and extent to which such alternatives or risks were disclosed to the patient because he reasonably believed the manner and extent of such disclosure could reasonably be expected to adversely and substantially affect the patient's condition.

Thus, a plaintiff must prove that

(i) defendant failed to disclose the material risks, benefits, and alternatives to the procedure at issue which a reasonable medical practitioner "under similar circumstances would have disclosed, in a manner permitting [the plaintiff] to make a knowledgeable evaluation"; and

(ii) a reasonably prudent person in the plaintiff's position would not have undergone the surgery if he or she had been fully informed. Dunlop v. Sivaraman, 272 A.D.2d 570, 709 N.Y.S. 419 (2d Dep't 2000); Faulknor v. Shnayerson, 273 A.D.2d 271, 709 N.Y.S.2d 848 (2d Dep't 2000); Davis v. Nassau Ophthalmic Svces., 232 A.D.2d 358, 648 N.Y.S.2d 454 (2d Dep't 1996) (citations omitted); and

(iii) the alleged injury in fact was proximately caused by the procedure. Santilli v. CHP, 274 A.D.2d 905, 711 N.Y.S. 249 (3d Dep't 2000); Tibodeau v. Keeley, 208 A.D.2d 610, 617 N.Y.S.2d 183 (2d Dep't 1994); Eppel v. Fredericks, 203 A.D.2d 152, 610 N.Y.S.2d 254 (1st Dep't 1994); Flores v. Flushing Hosp. Ctr., 109 A.D.2d 198, 490 N.Y.S.2d 770 (1st Dep't 1985).

The first element under CPLR §4401-a, the alleged "qualitative insufficiency" of the consent, must be supported by expert medical testimony. King v. Jordan, 265 A.D.2d 619, 696 N.Y.S.2d 280 (3d Dep't 1999); Hylick v. Halweil, 112 A.D.2d 400, 492 N.Y.S.2d 57 (2d Dep't 1985). A plaintiff is **not** required to adduce expert medical testimony to prove the second element, that a reasonably prudent person in plaintiff's position would not have undergone the procedure if the risks had been fully disclosed. Anderson v. Delaney, 269 A.D.2d 193, 703 N.Y.S.2d 714 (1st Dep't 2000) (plaintiff's affidavit stating that she would not have undergone the procedure was sufficient on its own to raise a question of fact); Laribee v. City of Rome, 254 A.D.2d 805, 678 N.Y.S.2d 565 (4th Dep't 1998); Hardt v. LaTrenta, 251 A.D.2d 174, 674 N.Y.S.2d 335 (1st Dep't 1998) (plaintiff was not required to adduce an expert medical testimony regarding the reasonably prudent person element of §2805-d); Osorio v. Brauner, 242 A.D.2d 511, 662 N.Y.S.2d 488 (1st Dep't 1997).

A recent Court of Appeals decision of note is Lynn G. v. Hugo 96 N.Y.2d 306, 752 N.E.2d 250, 728 N.Y.S.2d 121 (2001). There, plaintiff argued she was not competent to consent to a full abdominoplasty or "tummy tuck" because she suffered from Body Dysmorphic Disorder (BDD), which rendered her incapable of assessing whether the benefits outweighed the risks of such surgery. She claimed that because she had visited her plastic surgeon approximately fifty times in the six years prior to the surgery, and she had told him she was taking anti-depressants, her surgeon should have inquired into her mental health before obtaining her consent. The Court of Appeals held that the record did not reveal that plaintiff suffered this condition or that the surgeon had any reason to suspect it.

IV. WRONGFUL DEATH

Wrongful Death is governed by statute in New York. It is a separate cause of action for the statutory survivors of the decedent. It allows for the recovery of pecuniary damages only; it prevents recovery (under this theory) for the pain and suffering of the decedent and for loss of consortium to the survivors.

A. Elements of a Statutory Cause of Action

The elements of the New York wrongful death cause of action are:

(1) the death of a human being born alive. Endresz v. Friedberg, 24 N.Y.2d 478, 248 N.E.2d 901, 301 N.Y.S.2d 65 (1969);
(2) caused by the wrongful act or omission of a person or corporation who, by reason of the wrongful act or omission, would have been liable to the deceased for injury had death not ensued;
(3) the existence at the time of death of statutory distributees who have sustained a pecuniary loss by reason of decedent's death; and
(4) the appointment of a personal representative who alone may bring suit. See EPTL §5-4.1(1)

B. Damages Must Be Pecuniary

EPTL 5-4.3 limits an award of damages in a wrongful death case to the fair and just compensation for the pecuniary injuries resulting from the death of the decedent "to the persons for whose benefit the action is brought." The New York wrongful death statute only permits recovery of pecuniary damages such as loss of services and lost earnings. It does not permit recovery for grief of the survivors, the loss of their decedent's love, companionship and society, or the surviving spouse's loss of consortium. In re Acquafredda, 189 A.D.2d 504, 596 N.Y.S.2d 839 (2d Dep't 1993);

Garland v. Herrin, 724 F.2d 16 (2d Cir. 1983); Smith v. Lehigh Valley R.Co., 177 N.Y. 379, 69 N.E.2d 729 (1904); Tilley v. Hudson Riv. R.R.Co., 24 N.Y. 471, 23 How. Pr. 363 (1862). The Court of Appeals has refused to supplement the statutory wrongful death act with a common law remedy that would provide such non-pecuniary damages. See Gonzalez v. N.Y. City Hous. Auth., 77 N.Y.2d 663, 572 N.E.2d 598, 569 N.Y.S.2d 915 (1991); Johnson v. Manhattan & Bronx Surface Transit Operating Auth., 71 N.Y.2d 198, 519 N.E.2d 326 (1988); Lift v. Schildkrout, 49 N.Y.2d 622, 404 N.E.2d 1288, 427 N.Y.S.2d 746 (1980).

Also recoverable is the value of parental care and guidance and services provided by a parent or grandparent, regardless of the fact that the child or grandchild may be an adult with independent means of support. See Gonzalez, 77 N.Y.2d at 668-69, 572 N.E.2d at 601, 569 N.Y.S.2d at 918. These have been deemed a pecuniary interest of the survivors because replacement of such services and guidance carry an objectively discoverable cost. This factor seems to be the defining characteristic of any included damage award and an argument against inclusion of a particular damage claim would be best served by showing the subjective gray area of a claim.

V. NON-PARTY MEDICAL EXPERTS AND SUBSEQUENT TREATING PHYSICIANS

This section discusses New York's unique rules regarding disclosure of retained experts and recent developments with respect to *ex parte* interviews of non-party treating physicians.

A. Disclosure under CPLR §3101(d).

New York places severe limits on expert disclosure. It is one of the few jurisdictions that does not allow pretrial depositions of experts. In addition, under an unproven theory that expert physicians in medical malpractice cases are susceptible to coercion from other physicians not to testify against their colleagues, their identities may be kept hidden until they take the stand at trial.

Section 3101(d)(1)(i) of the CPLR provides as follows:

> Upon request, each party shall identify each person whom the party expects to call as an expert witness at trial and shall disclose in *reasonable detail the subject matter* on which each expert is expected to testify, the *substance of the facts and opinions on which each expert is expected to testify*, the *qualifications* of each expert witness and a *summary of the grounds for each expert's opinion*. However, where a party for good cause shown retains an expert an insufficient period of time before the commencement of trial to give appropriate notice thereof, the party shall not thereupon be precluded from introducing the expert'stestimony at the trial solely on the grounds of noncompliance with this paragraph. In that instance, upon motion of any party, made before or at trial, or on its own initiative, the court may make whatever order may be just. *In an action for medical, dental, or podiatric malpractice, a party, in responding to a request, may omit the names of medical, dental, or podiatric experts* but shall be required to disclose all other information concerning such experts otherwise required by this paragraph.[5]

1. Expert Disclosure Must Be Requested

Expert disclosure is required only upon request. If the opposing party fails to serve a demand for expert disclosure during discovery, a party has no obligation to comply with CPLR 3101(d)(1)(i) and will not be precluded from introducing expert testimony at trial for having failed to do so. See Collins v. Greater N.Y. Sav. Bank, 194 A.D.2d 514, 598 N.Y.S.2d 544 (2d Dep't 1993).

---

[5] The statute's effective date was July 1, 1985, and it does not apply retroactively to actions commenced prior to that date. See Estate of Flynn, 130 Misc. 2d 301, 496 N.Y.S.3d 653 (Sur. Ct., Bronx County 1985). The former version of CPLR 3101(d) specifically provided that the opinion of an expert, prepared for litigation, was not subject to disclosure. See Jasopersaud v. Rho, 169 A.D.2d 184, 186, 572 N.Y.S.2d 700, 702 (2d Dep't 1991). CPLR 3101(d)(1)(ii) sets forth the procedures for the taking of expert witness examinations before trial in medical malpractice actions. This section is rarely invoked because it requires the agreement of all parties to produce their respective experts for depositions. Such unanimity is rarely achieved. In addition, CPLR 3101(d)(1)(iii) permits the court to order further disclosure concerning the expected testimony of any expert based upon a showing of "special circumstances". These exist where "material or physical evidence underlying a claim is lost or destroyed" after the expert had examined it or where "some other unique factual situation exists." Hallahan v. Ashland Chem. Co., 237 A.D.2d 697, 698, 654 N.Y.S.2d 443, 445 (3d Dep't 1997).

On the other hand, a party upon whom a demand for expert disclosure is made may not elect not to respond in any manner, without having moved for a protective order, simply because he or she believes that the discovery demand is overbroad. This can result in preclusion of the expert's testimony at trial. See Morris v. Clements, 228 A.D.2d 990, 644 N.Y.S.2d 850 (3d Dep't 1996); Howarth v. O'Daly, 221 A.D.2d 318, 633 N.Y.S.2d 385 (2d Dep't 1995). Furthermore, if a plaintiff does not move for a timely protective order with respect to defendant's expert witness demands for disclosure, the court will require the plaintiff to provide such responses. Morabito v. Hudson Valley Plastic Surgeons, 286 A.D.2d 485, 729 N.Y.S.2d 634 (2d Dep't 2001). In addition, a party must amend or supplement its expert disclosure when the information previously supplied is no longer correct and complete and if the failure to do so would be materially misleading. CPLR 3101(h).

2. Redaction of Expert's Identity in Medical Malpractice Actions

The statute makes clear that in medical, dental and podiatric malpractice cases, the actual identity of the expert need not be disclosed. This exception was added because of the "perceived problem of the exertion of direct or indirect pressure by some physicians to discourage their colleagues from giving expert testimony against them." Rubenstein v. Columbia Presbyterian Med. Ctr., 139 Misc. 2d 349, 352, 527 N.Y.S.2d 680, 683 (Sup. Ct., N.Y. County 1988).

Whether such coercion actually occurs is debatable. Moreover, redaction is not foolproof because computerized medical directories allow parties to identify opposing experts according to various criteria, including medical school attended, residencies, licenses and so on. Not surprisingly, various bar groups have lobbied for an amendment to CPLR 3101(d)(1)(i) to bring it in line with federal procedure which requires the parties to identify their experts and produce them for depositions. FRCP 26(a).

It is settled that a party may successfully oppose a summary judgment motion without disclosing the names of the party's expert witnesses, provided that a redacted copy of the expert's affirmation is made available to the court for *in camera* inspection. See Napiersiki v. Finn, 229 A.D.2d

869, 646 N.Y.S.2d 415 (3d Dep't 1996). In contrast, the Appellate Division, Second Department has held that this protection is not available to a defendant who submits an expert affidavit in *support* of a motion for summary judgment. In Marano v. Mercy Hospital, 241 A.D.2d 48, 670 N.Y.S.2d 570 (2d Dep't 1998), the court held that a summary judgment *movant*, who bears the initial burden of establishing entitlement to judgment as a matter of law, may not rely on a redacted expert affidavit.

However, when the movant has met its threshold burden, regardless of whether the cause of action sounds in medical malpractice, strict products liability, traditional tort or other ground, affirmative proof in *admissible form* must be offered to raise an issue for the trier of fact. At that juncture, rules concerning pretrial disclosure are inapplicable. As aforesaid, such a motion is, procedurally, duplicative of an actual trial. The sanctioning of the procedural gymnastics envisioned by would be the equivalent to allowing plaintiff's expert to testify from behind a screen at trial. Such a procedure does nothing to advance the truth-determining function of our system of jurisprudence, nor is it authorized by statute. Nandy v. Albany Med. Ctr. Hosp., 140 Misc. 2d 693, 532 N.Y.S.2d 41 (3d Dep't 1988) (But see McCarty v. Cmty. Hosp., 203 A.D.2d 432, 610 N.Y.S.2d 588 (2d Dep't 1994) (criticizing Nandy and determining that an in camera review of the expert testimony is the proper procedure).

In Wagner v. Kingston Hospital, 182 A.D.2d 616, 582 N.Y.S.2d 214 (2d Dep't 1992), and Ryan v. Michelson, 241 A.D.2d 434, 660 N.Y.S.2d 435 (1st Dep't 1997), the First and Second Departments held that a plaintiff may redact identifying information in a physical examination report disclosed pursuant to CPLR 3121(b) if the plaintiff intends to use the examining physician as his or her expert at trial. The courts reasoned that permitting service of redacted physical examination report is an appropriate accommodation of the competing purposes of broad disclosure under CPLR 3121(b) and protection of the expert's identity under CPLR 3101(d)(1)(i).

3. What is Adequate Disclosure?

The statute is not explicit as to the timing and breadth of expert disclosure required short of identifying the expert; it merely directs disclosure in "reasonable detail" of the subject matter of the expert's expected testimony, the "substance of the facts and opinions on which each expert is expected to testify" and the qualifications of each expert. CPLR 3101(d)(1)(i). The statute merely directs disclosure in "reasonable detail" of the "subject matter" of the expert's expected testimony, the "substance of the facts and opinions on which each expert is expected to testify", and the "qualifications" of each expert. At the same time it allows medical malpractice parties to withhold their expert's identities, apparently a legislative response to the perception that some physicians would discourage their colleagues from giving expert testimony against them if they knew their identities.

For more than a decade Jasopersaud v. Rho, 169 A.D.2d 184, 572 N.Y.S.2d 700 (2d Dep't 1991), was the defining case in New York regarding the adequate level of disclosure. The Appellate Division held that a party fulfills the "qualifications" requirement if he or she discloses the (1) medical school attended by the expert, (2) the expert's board certifications, (3) areas of special expertise, (4) jurisdictions of licensure and the (5) locations of internships, residencies and/or fellowships. The court ruled that the dates associated with attainment of these qualifications (for instance, the year of medical school graduation) and the expert's present hospital affiliations were not discoverable because such information would tend to reveal the identity of the witness, defeating the legislative policy underlying the statutory exception.

In 2002, the Second Department specifically overruled Jasopersaud with its decision in Thomas v. Alleyne, 302 A.D.2d 36, 752 N.Y.S.2d 362 (2d Dep't 2002). The court held that:

> defendants in medical malpractice actions are presumptively entitled to a statement of the plaintiff's expert's qualifications in "reasonable detail" (CPLR 3101 [d] [1] [i]), as the statute commands, and that the plaintiffs in such cases may avoid compliance with this obligation only upon production of proof sufficient to sustain findings (a) that there is a reasonable probability that such compliance would lead to the disclosure of the actual identity of their expert or experts, and (b) that there is a reasonable probability that such disclosure would cause such expert or experts to be subjected to "unreasonable annoyance, expense, embarrassment, disadvantage, or other prejudice" (CPLR 3103 [a]).

Id. at 37-38, 752 N.Y.S.2d at 362.

The trend towards increased disclosure began with Duran v. New York City Health & Hospital Corporation, 182 Misc. 2d 232, 696 N.Y.S.2d 795 (Sup. Ct. Bronx Cty. 1999), app. withdrawn, 282 A.D.2d 995, 723 N.Y.S.2d 422 (1st Dep't 2001). In Duran, the Supreme Court, Bronx County granted plaintiff a protective order allowing plaintiff to disclose no more than the expert's state of licensure and board certification. The court reasoned that Jasopersaud and Yablon were premised on the unlikelihood, at the time those cases were decided, that disclosure of the expert's medical school, residency and fellowships of plaintiff's expert and the States in which the expert was licensed would lead to identification of the expert's name. The Duran plaintiff, however,

> presented an example of how one could easily identify an expert by using the information provided in an expert response pursuant to *Jasopersaud (supra)*. The search is conducted as follows: First one would select the GENMED library from the list provided by LEXIS-NEXIS. Next, one would choose the file entitled ABMS Board Certified Physicians. From the ABMS file one would pick instruction to conduct a full text search. Finally, by searching with particular words and phrases, such as the State of licensure, board certification, medical school and internship, one can find the identity of a doctor. Using this method, plaintiff demonstrated how that particular expert was easily identified. However, plaintiff found that the only search that did not enable her to narrow down the possibilities in order to identify the physician was a search using only the location of licensure and board certification.

Duran, 182 Misc. 2d at 234, 696 N.Y.S.2d at 796. Based on that showing, the court granted a protective order limiting expert disclosure.

Similarly, in Deitch v. May, 185 Misc. 2d 484, 713 N.Y.S.2d 278 (Sup. Ct. Rockland Cty. 2000), the Supreme Court, Rockland County denied a motion to preclude the testimony of an expert witness based on inadequate disclosure under CPLR 3101(d)(1). The disclosure stated only that the witness was "licensed to practice medicine in New York State and board certified in neurosurgery" and that the "expert is in private practice and affiliated with a teaching hospital in the New York metropolitan area." Deitch, 185 Misc. 2d at 488, 713 N.Y.S.2d at 281. The court agreed that any more specific disclosure would have enabled the other side to identify the witness using computer technology. It held that Jasopersaud is "stale law" given the advances in technology since that case was decided. Id.

In Thompson v. Swiantek, 291 A.D.2d 884, 736 N.Y.S.2d 819 (4th Dep't 2002), plaintiffs disclosed merely that their expert is a board certified neurologist who is licensed to practice in Pennsylvania and New Jersey, and that he is a professor of urology in New Jersey. Citing Duran, the Fourth Department declined to require plaintiff to disclose more information on the ground that such disclosure would effectively lead to disclosure of the expert's identity. Thompson is significant because it appears to be the first appellate decision rejecting Jasopersaud.

4. What is Timely Disclosure?

The statute is silent as to precisely when expert disclosure must occur, but it states that preclusion of an expert will not result if the disclosure is made, for good cause shown, an "insufficient" amount of time before trial. CPLR 3101(d)(1)(i). As with inadequate disclosure, untimely disclosure rarely results in preclusion, even where disclosure is made on the eve of trial, as long as the party shows good cause of the delay or that he or she did not intentionally withhold disclosure. Compare Silverberg v. Cmty. Gen. Hosp. of Sullivan Cty., 290 A.D.2d 788, 736 N.Y.S.2d 758 (3d Dep't 2002) (court must look at the reasonableness for non-compliance before taking such a drastic step as preclusion) with Meyer v. Zeichner, 263 A.D.2d 597, 693 N.Y.S.2d 274 (3d Dep't 1999) (burden for showing good cause for non compliance falls on the non-complying party). The preferred relief is to allow the opposing party a short continuance to research the expert's background, see Gallo v. Linkow, 255 A.D.2d 113, 679 N.Y.S.2d 377 (1st Dep't 1996), or, in rare cases, to impose a monetary sanction against counsel for the offending party (see Tamborino v. Burkakoff, 224 A.D.2d 609, 638 N.Y.S.2d 697 (2d Dep't 1996); Aversa v. Taubes, 194 A.D.2d 580, 598 N.Y.S.2d 801 (2d Dep't 1993)).

B. Interviews Of Subsequent Treating Physicians Under Arons v. Jutkowitz

In medical malpractice cases, both sides have an interest in securing the cooperation and testimony of physicians who were involved in the plaintiff's care and treatment.

In Arons, the Court of Appeals resolved a dispute over whether defendants have a right to interview non-party treating physicians ex parte in light of the HIPAA privacy rule. When the plaintiffs refused to supply HIPAA-compliant authorizations for these interviews, defendants sought an order to compel the authorizations under 45 C.F.R. §§ 164.512(e)(1)(i) and 164.508. The trial court granted the order, but the decision was reversed on appeal. Ultimately, the Court of Appeals found that non-party treating physicians could be interviewed off the record.

The Court of Appeals ruled that plaintiff waived the physician-patient privilege when he commenced suit. Arons v. Jutkowitz, 9 N.Y.3d 393,409, 880 N.E.2d 831, 2007 N.Y. LEXIS 3355, 850 N.Y.S.2d 345, 2007 NY Slip Op 9309 (2007) quoting Dillenbeck v Hess, 73 NY2d 278, 287, 536 NE2d 1126, 539 NYS2d 707 (1989). It noted the inequity in allowing a party to commence suit because of a medical condition while at the same time asserting the physician-patient privilege to thwart the defending party from uncovering critical facts. Id, quoting Dillenback, supra. The Court understood that ex-parte communications are important to streamline the discovery process and have the potential to lead to the prompt resolution of claims. Arons, 9 N.Y.3d 393 at 408.

Despite this holding, there are important limitations to the defendant's right to conduct ex parte interviews with non-party treating physicians. The interviewing attorney must reveal the interest and patient in question in order to prevent the disclosure of confidential or privileged information. Arons, 9 N.Y.3d 393 at 410. Additionally, the discussion is entirely voluntary as the disclosure is permissive under 45 CFR 164.502(a)(1). Id.

Arons has spawned intense legislative lobbying by the plaintiffs' bar in Albany and an "anti-Arons" bill (S5256B) to prohibit *ex parte* interviews. The bill is pending.[6]

Courtesy of Charles L. Bach Jr., Heidell Pittoni Murphy & Bach LLP

[6] The author gratefully acknowledges the valuable assistance of summer associate Brian McGaughan in creating this treatise.

APPENDIX B

ILLUSTRATIONS OF MEDICAL PROBLEMS AND CONDITIONS

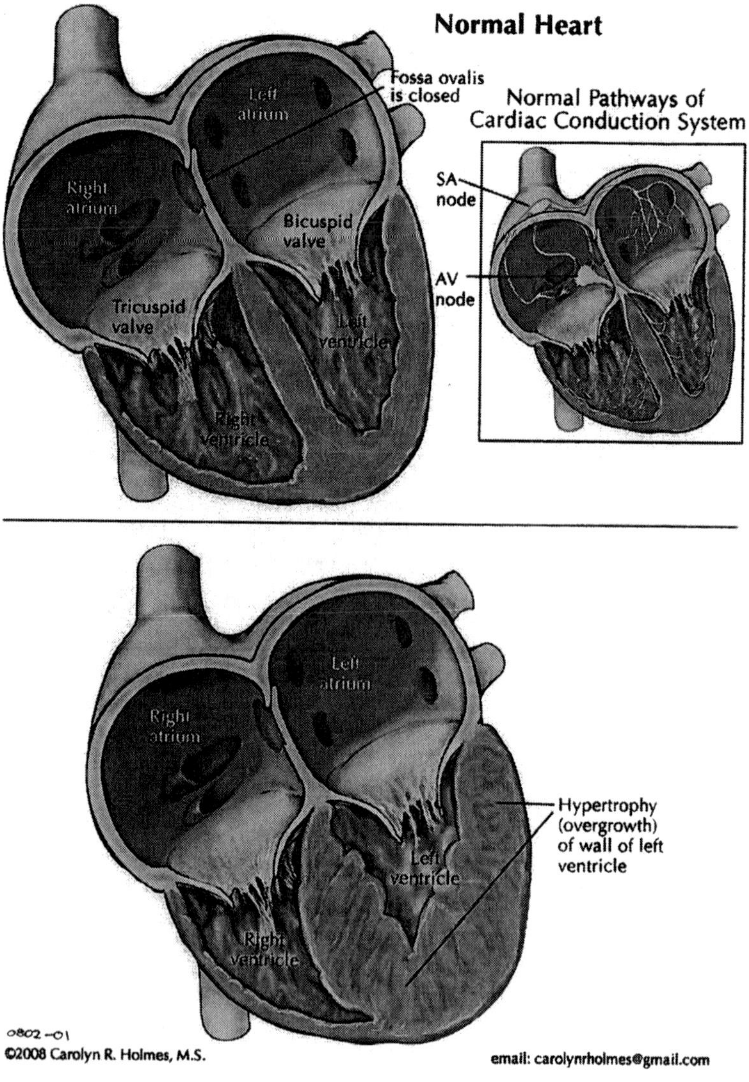

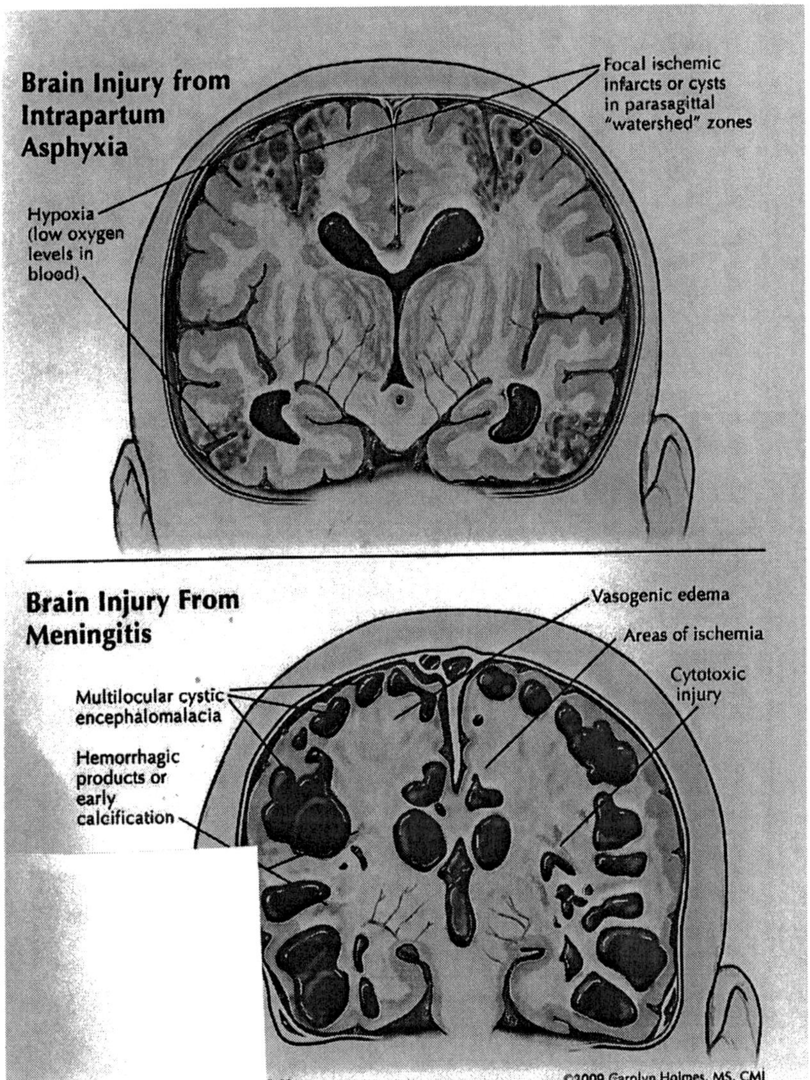
Brain Injury from Intrapartum Asphyxia
Focal ischemic infarcts or cysts in parasagittal "watershed" zones
Hypoxia (low oxygen levels in blood)
Brain Injury From Meningitis
Vasogenic edema
Areas of ischemia
Cytotoxic injury
Multilocular cystic encephalomalacia
Hemorrhagic products or early calcification
5-03
©2009 Carolyn Holmes, MS, CMI

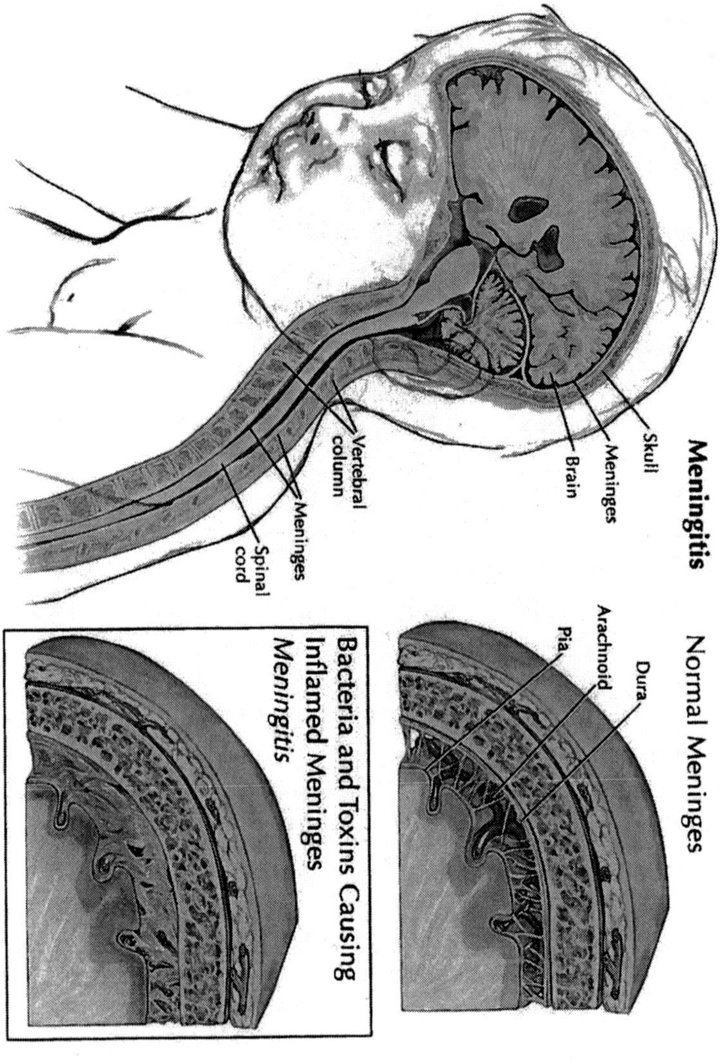
Meningitis
Skull
Meninges
Brain
Vertebral column
Meninges
Spinal cord
Normal Meninges
Dura
Arachnoid
Pia
Bacteria and Toxins Causing Inflamed Meninges
Meningitis

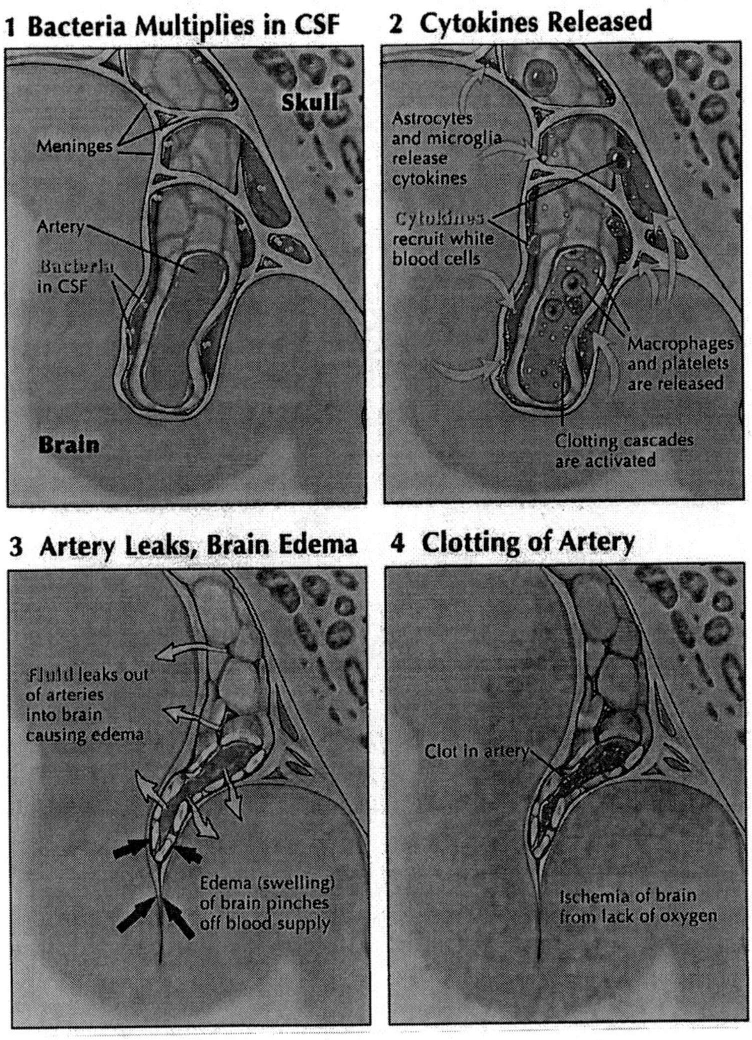
1 Bacteria Multiplies in CSF
Skull
Meninges
Artery
Bacteria in CSF
Brain
2 Cytokines Released
Astrocytes and microglia release cytokines
Cytokines recruit white blood cells
Macrophages and platelets are released
Clotting cascades are activated
3 Artery Leaks, Brain Edema
Fluid leaks out of arteries into brain causing edema
Edema (swelling) of brain pinches off blood supply
4 Clotting of Artery
Clot in artery
Ischemia of brain from lack of oxygen

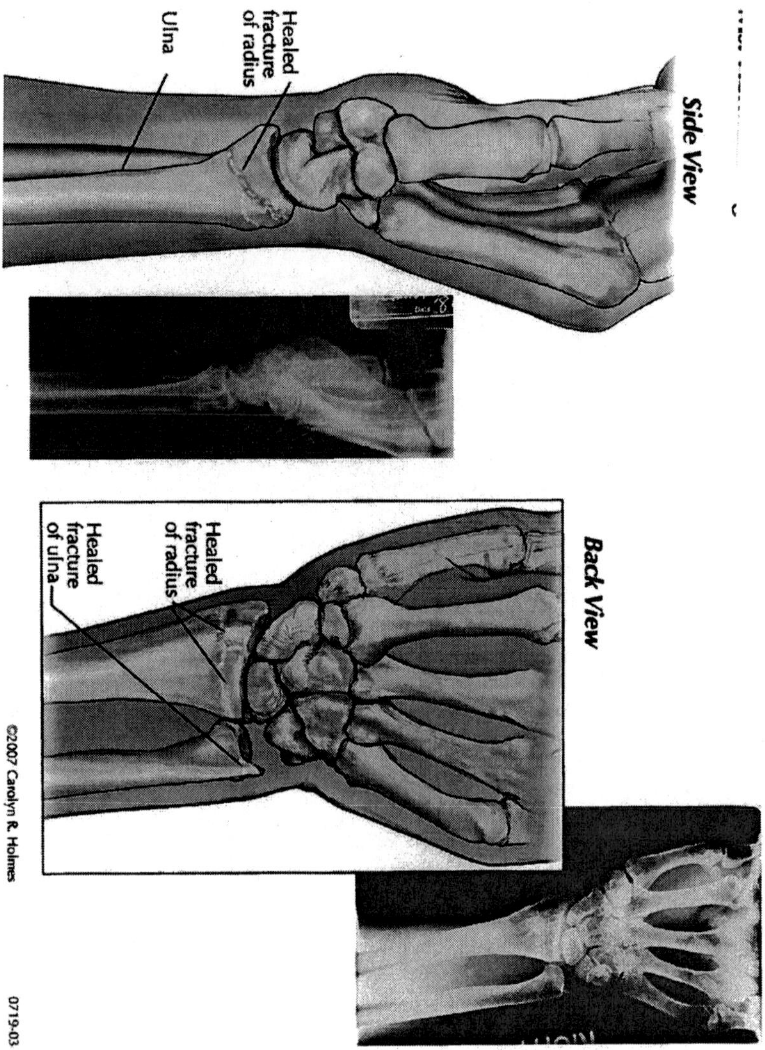
Side View
Healed fracture of radius
Ulna
Back View
Healed fracture of radius
Healed fracture of ulna
©2007 Carolyn R. Holmes
0719-03

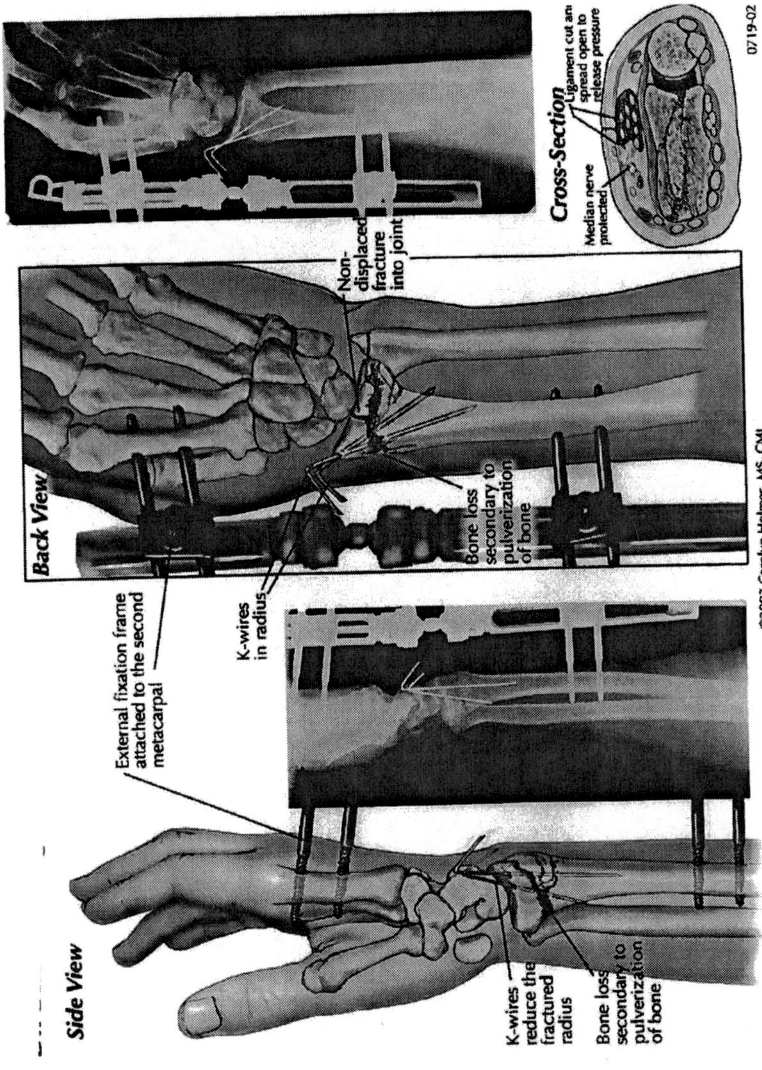
Side View
Back View
Cross-Section
External fixation frame attached to the second metacarpal
K-wires in radius
Non-displaced fracture into joint
Bone loss secondary to pulverization of bone
K-wires reduce the fractured radius
Bone loss secondary to pulverization of bone
Median nerve protected
Ligament cut and spread open to release pressure
0719-02
©2007 Carolyn Holmes, MS, CMI

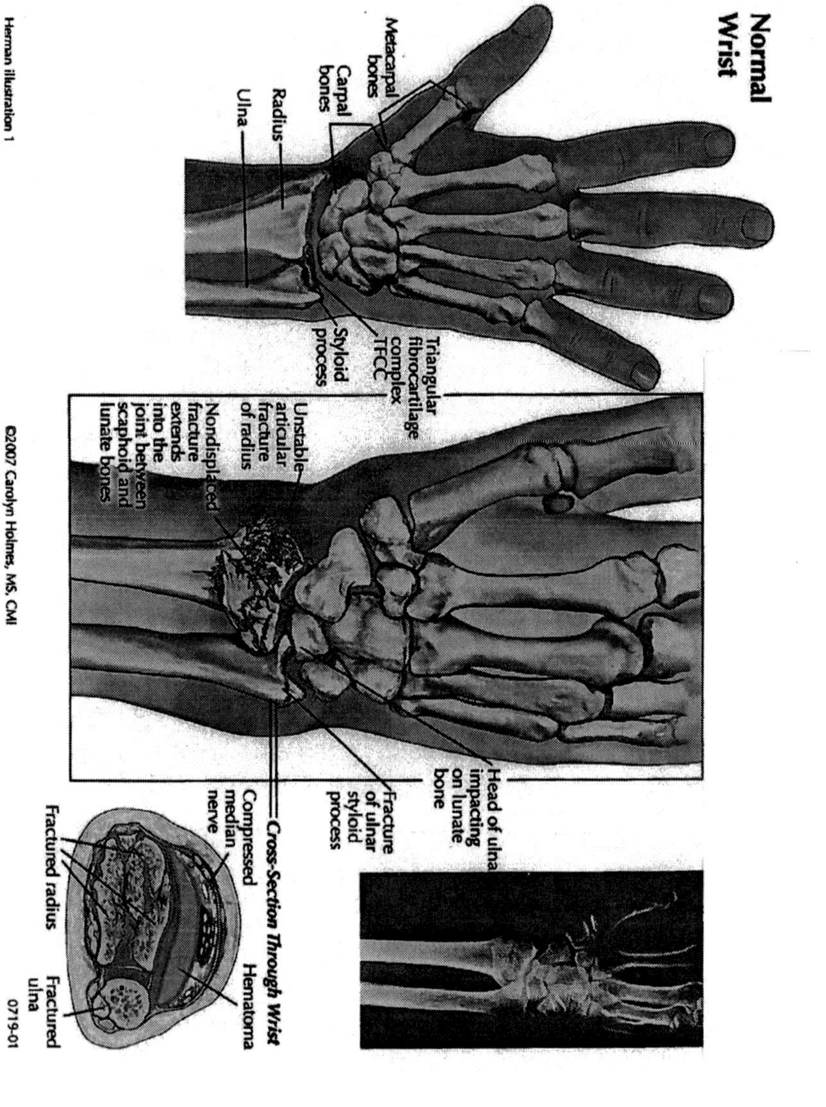

Courtesy of Charles L. Bach Jr., Heidell Pittoni Murphy & Bach LLP

APPENDIX C

RICHARDS ET AL. v. U.S.

Supreme Court of the United States
Suzanne Thomas **RICHARDS**, etc., et **al.**, Petitioners,
v.
UNITED STATES of America et **al.**

No. 59.
Argued Nov. 15, 1961.
Decided Feb. 26, 1962.

Actions under the Federal Tort Claims Act and under the Oklahoma Wrongful Death Act, for death of passengers who lost their lives when an aircraft operated by an airline subject to federal regulation crashed in Missouri. The government asserted a right of indemnity against the airline. The United States District Court for the Northern District of Oklahoma entered judgment dismissing the action and appeals were taken. The Court of Appeals, 285 F.2d 521, affirmed, and certiorari was granted. The Supreme Court, Mr. Chief Justice Warren, held that complaints failed to state claims upon which relief could be granted under the Federal Tort Claims Act or under Oklahoma Wrongful Death Act, where act of negligence allegedly occurred in Oklahoma, and death in Missouri, and plaintiffs received maximum amount recoverable under Missouri Death Act.

Affirmed.

West Headnotes

[1] Federal Courts 170B ⚿457

170B Federal Courts
170BVII Supreme Court
170BVII(B) Review of Decisions of Courts of Appeals
170Bk455 Decisions Reviewable and Grounds for Issuance
170Bk457 k. Conflicting Decisions of Courts of Appeals.
(Formerly 106k383(4), 106k383(1))

Certiorari would be granted to resolve a conflict between circuits as to law a federal district court should apply in an action brought under the Federal Tort Claims Act where an act of negligence occurs in one state and results in an injury and death in another state, and to enunciate a rule that could be applied uniformly in Federal Tort Claims Act cases. 28 U.S.C.A. §§ 1346(b), 2674.

[2] United States 393 ⚷78(2)

393 United States
393V Liabilities
393k78 Torts
393k78(2) k. Statutory Provisions.

United States 393 ⚷78(3)

393 United States
393V Liabilities
393k78 Torts
393k78(3) k. Private Person's Liability as Measure.

The Federal Tort Claims Act was designed primarily to remove sovereign immunity of the United States from suits in tort, and with certain specific exceptions to render the Government liable in tort as a private individual would be under like circumstances. 28 U.S.C.A. §§ 1346(b), 2674.

[3] United States 393 ⚷78(2)

393 United States
393V Liabilities
393k78 Torts
393k78(2) k. Statutory Provisions.

The Federal Tort Claims Act was not patterned to operate with complete independence from principles of law developed in common law and refined by statute, but was designed to build upon legal relationships formulated and characterized by the states. 28 U.S.C.A. §§ 1346(b), 2674.

[4] Statutes 361 ⚷212.6

361 Statutes
361VI Construction and Operation
361VI(A) General Rules of Construction
361k212 Presumptions to Aid Construction
361k212.6 k. Words Used.

It is assumed that legislative purpose is expressed by ordinary meaning of words used.

[5] United States 393 ⚷78(14)

393 United States
393V Liabilities
393k78 Torts
393k78(14) k. Place of Injury and Law Governing.

The Federal Tort Claims Act requires federal courts, in multistate tort actions, to look in the first instance to law of the place where the acts of negligence took place, and does not, through use of the words "act or omission," refer to the place where the negligence had its operative effect. 28 U.S.C.A. §§ 1346(b), 2674.

[6] Statutes 361 ⚷184

361 Statutes
361VI Construction and Operation
361VI(A) General Rules of Construction
361k180 Intention of Legislature
361k184 k. Policy and Purpose of Act.

Statutes 361 ⚷206

361 Statutes
361VI Construction and Operation
361VI(A) General Rules of Construction
361k204 Statute as a Whole, and Intrinsic Aids to Construction
361k206 k. Giving Effect to Entire Statute.

Statutes 361 ⚷208

361 Statutes
361VI Construction and Operation
361VI(A) General Rules of Construction
361k204 Statute as a Whole, and Intrinsic Aids to Construction
361k208 k. Context and Related Clauses.

A section of a statute should not be read in isolation from context of the whole act, and in interpreting legislation, Supreme Court must not be guided by a single sentence or member of a sentence, but should look to provisions of the whole law and to its object and policy.

[7] United States 393 ⚷78(14)

393 United States
393V Liabilities
393k78 Torts
393k78(14) k. Place of Injury and Law Governing.

A federal district court should apply the whole law, including choice-of-law rules of the state where the negligent act or omission occurred, in an action brought under the Federal Tort Claims Act, where negligence occurs in one state and results in injury and death in another state, and the court should not apply merely internal law of place where operative effect of the negligence took place. 28 U.S.C.A. §§ 1346(b), 2674.

[8] States 360 ⚷5(2)

360 States
360I Political Status and Relations
360I(A) In General
360k5 Relations Among States Under Constitution of United States
360k5(2) k. Full Faith and Credit in Each State to the Public Acts, Records, Etc. of Other States.
(Formerly 360k51/2, 360k5)

If more than one state has sufficiently substantial contact with an activity, the forum state, by analysis of the interests possessed by the states involved, could constitutionally apply to decision of the case the law of one or another state having such an interest in the multistate activity.

[9] Negligence 272 🗝204

272 Negligence
272I In General
272k204 k. What Law Governs.
(Formerly 272k103.5, 272k1031/2)

An Oklahoma state court was free to apply either its own law, the place where the negligence occurred, or the law of Missouri, the place where the injury occurred, to an action brought in its court and involving such factual situation.

[10] Death 117 🗝8

117 Death
117III Actions for Causing Death
117III(A) Right of Action and Defenses
117k8 k. What Law Governs.

Death 117 🗝96

117 Death
117III Actions for Causing Death
117III(H) Damages or Compensation
117k94 Measure and Amount Awarded
117k96 k. Statutory Limitations.

United States 393 🗝78(14)

393 United States
393V Liabilities
393k78 Torts
393k78(14) k. Place of Injury and Law Governing.

Under Oklahoma law, an action for wrongful death is based on statute of the place where the injury occurred that caused the death, and therefore,

Missouri wrongful death statute controlled maximum recovery in a wrongful death action brought under the Federal Tort Claims Act, and under Oklahoma Wrongful Death Act, where act of negligence occurred in Oklahoma, and injury that caused the death occurred in Missouri. V.A.M.S. § 537.090; 28 U.S.C.A. §§ 1346(b), 2674.

[11] Federal Courts 170B ⚷460.1

170B Federal Courts
 170BVII Supreme Court
  170BVII(B) Review of Decisions of Courts of Appeals
   170Bk460 Review on Certiorari
    170Bk460.1 k. In General.
 (Formerly 170Bk460, 106k383(7))

Supreme Court ordinarily accepts determinations of Courts of Appeal on questions of state law, and would do so where petitioners seeking certiorari did not contend there was an erroneous interpretation of state law.

[12] United States 393 ⚷140

393 United States
 393IX Actions
  393k140 k. Pleading.

Complaints for wrongful death of plaintiffs' decedents, under the Federal Tort Claims Act, and under the Oklahoma Wrongful Death Act failed to state claims upon which relief could be granted, where act of negligence allegedly occurred in Oklahoma, and death in Missouri, and plaintiffs received maximum amount recoverable under the Missouri Death Act. V.A.M.S. § 537.090; 28 U.S.C.A. §§ 1346(b), 2674.

[13] Death 117 ⚷96

117 Death
 117III Actions for Causing Death
  117III(H) Damages or Compensation
   117k94 Measure and Amount Awarded
    117k96 k. Statutory Limitations.

Payment of maximum amounts recoverable under Missouri statute for wrongful deaths which occurred in Missouri precluded recovery under the Federal Tort Claims Act and under Oklahoma Death Act, even though acts of negligence which caused the fatal accident allegedly occurred in Oklahoma. V.A.M.S. § 537.090; 12 O.S.1951 §§ 1051-1054; 28 U.S.C.A. §§ 1346(b), 2674.

****587 *2** Truman B. Rucker, Tulsa, Okl., for petitioners.

Richard J. Medalie, Washington, D.C., for respondent, the United States.

W. B. Patterson, Dallas, Tex., for respondent, American Airlines, Inc.

Mr. Chief Justice WARREN delivered the opinion of the Court.

The question to be decided in this case is what law a Federal District Court should apply in an action brought under the Federal Tort Claims Act[FN1] where an act of negligence occurs in one State and results in an injury and death in another State. The basic provision of the Tort Claims Act states that the Government shall be liable for tortious conduct committed by its employees acting within the scope of their employment 'under circumstances where the United States, if a private person, would be liable to the claimant in accordance with the ***3** law of the place where the act or omission occurred.' [FN2] The parties urge that the alternatives in selecting the law to determine liability under this statute are: (1) the internal law of the place where the negligence occurred, or (2) the whole law (including choice-of-law rules) of the place where the negligence occurred, or (3) the internal law of the place where the operative effect of the negligence took place.

FN1. The provisions of the Tort Claims Act are now found in 28 U.S.C. ss 1291, 1346, 1402, 1504, 2110, 2401, 2402, 2411, 2412, and 2671-2680, 28 U.S.C.A. ss 1291, 1346, 1402, 1504, 2110, 2401, 2402, 2411, 2412, 2671-2680.

FN2. 28 U.S.C. s 1346(b), 28 U.S.C.A. s 1346(b).

Although the particular facts of this case are relatively unimportant in deciding the question before us, a brief recitation of them is necessary to set the context for our decision. The petitioners are the personal representatives of passengers killed when an airplane, owned by the respondent American Airlines, crashed in Missouri while en route from Tulsa, Oklahoma, to New York City. Suit was brought by the petitioners**588 against the United States in the Federal District Court for the Northern District of Oklahoma, on the theory that the Government, through the Civil Aviation Agency, had 'negligently failed to enforce the terms of the Civil Aeronautics Act and the regulations thereunder which prohibited the practices then being used by American Airlines, Inc., in the overhaul depot of Tulsa, Oklahoma.'FN3 The petitioners in each case either had already received a $15,000 settlement from the Airlines, the maximum amount recoverable under the Missouri Wrongful Death Act,FN4 amount had been tendered that amount. They sought additional amounts from the United States under the Oklahoma Wrongful ***4** Death ActFN5 which contains no limitation on the amount a single person may recover from a tortfeasor. The Government filed a third-party complaint against American Airlines, seeking reimbursement for any amount that the petitioners might recover against the United States.

FN3. Under 72 Stat. 778, 49 U.S.C. s 1425, 49 U.S.C.A. s 1425, the Administrator of the Federal Aviation Agency is charged with the responsibility of enforcing rules and regulations controlling inspection, maintenance, overhaul and repair of all equipment used in air transportation.

FN4. Mo.Rev.Stat.1949, s 537.090, V.A.M.S. Subsequent to the origination of these actions the Missouri Code was amended to provide for maximum damages of $25,000. Mo.Rev.Stat.1959, s 537.090.

FN5. Okl.Stat., 1951, Tit. 12, ss 1051-1054.

After a pretrial hearing, the District Court ruled that the complaints failed to state claims upon which relief could be granted under the Oklahoma Act since that statute could not be applied extraterritorially 'where an act or omission occurring in Oklahoma results in injury and death in the State of Missouri.' FN6 Alternatively, the court noted that if Oklahoma law was applicable under the Federal Tort Claims Act, 'then the general law of

Oklahoma, including its conflicts of law rule, is applicable thereunder,' thus precluding further recovery since the Oklahoma conflicts rule would refer the court to the law of Missouri, the place where the negligence had its operative effect.FN7 In dismissing the petitioners' complaints against the United States, the court found it unnecessary to pass upon the third-party complaint asserted by the Government against American. On appeal, the Court of Appeals for the Tenth Circuit affirmed the judgment by a divided vote,FN8 the majority agreeing with the lower court that the complaints failed to state a cause of action upon which relief could be based under either the Oklahoma or the Missouri Wrongful Death Act. In dissent, the chief judge, believing that Congress intended the internal law of the place where the act or omission occurred to control the rights and liabilities of the parties, stated that he thought it was error to apply the Oklahoma ***5** conflict-of-laws rule, and would have remanded the case for a determination of liability under the Oklahoma Act.

FN6. The opinion of the District Court is not reported.

FN7. Gochenour v. St. Louis-San Francisco R. Co., 205 Okl. 594, 239 P.2d 769.

FN8. 285 F.2d 521.

[1] That the question confronting us is an important one and of a recurring nature is made apparent by the conflicting views expressed in its solution by the lower federal courts. In the five circuits in which it has arisen, resolution of the question has been reached by adoption of one or another of the alternatives urged upon us by the parties to this suit. The petitioners' contention, that the reference in Section 1346(b) to the 'place where the act or omission occurred' directs application of only the internal law of that State-here, Oklahoma-is supported by the Seventh Circuit's decision in ****589**Voytas v. United States, 256 F.2d 786, and by the District of Columbia Circuit in Eastern Air Lines v. Union Trust Co., 95 U.S.App.D.C. 189, 221 F.2d 62, as well as by the dissenting judge of the Tenth Circuit in the instant case. The Government's interpretation of the Act, that in order also to give effect to Section 2674,FN9 providing that the United States shall be liable in the same manner as a private individual, a court must refer to the whole law of the State where the act or omission occurred, was adhered

to by the Second Circuit in Landon v. United States, 197 F.2d 128, as well as by the Tenth Circuit in the case at bar. American Airlines, although willing to abide by the interpretation advanced by the Government, suggests, as an alternative, that the internal law of the place where the negligence had its operative effect-here, Missouri-should control. This construction of the Act is supported by the Ninth Circuit's decision in United States v. Marshall, 230 F.2d 183, and by the dissenting opinion in the Union Trust case, supra. It was to resolve the three-fold conflict and to enunciate a rule that can be applied uniformly in Tort Claims Act cases that we granted certiorari. 366 U.S. 916, 81 S.Ct. 1093, 6 L.Ed.2d 240.

FN9. 28 U.S.C. s 2674, 28 U.S.C.A. s 2674.

***6** I.

The principal provision of the Federal Tort Claims Act, originally enacted as Title IV of the Legislative Reorganization Act of 1946,[FN10] is Section 1346(b), reading in pertinent part:

FN10. 60 Stat. 842 (1946).

'* * * the district courts * * * shall have exclusive jurisdiction of civil actions on claims against the United States, for money damages * * * for injury or loss of property, or personal injury or death caused by the negligent or wrongful act or omission of any employee of the Government while acting within the scope of his office or employment, under circumstances where the United States, if a private person, would be liable to the claimant in accordance with the law of the place where the act or omission occurred.'

Section 2674, also relevant to our decision, provides:

'The United States shall be liable, respecting * * * tort claims, in the same manner and to the same extent as a private individual under like circumstances, but shall not be liable for interest prior to judgment or for punitive damages.'

[2][3] The Tort Claims Act was designed primarily to remove the sovereign immunity of the United States from suits in tort and, with certain specific exceptions, to render the Government liable in tort as a private individual

would be under like circumstances.FN11 It is evident that the Act was not patterned to operate with complete independence ***7** from the principles of law developed in the common law and refined by statute and judicial decision in the various States. Rather, it was designed to build upon the legal relationships formulated and characterized by the States, and, to that extent, the statutory scheme is exemplary of the generally interstitial character of federal law. If Congress had meant to alter or supplant the legal relationships developed by the States, it could specifically have done so to further the limited objectives of the Tort Claims Act. That is, notwithstanding the generally interstitial character of the law, Congress, in waiving the immunity of the Government for tortious conduct of its employees, could have imposed restrictions****590** and conditions on the extent and substance of its liability.FN12 We must determine whether, and to what extent, Congress exercised this power in selecting a rule for the choice of laws to be applied in suits brought under the Act. And, because the issue of the applicable law is controlled by a formal expression of the will of Congress, we need not pause to consider the question whether the conflict-of-laws rule applied in suits where federal jurisdiction rests upon diversity of citizenship shall be extended to a case such as this, in which jurisdiction is based upon a federal statute. FN13 In addition, and even though Congress has left to judicial implication the task of giving content to its will in selecting the controlling law, because of the formal expression found in the Act itself, we are presented with a situation wholly distinguishable from those cases in which our initial inquiry has been whether the appropriate rule should be the simple adoption of state ***8** law.FN14 Here, we must decide, first, to which State the words 'where the act or omission occurred' direct us, and, second, whether application of the internal law or the whole law of that State would be most consistent with the legislative purpose in enacting the Tort Claims Act.

FN11. See Feres v. United States, 340 U.S. 135, 71 S.Ct. 153, 95 L.Ed. 152, for a detailed analysis of the purposes of the Federal Tort Claims Act in the context of its legislative history.

FN12. Soriano v. United States, 352 U.S. 270, 77 S.Ct. 269, 1 L.Ed.2d 306; United States v. Sherwood, 312 U.S. 584, 61 S.Ct. 767, 85 L.Ed. 1058.

FN13. Klaxon Co. v. Stentor Electric Mfg. Co., 313 U.S. 487, 61 S.Ct. 1020, 85 L.Ed. 1477. See Vanston Bondholders Protective Committee v. Green, 329 U.S. 156, 67 S.Ct. 237, 91 L.Ed. 162; McKenzie v. Irving Trust Co., 323 U.S. 365, 65 S.Ct. 405, 89 L.Ed. 305; D'Oench, Duhme & Co. v. Federal Deposit Ins. Corp., 315 U.S. 447, 62 S.Ct. 676, 86 L.Ed. 956.

FN14. See, e.g., Holmberg v. Armbrecht, 327 U.S. 392, 66 S.Ct. 582, 90 L.Ed. 743; Clearfield Trust Co. v. United States, 318 U.S. 363, 63 S.Ct. 573, 87 L.Ed. 838; D'Oench, Duhme & Co. v. Federal Deposit Ins. Corp., 315 U.S. 447, 62 S.Ct. 676, 86 L.Ed. 956; Royal Indemnity Co. v. United States, 313 U.S. 289, 61 S.Ct. 995, 85 L.Ed. 1; Board of Com'rs of Jackson County v. United States, 308 U.S. 343, 60 S.Ct. 285, 84 L.Ed. 313. See also discussion in Hart and Wechsler, The Federal Courts and the Federal System, 679 et seq.

II.

The legislative history of the Act, although generally extensive,FN15 is not, except in a negative way, helpful in solving the problem of the law to be applied in a multistate tort action such as is presented by the facts of this case. It has been repeatedly observed that Congress did not consider choice-of-law problems during the long period that the legislation was being prepared for enactment.FN16 The concern of Congress, as illustrated by the legislative history,FN17 was the problem of a person injured by an employee operating a government vehicle or otherwise acting within the scope of his employment, situations ***9** rarely involving a conflict-of-laws question. FN18 In these instances,****591** where the negligence and the injury normally occur simultaneously and in a single jurisdiction, the law to be applied is clear, and no solution to the meaning of the words 'the law of the place where the act or omission occurred' is required. Here, however, we are faced with events touching more than one 'place'-a problem which Congress apparently did not explicitly consider-and, thus, we are compelled to give content to those critical words.

FN15. Hearings before House Committee on the Judiciary on H.R. 5373 and H.R. 6463, 77th Cong., 2d Sess.; S.Rep. No. 1196, 77th Cong., 2d Sess.; H.R.Rep. No. 2245, 77th Cong., 2d Sess.; No. 1287, 79th Cong., 1st Sess.

FN16. See, e.g., 68 Harv.L.Rev. 1455 (1955); 45 Iowa L.Rev. 125 (1959); 6 N.Y.L.F. 484, 488-490 (1960).

FN17. See H.R.Rep. No. 2428, 76th Cong., 3d Sess. 3; Hearings on H.R. 5373 and H.R. 6463, note 15, supra, 39, 66; Hearings before a Subcommittee of the House Committee on the Judiciary on H.R. 7236, 76th Cong., 3d Sess. 7, 16; Hearings before a Subcommittee of the Senate Committee on the Judiciary on S. 2690, 76th Cong., 3d Sess. 9; 69 Cong.Rec. 2192, 2193, 3118; 86 Cong.Rec. 12024.

FN18. See, e.g., Knecht v. United States, 3 Cir., 242 F.2d 929; Irish v. United States, 9 Cir., 225 F.2d 3; United States v. Praylou, 4 Cir., 208 F.2d 291; Somerset Seafood Co. v. United States, 4 Cir., 193 F.2d 631; D'Anna v. United States, 4 Cir., 181 F.2d 335; Olson v. United States, 8 Cir., 175 F.2d 510; Modla v. United States, D.C., 151 F.Supp. 198; Irvin v. United States, D.C., 148 F.Supp. 25.

[4][5] In the Tort Claims Act Congress has expressly stated that the Government's liability is to be determined by the application of a particular law, the law of the place where the act or omission occurred,[FN19] and we must, of course, start with the assumption that the legislative purpose is expressed by the ordinary meaning of the words used. We believe that it would be difficult to conceive of any more precise language Congress could have used to command application of the law of the place where the negligence occurred than the words it did employ in the Tort Claims Act. Thus we first reject the alternative urged by American Airlines. The legislative materials cited to us by American[FN20] not only lack probative force ***10** in a judicial sense, but they are completely unpersuasive to support the argument that Congress intended the words 'act or omission' to refer to the place where the negligence had its operative effect. The ease of application inherent in the rule urged by American lends a certain attractiveness, but we are bound to operate within the framework of the words chosen by Congress and not to question the wisdom of the latter in the process of construction. We conclude that Congress has, in the Tort Claims Act, enacted a rule which requires federal courts, in multistate tort actions, to look in the first instance to the law of the place where the acts of negligence took place.

FN19. 28 U.S.C. s 1346(b), 28 U.S.C.A. s 1346(b).

FN20. Hearings before House Committee on the Judiciary on H.R. 5373 and H.R. 6463, 77th Cong., 2d Sess. 9, 30. American suggests that support for its argument is found in the testimony of Mr. Francis Shea, then Assistant Attorney General of the United States, before the House Committee on the Judiciary, who stated, when asked where a claimant might bring suit under the Act, that the venue provision allowed suit to be brought either where the claimant resides or where the injury took place. Because the venue provision of the Act also contains the words 'wherein the act or omission complained of occurred' (28 U.S.C. s 1402(b)), 28 U.S.C.A. s 1402(b), American contends that the reference to the place where the injury occurred should control the meaning of the 'act or omission' language in Section 1346(b). In addition to the fact that this testimony bears no relation to the choice-of-laws problems, and that considerations underlying the problem of venue are substantially different from those determining applicable law, we are not persuaded to allow an isolated piece of legislative history to detract from the Act the words Congress expressly employed.

III.

However, our task is not completed. Having rejected the third alternative stated initially as inconsistent with the express terminology of the Act, we must now determine the reach of the words 'law of the place.' Do they embrace the whole law of the place where the negligence occurred, or only the internal law of that place? This problem, unlike the initial question discussed under II, supra, has not been dealt with by any formal expression of Congress and we must therefore establish the rule to be applied uniformly by lower federal courts, with due regard to the variant interests and policies expressed by the Tort Claims Act legislation.

***11** [6][7] We believe it fundamental that a section of a statute should not be read ****592** in isolation from the context of the whole Act, FN21 and that in fulfilling our responsibility in interpreting legislation, 'we must not be guided by a single sentence or member of a sentence, but (should) look to the provisions of the whole law, and to its object and policy.'FN22 We should not assume that Congress intended to set the courts completely adrift from state law with regard to questions for which it has not provided a specific and definite answer in an act such as the one before us which, as we have indicated, is so intimately related to state law. Thus, we conclude that a reading of the statute as a whole, with due regard to its purpose, requires application of the whole law of the State where the act or omission occurred.

> FN21. National Labor Relations Board v. Lion Oil Co., 352 U.S. 282, 288, 77 S.Ct. 330, 333, 1 L.Ed.2d 331; Cherokee Intermarriage Cases, 203 U.S. 76, 89, 27 S.Ct. 29, 34, 51 L.Ed. 96; Panama Refining Co. v. Ryan, 293 U.S. 388, 439, 55 S.Ct. 241, 256, 79 L.Ed. 446 (Cardozo, J., dissenting).

> FN22. Mastro Plastics Corp. v. National Labor Relations Board, 350 U.S. 270, 285, 76 S.Ct. 349, 359, 100 L.Ed. 309, quoting from United States v. Boisdore's Heirs, 8 How. 113, 122, 12 L.Ed. 1009.

We are led to our conclusion by other persuasive factors notwithstanding the fact that the very conflict among the lower federal courts that we must here resolve illustrates the also reasonable alternative view expressed by the petitioners. First, our interpretation enables the federal courts to treat the United States as a 'private individual under like circumstances,' and thus is consistent with the Act considered as a whole.FN23 The general conflict-of-laws rule, followed by a vast majority of the States,FN24 is to apply the law of the place of injury to the ***12** substantive rights of the parties. Therefore, where the forum State is the same as the one in which the act or omission occurred, our interpretation will enable the federal courts to treat the United States as an individual would be treated under like circumstances. FN25 Moreover, this interpretation of the Act provides a degree of flexibility to the law to be applied in federal courts that would not be possible under the view advanced either by the petitioners or by American. Recently there has been a tendency on the part of some States to depart from the general conflicts rule in order to take into account the interests of the State having significant contact with the parties to the litigation.FN26 We can see ****593** no compelling reason to saddle the Act with an interpretation that would ***13** prevent the federal courts from implementing this policy in choice-of-law rules where the State in which the negligence occurred has adopted it. Should the States continue this rejection of the older rule in those situations where its application might appear inappropriate or inequitable,FN27 the flexibility inherent in our interpretation will also be more in step with that judicial approach, as well as with the character of the legislation and with the purpose of the Act considered as a whole.

FN23. 28 U.S.C. s 2674, 28 U.S.C.A. s 2674, quoted in the text, supra, as well as 28 U.S.C. s 1346(b), 28 U.S.C.A. s 1346(b), provides that the United States should be treated as an individual defendant would be under like circumstances.

FN24. Restatement, Conflict of Laws, ss 377, 378 and 391. This rule has been repeated so frequently that a citation of cases here would serve no purpose. For a collection of cases, see Goodrich, Conflict of Laws, 263-264; Stumberg, Conflict of Laws, 182-187; 25 C.J.S. Death s 28, nn. 27-30.

FN25. For example, had the petitioners in the instant case brought suit against American as well as the United States, the petitioners' interpretation of the Act would have the District Court determine the American's liability by the law of Missouri and the United States' by the law of Oklahoma. Under our construction of the Act, however, both defendants' liability would be determined by the law of Missouri. However, because of the venue provision in the statute, allowing suit to be brought where all the plaintiffs reside as well as where the act or omission occurred (28 U.S.C. s 1402(b), 28 U.S.C.A. s 1402(b); see Knecht v. United States, 3 Cir., 242 F.2d 929; Olson v. United States, 8 Cir., 175 F.2d 510), a situation may arise where a District Court could not determine the Government's and a private individual's liability in exactly the same manner.

FN26. Grant v. McAuliffe, 41 Cal.2d 859, 264 P.2d 944, 42 A.L.R.2d 1162; Schmidt v. Driscoll Hotel, Inc., 249 Minn. 376, 82 N.W.2d 365; Haumschild v. Continental Casualty Co., 7 Wis.2d 130, 95 N.W.2d 814. See Currie, Survival of Actions: Adjudication versus Automation in the Conflict of Laws, 10 Stan.L.Rev. 205 (1958). Cf. Vrooman v. Beech Aircraft Corp., 10 Cir., 183 F.2d 479; Levy v. Daniels' U-Drive Auto Renting Co., 108 Conn. 333, 143 A. 163, 61 A.L.R. 846; Caldwell v. Gore, 175 La. 501, 143 So. 387; Burkett v. Globe Indemnity Co., 182 Miss. 423, 181 So. 316.

FN27. In addition to the cases cited in note 26, supra, see the opinion by Mr. Justice Black in Vanston Bondholders Protective Committee v. Green, 329 U.S. 156, 161-162, 67 S.Ct. 237, 239, 91 L.Ed. 162, where it is stated in context to a different but analogous problem:

> 'In determining which contact is the most significant in a particular transaction, courts can seldom find a complete solution in the mechanical formulae of the conflicts of law. Determination requires the exercise of an informed judgment in the balancing of all the interests of the states with the most significant contacts in order best to accommodate the equities among the parties to the policies of those states.'

In the absence of persuasive evidence to the contrary, we do not believe that Congress intended to adopt the inflexible rule urged upon us by the petitioners. Despite the power of Congress to enact for litigation of this type a federal conflict-of-laws rule independent of the States' development of such rules, we should not, particularly in the type of interstitial legislation involved here, assume that it has done so. Nor are we persuaded to require such an independent federal rule by the petitioners' argument that there are other instances, specifically set forth in the Act,[FN28] where the liability of the United States is not coextensive***14** with that of a private person under state law. It seems sufficient to note that Congress has been specific in those instances where it intended the federal courts to depart completely from state law and, also, that this list of exceptions contains no direct or indirect modification of the principles controlling application of choice-of-law rules. Certainly there is nothing in the legislative history that even remotely supports the argument that Congress did not intend state conflict rules to apply to multistate tort actions brought against the Government.[FN29]

> FN28. The Act permits claimants to sue only in the federal courts, and not in the state courts which are available in actions against a private individual, s 1346(b); the Act prescribes its own period of limitations which may be shorter or longer than that of the State, s 2401(b); the claimant cannot obtain a trial by jury under the Act, although he could against a private individual, s 2402; the claimant cannot obtain interest prior to judgment in suits under the Act regardless of the state rule governing private individuals, s 2674; the claimant cannot obtain punitive damages under the Act, even though state law may provide for it as against a private defendant, s 2674; the claimant cannot recover any damages against the United States on any claim arising out of assault, battery, false imprisonment, false arrest, malicious prosecution, abuse of process,

libel, slander, misrepresentation, deceit, or interference with contract rights, whereas he could recover such damages against a private individual, s 2680(h); the claimant cannot obtain any recovery against the United States on a claim arising in a foreign country, although he could against a private individual, s 2680(k); and the Act exempts the Government from liability for claims based on various types of activities, although a private individual would be liable in the same circumstances, s 2680.

FN29. In fact, despite the ambiguity that exists in the history due to the fact that Congress did not specifically consider the choice-of-laws problem, the legislative material indicates that Congress thought in terms of state law being applicable. The term 'law of the place where the act or omission occurred' was particularized as (1) the law of the situs of the wrongful act or omission. Hearings before House Committee on the Judiciary on H.R. 5373 and H.R. 6463, 77th Cong., 2d Sess. 35; (2) local law, id., at 26, 27, 30, 59 and 61; S.Rep. No. 1196, 77th Cong., 2d Sess. 6; H.R.Rep. No. 2245, 77th Cong., 2d Sess. 9; H.R.Rep. No. 1287, 79th Cong., 1st Sess. 4; S.Rep. No. 1400, 79th Cong., 2d Sess. 32; (3) local tort law. Hearings before House Committee on the Judiciary on H.R. 5373 and H.R. 6463, 77th Cong., 2d Sess. 30; (4) the law of the situs of the alleged tort. Hearings before a Subcommittee of the Senate Committee on the Judiciary on S. 2690, 76th Cong., 3d Sess. 44; and (5) the locale of the injury or damage. Hearings before the House Committee on the Judiciary on H.R. 5373 and H.R. 6463, 77th Cong., 2d Sess. 9.

****594 *15** Under our interpretation of the Act we find it unnecessary to judge the effect of the Oklahoma courts' pronouncements that the Oklahoma Wrongful Death Act cannot be given extra-territorial effect.[FN30]

FN30. Gochenour v. St. Louis-San Francisco R. Co., 205 Okl. 594, 239 P.2d 769. See Fenton v. Sinclair Refining Co., 206 Okl. 19, 240 P.2d 748.

IV.

[8][9][10][11][12][13] Our view of a State's power to adopt an appropriate conflict-of-laws doctrine in a situation touching more than one place has

been indicated by our discussion in Part III of this opinion. FN31 Where more than one State has sufficiently substantial contact with the activity in question, the forum State, by analysis of the interests possessed by the States involved, could constitutionally apply to the decision of the case the law of one or another state having such an interest in the multistate activity.FN32 Thus, an Oklahoma state court would be free to apply either its own law, the law of the place where the negligence occurred, or the law of Missouri, the law of the place where the injury occurred, to an action brought in its courts and involving this factual situation.FN33 Both the ***16** Federal District Court sitting in Oklahoma, and the Court of Appeals for the Tenth Circuit, have interpreted the pertinent Oklahoma decisions,FN34 which we have held are controlling, to declare that an action for wrongful death is based on the statute of the place where the injury occurred that caused the death.FN35 Therefore,****595** Missouri's statute controls the case at bar. It is conceded that each petitioner has received $15,000, the maximum amount recoverable under the Missouri Act, and the petitioners thus have received full compensation for their claims. Accordingly, the courts below were correct in holding that, in accordance with Oklahoma law, petitioners had failed to state claims upon which relief could be granted. The judgment is affirmed.

FN31. Supra, 369 U.S., pp. 12-13, 82 S.Ct., pp. 593-594 and cases cited. See also Carroll v. Lanza, 349 U.S. 408, 75 S.Ct. 804, 99 L.Ed. 1183; Watson v. Employers Liability Corp., 348 U.S. 66, 75 S.Ct. 166, 99 L.Ed. 74; Pacific Employers Ins. Co. v. Industrial Accident Comm., 306 U.S. 493, 59 S.Ct. 629, 83 L.Ed. 940. Cf. Hartford Accident & Indemnity Co. v. Delta & Pine Land Co., 292 U.S. 143, 54 S.Ct. 634, 78 L.Ed. 1178; Home Insurance Co. v. Dick, 281 U.S. 397, 50 S.Ct. 338, 74 L.Ed. 926.

FN32. See, e.g., the cases cited in note 26, supra.

FN33. Alabama G.S.R. Co. v. Carroll, 97 Ala. 126, 11 So. 803, 18 L.R.A. 433; Otey v. Midland Valley R. Co., 108 Kan. 755, 197 P. 203; Connecticut Valley Lumber Co. v. Maine Central R. Co., 78 N.H. 553, 103 A. 263; El Paso & N.W.R. Co. v. McComus, 36 Tex.Civ.App. 170, 81 S.W. 760 (holding that the law of the place of injury controls) and Schmidt v. Driscoll Hotel, Inc., 249 Minn. 376,

82 N.W.2d 365 (holding that the law of the place of negligence controls). See also Hunter v. Derby Foods, 2 Cir., 110 F.2d 970, 133 A.L.R. 255; 35 Col.L.Rev. 202.

FN34. Gochenour v. St. Louis-San Francisco R. Co., 205 Okl. 594, 239 P.2d 769; Miller v. Tennis, 140 Okl. 185, 282 P. 345. See Fenton v. Sinclair Refining Co., 206 Okl. 19, 240 P.2d 748.

FN35. We are aware that in the Oklahoma cases cited in note 34, supra, both the injury and negligence occurred in the same sister State, and that the two courts below relied largely on dictum in those cases to conclude that Oklahoma would follow the general rule that the law of the place of injury would control even had the negligence that caused the injury taken place in Oklahoma. The petitioners here do not contend that this was an erroneous interpretation of state law. We ordinarily accept the determinations of Courts of Appeals on questions of state law and do so here under the circumstances presented. General Box Co. v. United States, 351 U.S. 159, 165, 76 S.Ct. 728, 732, 100 L.Ed. 1055; Estate of Spiegel v. Commissioner, 335 U.S. 701, 707-708, 69 S.Ct. 301, 303-304, 93 L.Ed. 330; Huddleston v. Dwyer, 322 U.S. 232, 237, 64 S.Ct. 1015, 1018, 88 L.Ed. 1246.

Affirmed.

U.S.Okl. 1962.
Richards v. U.S.
369 U.S. 1, 82 S.Ct. 585, 7 L.Ed.2d 492

END OF DOCUMENT

Courtesy of Robert W. Frank, Neil Dymott Frank McFall and Trexler APC

APPENDIX D

SAMPLE PATIENT/FAMILY ERROR FOLLOW-UP LETTER

Dear patient/family member

I wanted to send you this brief note to follow up on our recent discussion on (date), again expressing my sympathy and concern for the unexpected_________. I'm sure this must be a difficult time for you. Rest assured my physician colleagues, our staff and I will be working hard to help and take care of you as best we can. I/Dr_______ will be available to answer any further questions you or your family may have. Please realize I am concerned about your condition and regret that your/the treatment has not turned out as we desired at this point. Thank you for allowing me the opportunity to take care of you.

Sincerely,

Courtesy of Robert W. Frank, Neil Dymott Frank McFall and Trexler APC

APPENDIX E

POWERPOINT PRESENTATION:
HOW TO APOLOGIZE WITHOUT ADMITTING FAULT

Evidence Code 1160

The portion of statements, writings, or benevolent gestures expressing sympathy or a general sense of benevolence relating to the pain, suffering or death of a person involved in an accident and made to that person shall be inadmissible as evidence of an admission of liability in a civil action. A statement of fault, however, which is part of, or in addition to, any of the above shall not be inadmissible pursuant to this section. (Relevant section)

Key Points of an Apology

- Apologize for the experience or outcome – NOT the process
- Have someone else present when the apology is made
- Document the substance of the communicated apology
- Prepare a follow-up letter after checking with Risk Management
- Visit the patient periodically during the remaining hospitalization to show concern and compassion

Sample Apologies

- I am sorry you have had this unintended experience/complication
- This must be a difficult time, know that my colleagues, staff and I will be working to help you through this as best we can
- I am saddened for your loss and extend my sincere condolences and concern for you and your family

What NOT to Say

- It was my fault / error / mistake
- It was the someone else's fault / error / mistake
- This never should have happened
- I was wrong, I misjudged ________
- I made a mistake, sorry

More on Documenting & Follow-Up

- Document ONLY the facts (who, what, where and when)
- Do not include how and why unless you know for CERTAIN
- Do not include impressions, assumptions, speculations or probabilities

Documenting the Apology Conversation

- Identify the witnesses present
- Identify that you offered condolences, concern and/or sympathy
- Include your offer to answer questions and to ensure ongoing care as needed will be provided

The Follow-up Apology Letter

Sample Patient/Family Follow Up Letter

Dear patient/family member:

I wanted to send you this brief note to follow up on our recent discussion on (date), again expressing my sympathy and concern for the unexpected__________. I'm sure this must be a difficult time for you. Rest assured my physician colleagues, our staff and I will be working hard to help and take care of you as best we can. I/Dr________ will be available to answer any further questions you or your family may have. Please realize I am concerned about your condition and regret that your/the treatment has not turned out as we desired at this point. Thank you for allowing me the opportunity to take care of you.

Sincerely,

Sample Situations You May Encounter

- Medication Errors
- Anesthesia Awareness
- OB Complications
- Esophageal Intubations with Complications

Medication Error Reporting Requirements for the Pharmacy

Pharmacy Board Regulations
Title 16, section 1711

When a pharmacist determines that a medication error has occurred, a pharmacist shall as soon as possible:

** Communicate to the patient or the patient's agent the fact that a medication error has occurred and the steps required to avoid injury or mitigate the error.

** Communicate to the prescriber the fact that a medication error has occurred.

The communication requirement shall only apply to medication errors if the drug was administered to or by the patient, or if the medication error resulted in a clinically significant delay in therapy.

An investigation of each medication error shall commence as soon as is reasonably possible, but no later than 2 business days from the date the medication error is discovered.

Courtesy of Robert W. Frank, Neil Dymott Frank McFall and Trexler APC

APPENDIX F

WANG v. HECK

Court of Appeal, Second District, Division 4, California.
CANG **WANG** et al., Plaintiffs and Appellants,
v.
Christianne N. **HECK**, M.D., et al., Defendants and Respondents.

No. B228191.
Jan. 25, 2012.

Background: Motorists, injured when struck by a car being operated by epilepsy patient who suffered an epileptic seizure and lost consciousness, brought action against patient's neurologist and neurologist's employer, alleging medical negligence. The Superior Court, Los Angeles County, No. SC101283,Lisa Hart Cole, J., entered summary judgment in favor of defendants. Motorists appealed.

Holdings: The Court of Appeal, Willhite, J., held that:
(1) litigation privilege applied to neurologist who prepared a medical evaluation form for patient, communicating to the Department of Motor Vehicles (DMV) that patient's epilepsy did not affect his ability to drive safely, and
(2) litigation privilege extended to neurologist's noncommunicative conduct prior to completing DMV form.

Affirmed.

West Headnotes

[1] Torts 379 ⚿122

379 Torts
  379I In General
    379k120 Defenses and Mitigating Circumstances
      379k122 k. Litigation Privilege; Witness Immunity.

The litigation privilege is not limited to statements made during a trial or other proceedings, but may extend to steps taken prior thereto, or afterwards. West's Ann.Cal.Civ.Code § 47(b).

[2] Torts 379 ⚷122

379 Torts
379I In General
379k120 Defenses and Mitigating Circumstances
379k122 k. Litigation Privilege; Witness Immunity.

The litigation privilege is broadly applied, and doubts are resolved in favor of the privilege. West's Ann.Cal.Civ.Code § 47(b).

[3] Health 198H ⚷752

198H Health
198HV Malpractice, Negligence, or Breach of Duty
198HV(D) Duties and Liabilities to Non-Patients
198Hk752 k. Acts of Patients in General.

Litigation privilege applied to neurologist who prepared a medical evaluation form for patient, communicating to the Department of Motor Vehicles (DMV) that patient's epilepsy did not affect his ability to drive safely, and thus neurologist was relieved of liability in medical negligence action brought by motorists who were injured in an automobile accident that occurred when patient suffered an epileptic seizure and lost consciousness while driving; neurologist was a professional whose role as to the DMV hearing was limited to evaluating patient's fitness for driving, the form was used in administrative proceeding in order for DMV hearing officer to determine whether to reinstate patient's suspended driver's license, and form was completed in order to achieve the object of the DMV hearing. West's Ann.Cal.Civ.Code § 47(b).

See Cal. Jur. 3d, Healing Arts and Institutions, § 456; Cal. Civil Practice (Thomson Reuters 2011) Torts, § 32:75; Flahavan et al., Cal. Practice Guide: Personal Injury (The Rutter Group 2011) ¶ 2:3202 (CAPI Ch. 2(IV)-A); 5 Witkin, Summary of Cal. Law (10th ed. 2005) Torts, § 131.

[4] Torts 379 ⚷122

379 Torts
379I In General

379k120 Defenses and Mitigating Circumstances
379k122 k. Litigation Privilege; Witness Immunity.

The protective mantle of the litigation privilege embraces not only the courtroom testimony of witnesses, but also protects prior preparatory activity leading to the witnesses' testimony. West's Ann.Cal.Civ.Code § 47(b).

[5] Health 198H ⚷752

198H Health
198HV Malpractice, Negligence, or Breach of Duty
198HV(D) Duties and Liabilities to Non-Patients
198Hk752 k. Acts of Patients in General.

Litigation privilege applicable to neurologist who prepared a medical evaluation form for patient, communicating to the Department of Motor Vehicles (DMV) that patient's epilepsy did not affect his ability to drive safely, extended to neurologist's conduct prior to completing the DMV evaluation form, in reaching her conclusion that it was safe for patient to drive and in failing to warn patient not to drive, and thus neurologist was relieved of liability in medical negligence action brought by motorists who were injured in an automobile accident that occurred when patient suffered an epileptic seizure and lost consciousness while driving; neurologist's conclusions were the basis of her communication, gravamen of the action was neurologist's completion of the DMV evaluation form, and neurologist's noncommunicative conduct prior to completing the DMV evaluation form was necessarily related to the form itself.

[6] Torts 379 ⚷122

379 Torts
379I In General
379k120 Defenses and Mitigating Circumstances
379k122 k. Litigation Privilege; Witness Immunity.

If the gravamen of the action is communicative, the litigation privilege extends to noncommunicative acts that are necessarily related to the communicative conduct; to show that the litigation privilege does not apply, the plaintiff must demonstrate that an independent, noncommunicative, wrongful act was the gravamen of the action. West's Ann.Cal.Civ.Code § 47(b).

James L. Pocrass Law Corporation, James L. Pocrass, Los Angeles, and Keith A. Lovendosky, Santa Monica, for Plaintiffs and Appellants.

Fonda & Fraser, Los Angeles, Stephen C. Fraser and Alexander M. Watson; Horvitz & Levy, Encino, S. Thomas Todd and Wesley T. Shih for Defendants and Respondents.

WILLHITE, J.

***1** Appellants Cang Wang and Xiaofen Wang were critically injured when they were struck by a car being driven by Amr Sarieh, who suffered an epileptic seizure and lost consciousness. Appellants filed a complaint against Sarieh's neurologist, Christianne N. Heck, M.D. (Heck) and Heck's employer, the University of Southern California (USC) (collectively, respondents).FN1 The trial court granted summary judgment in favor of respondents on the basis that Heck's communication to the Department of Motor Vehicles (DMV) that Sarieh's epilepsy did not affect his ability to drive safely was privileged pursuant to Civil Code section 47, subdivision (b).FN2 We affirm.

FACTUAL AND PROCEDURAL BACKGROUND

Sarieh was born in 1971 and has had seizures since the age of 13. The seizures occurred every one or two weeks and caused Sarieh to black out for about three minutes. In 2001, a neurologist at USC examined Sarieh and noted that he was experiencing about one seizure per week or month.

Sarieh's driver's license was suspended for three years in 2001 or 2002 when he suffered a seizure and hit a lamp post. His license was suspended again when he had another seizure-related accident in 2007, but his license was reinstated in October 2008 after Heck wrote a favorable report to DMV, which we discuss more fully below.

Heck began treating Sarieh in 2003, when Sarieh enrolled in a research study regarding the use of a procedure called gamma knife radiosurgery to treat epileptic seizures. Heck was the principal investigator of the study at

USC, so she took over Sarieh's care from a colleague so that Sarieh could participate in the gamma knife radiosurgery trial.

Sarieh underwent the gamma knife radiosurgery at USC in June 2003. He was randomly placed in a group that received low dose radiosurgery, a procedure that ultimately was set aside because it was less effective than the high dose radiosurgery. Heck thought that Sarieh did not improve much after undergoing the surgery and that he would benefit from a standard type of epilepsy surgery, but Sarieh did not want to undergo the standard surgery. She also knew that he suffered seizures when he did not take his medication.

On November 5, 2007, Sarieh told Heck that he had a seizure resulting in a trip to the emergency room on October 19, 2007, and that he was averaging about one seizure per month. Heck again discussed epilepsy surgery with Sarieh, but he expressed fear of undergoing the surgery. Heck "made it clear he is not to drive" because he posed a risk of injury to himself and others, and she noted that she had reported Sarieh to the Department of Public Health.

In a letter dated January 16, 2008, Dr. Charles Liu told Heck that he had seen Sarieh in the neurosurgery clinic. Liu wrote that, although Sarieh's condition had improved, he continued to have persistent seizures after the gamma knife radiosurgery, about one every other month. Liu stated that Sarieh was very anxious to drive again, as Heck and Liu had discussed, and that Liu told Sarieh he should not drive if he continued to have seizures. Liu also recommended surgery to Sarieh.

***2** On January 17, 2008, Sarieh told Heck that his epilepsy had improved since the surgery, but he continued to have "approximately one seizure every couple of months." He asked Heck to complete a driver medical evaluation form for the DMV so that he would be able to drive, but Heck advised him not to drive. Heck noted that she gave Sarieh "strict orders to refrain from driving" because he admitted to driving illegally.

In April 2008, Sarieh told Heck that he had had two seizures in the previous year, the most recent one in November 2007. He again asked Heck for the DMV evaluation form, on the basis of which the DMV could have lifted the suspension of his privilege to drive. Although Sarieh reported that he had been seizure-free for a few months, which Heck thought rendered him safe to drive, Heck did not feel comfortable giving him the form because she was concerned about his compliance with taking his medication. She therefore recommended that he be seizure-free for another three months before she would complete the DMV form. She also again recommended that he consider epilepsy surgery.

On September 2, 2008, Sarieh again asked Heck to complete the DMV evaluation form so that he could have his license reinstated, and Heck did so. Sarieh told her that he had been seizure free since November 2007, which he attributed to his improved compliance with his medication requirements. Sarieh agreed to remain compliant with his medication requirements in order to be allowed to drive again. In the form, Heck reported that Sarieh suffered from epileptic seizures, had epilepsy surgery, continued to take medications, and last had a seizure in November 2007. She reported Sarieh's prognosis as good and his condition as stable and opined that his medical condition did not affect safe driving, so long as he took the prescribed medication.

On October 22, 2008, the DMV interviewed Sarieh to determine whether to reinstate his license, which had been suspended on November 24, 2007. The DMV hearing officer relied on the evaluation form completed by Heck and noted that Heck had indicated that "everything is good" and had cleared Sarieh to drive. Sarieh told the officer that he was not having any complications from seizures. The officer decided to lift the suspension of Sarieh's license, and this was done.

On November 15, 2008, around 10:15 a.m., Sarieh was driving to a pharmacy to pick up medication for his stomach. He had a seizure, lost consciousness, and lost control of his car, hitting appellants. Appellants suffered serious injuries, "including bilateral traumatic amputation of Mr. Wang's legs, and a compound ankle fracture and traumatic brain injury to Mrs. Wang." Sarieh had not taken his seizure medication the night before the accident.

Appellants filed a complaint against Sarieh, respondents, and the DMV, for negligence, medical negligence, and government tort liability.

Respondents filed a motion for summary judgment. In support, respondents filed a declaration by Heck in which she stated that when she completed the DMV evaluation form, she believed Sarieh had not had a seizure since November 2007, and she relied on his statement that his seizures were under control and that he was taking the prescribed medication. Respondents also filed an expert declaration by Dr. Robert Fisher, who opined that Heck's recommendation that Sarieh could drive was appropriate, based on Sarieh's statement that he had been free of seizures for ten months.

***3** The operative pleading is appellants' second amended complaint (the complaint), filed in May 2010, alleging medical negligence by respondents. FN3 The complaint alleges that on September 2, 2008, Heck "negligently evaluated [Sarieh] and negligently concluded that he did not have any medical conditions that affect safe driving. The [DMV] relied on that medical evaluation in reinstating [Sarieh's] driver's license." The complaint further alleges that, prior to September 2, 2008, Heck "so negligently failed to exercise the proper degree of knowledge and skill in examining, diagnosing, treating, operating and caring for [Sarieh] that [Sarieh] was allowed to operate a motor vehicle and collide with [appellants] which caused [appellants] to suffer the injuries and damages hereinafter alleged. Specifically, [respondents] negligently evaluated [Sarieh] and negligently deemed him fit to operate a vehicle safely."

In opposition to the summary judgment motion, appellants filed an expert declaration by Dr. Ronald Fisk, a neurologist with expertise in epilepsy. Fisk reviewed all of Sarieh's medical, pharmacy, and dental records, as well as his DMV file, the depositions of Sarieh and Heck, and the declarations of Heck and Fisher. Fisk concluded that Heck's decision to approve the reinstatement of Sarieh's driving privileges fell below the applicable standard of care. In support of his conclusion, Fisk pointed out that Heck was aware of the following when she completed the DMV form: neuropsychological tests of Sarieh indicated his IQ was between 71 and 76, which is below the average range; Sarieh had a poor record of compliance with his medication requirements, and Heck had not obtained a lab test to monitor his compliance since November 2007, even though Heck had obtained lab reports approximately every four months prior to November 2007; Sarieh was very anxious to resume driving and knew he could do so only if he reported being free of seizures; Sarieh's experimental surgery was not successful, and Sarieh did not want to undergo the standard epilepsy surgery.

The trial court granted respondents' summary judgment motion on the ground that the suit was barred by the litigation privilege found in section 47(b). The court reasoned that the complaint was based on the DMV evaluation form Heck completed in September 2008, which the court found to be a privileged communication pursuant to the statute, and that treatment prior to the September 2008 form was privileged because it was performed in anticipation of the DMV hearing. The court thus found that appellants had presented no triable issue of material fact, granted summary judgment in favor of respondents, and entered judgment in their favor. Appellants filed a timely notice of appeal.

DISCUSSION

Appellants contend that the trial court erred in finding that they had presented no triable issue of material fact, relying on the declaration of Fisk that they submitted in opposition to summary judgment. They further contend that the trial court erred in finding their suit barred by the litigation privilege. Appellants argue that Heck's negligent conduct was her failure to warn Sarieh not to drive, which was independent of her completion of the DMV evaluation form, and that this conduct was not a communication within the meaning of section 47(b).

***4** We review the trial court's grant of summary judgment de novo, "viewing the evidence in a light favorable to the plaintiff as the losing party, liberally construing the plaintiff's evidentiary submission while strictly scrutinizing the defendant's own showing, and resolving any evidentiary doubts or ambiguities in the plaintiff's favor. [Citation.]" (*Weber v. John Crane, Inc.* (2006) 143 Cal.App.4th 1433, 1438, 50 Cal.Rptr.3d 71.) "A defendant moving for summary [judgment] meets its burden of showing that there is no merit to a cause of action if that party has shown that one or more elements of the cause of action cannot be established or that there is a complete defense to that cause of action. (Code Civ. Proc., § 437c, subds. (*o*)(2), (p)(2).) If the defendant does so, the burden shifts back to the plaintiff to show that a triable issue of fact exists as to that cause of action or defense. In doing so, the plaintiff cannot rely on the mere allegations or denial of her pleadings, 'but, instead, shall set forth the specific facts showing that a triable issue of material fact exists....' (Code Civ. Proc., § 437c, subd. (p)(2).)" (*Bisno v. Douglas Emmett Realty Fund 1988* (2009) 174

Cal.App.4th 1534, 1542–1543, 95 Cal.Rptr.3d 492.) " ' "[A]ny doubts as to the propriety of granting the motion" are resolved in the opponent's favor.' [Citation.]" (*Smith v. Freund* (2011) 192 Cal.App.4th 466, 471, 121 Cal.Rptr.3d 427.)

[1] "The litigation privilege, codified at Civil Code section 47, subdivision (b), provides that a 'publication or broadcast' made as part of a 'judicial proceeding' is privileged.... 'The usual formulation is that the privilege applies to any communication (1) made in judicial or quasi-judicial proceedings; (2) by litigants or other participants authorized by law; (3) to achieve the objects of the litigation; and (4) that [has] some connection or logical relation to the action.' [Citation.] The privilege 'is not limited to statements made during a trial or other proceedings, but may extend to steps taken prior thereto, or afterwards.' [Citation.] [¶] 'The principal purpose of [the litigation privilege] is to afford litigants and witnesses [citation] the utmost freedom of access to the courts without fear of being harassed subsequently by derivative tort actions. [Citations.]' [Citation.]" (*Action Apartment Assn., Inc. v. City of Santa Monica* (2007) 41 Cal.4th 1232, 1241, 63 Cal.Rptr.3d 398, 163 P.3d 89 (*Action Apartment*).)

[2] The litigation privilege " 'exists to protect citizens from the threat of litigation for communications to government agencies whose function it is to investigate and remedy wrongdoing. [Citation.]' [Citation.]" (*People ex rel. Gallegos v. Pacific Lumber Co.* (2008) 158 Cal.App.4th 950, 958, 70 Cal.Rptr.3d 501 (*Gallegos*).) The phrase, "judicial or quasi-judicial proceedings," has been "defined broadly to include 'all kinds of truth-seeking proceedings,' including administrative, legislative and other official proceedings. [Citation.]" (*Ibid.*) "The interpretation of section 47, subdivision (b) is a pure question of law which we review independently. [Citations.]" (*Rothman v. Jackson* (1996) 49 Cal.App.4th 1134, 1139–1140, 57 Cal.Rptr.2d 284.) "The litigation privilege is broadly applied [citation] and doubts are resolved in favor of the privilege [citation]." (*Ramalingam v. Thompson* (2007) 151 Cal.App.4th 491, 500, 60 Cal.Rptr.3d 11 (*Ramalingam*).)

***5** [3] The trial court here reasoned that the September 2, 2008 DMV evaluation form fell within the meaning of section 47(b) because it was prepared "for use in a quasi-judicial setting by a government agency for purposes of evaluation of the driving status of defendant, Amr Sarieh." The court further reasoned that any allegations in the complaint based on Heck's treatment of Sarieh prior to September 2, 2008, were barred because Heck's treatment prior to that date constituted statements preliminary to or in anticipation of the DMV hearing.

We conclude that the litigation privilege applies to Heck's September 2, 2008 communication to the DMV. None of appellants' causes of action can stand without relying on Heck's completion of the DMV medical evaluation form. We therefore conclude that all of appellants' causes of action are barred by the litigation privilege and that appellants accordingly have failed to present a triable issue of material fact.

In *Gootee v. Lightner* (1990) 224 Cal.App.3d 587, 274 Cal.Rptr. 697 (*Gootee*), the appellant sued the respondents for professional negligence after the respondents performed psychological testing on the appellant's family in order to testify in child custody proceedings. The appellant contended that the respondents had been negligent in performing the testing and had destroyed some data. The trial court granted summary judgment in favor of the respondents based on its conclusion that their conduct in performing the testing fell within the litigation privilege of former Civil Code section 47, subdivision (2), now section 47(b)(1).[FN4] On appeal, the court affirmed, holding that the privilege applied to the respondents' conduct because "the gravamen of appellant's claim relies on negligent or intentional tortious conduct committed by respondents in connection with the testimonial function." (*Id.* at p. 591, 274 Cal.Rptr. 697.) The court reasoned that "[f]reedom of access to the courts and encouragement of witnesses to testify truthfully will be harmed if neutral experts must fear retaliatory lawsuits from litigants whose disagreement with an expert's opinions perforce convinces them the expert must have been negligent in forming such opinions." (*Id.* at p. 593, 274 Cal.Rptr. 697.)

Similar to the respondents in *Gootee*, Heck was a professional whose role as to the DMV hearing was limited to evaluating Sarieh's fitness for driving. (See *Gootee, supra,* 224 Cal.App.3d at p. 591, 274 Cal.Rptr. 697 [noting that it was undisputed that the respondents' role was limited to "evaluat[ing] the partisans in the custody matter for purposes of testifying concerning the custody dispute"].) Although Heck did not complete the DMV evaluation form for purposes of testifying in judicial proceedings, the form was used in the DMV hearing in order for the DMV hearing officer to determine whether to reinstate Sarieh's license. Thus, the form was used in an administrative proceeding, which is a " 'truth-seeking proceeding[ ]' " for purposes of applying the litigation privilege. (*Gallegos, supra,* 158 Cal.App.4th at p. 958, 70 Cal.Rptr.3d 501.)

***6** There is no question that Heck was a participant authorized by law to complete the DMV evaluation form and that the form was completed in order to achieve the object of the DMV hearing—that is, to determine Sarieh's fitness for driving. (See *Action Apartment, supra,* 41 Cal.4th at p. 1241, 63 Cal.Rptr.3d 398, 163 P.3d 89 [listing the requirements for application of the litigation privilege].) Because Sarieh's license had been suspended, he needed Heck to complete the evaluation form in order for the DMV to determine whether the license should be reinstated. There can be no dispute that the form had " 'some connection or logical relation' " to the DMV hearing. (*Ibid.*) All four requirements of the litigation privilege accordingly are satisfied.

[4] Appellants attempt to avoid the application of the litigation privilege by arguing that it was not merely Heck's completion of the DMV medical evaluation form, but her treatment of Sarieh prior to September 2, 2008, and her failure to warn Sarieh not to drive that constituted medical negligence. However, "the protective mantle of the privilege embraces not only the courtroom testimony of witnesses, but also protects prior preparatory activity leading to the witnesses' testimony." (*Gootee, supra,* 224 Cal.App.3d at p. 594, 274 Cal.Rptr. 697.)

In *Block v. Sacramento Clinical Labs, Inc.* (1982) 131 Cal.App.3d 386, 182 Cal.Rptr. 438 (*Block*), the defendant toxicologist erroneously calculated and informed the district attorney's office of the amount of baby aspirin found in the plaintiff's deceased baby daughter, leading to murder charges against the plaintiff. After the error was discovered and the charges were dismissed, the plaintiff sued the toxicologist for professional negligence. The toxicologist asserted the litigation privilege. The plaintiff "attempted to avoid the privilege by arguing that recovery was sought based on defendant's *negligent conduct in reaching his conclusions,* rather than on the testimony itself." (*Gootee, supra,* 224 Cal.App.3d at p. 594, 274 Cal.Rptr. 697.) This argument was rejected because, " '[o]n any cognizable theory of duty, the negligent calculation formed the basis of [defendant's] communication and was privileged [citation].' [Citation.]" *(Ibid.)*

[5] Similarly here, appellants argue that their claims are based on Heck's negligent conduct in reaching her conclusion that it was safe for Sarieh to drive, rather than the conclusion itself. However, it is clear that Heck's conduct prior to completing the September 2, 2008 DMV evaluation form was the basis of her communication in completing the form. Although appellants attempt to characterize their claim as medical negligence by failing to warn Sarieh not to drive, the basis of their complaint is Heck's statement on the DMV medical evaluation form that Sarieh could drive safely. Because "[t]he offending conduct alleged by appellant[s] occurred during and as part of the preparatory activities which were directed toward and done in contemplation of" determining Sarieh's fitness to drive, this case "falls squarely within the rationale of [*Gootee*] and *Block.*" *(Gootee, supra,* 224 Cal.App.3d at p. 595, 274 Cal.Rptr. 697.)

***7** [6] Moreover, " '[i]f the gravamen of the action is communicative, the litigation privilege extends to noncommunicative acts that are necessarily related to the communicative conduct.... [Citations.]' [Citations.] To show that the litigation privilege does not apply, the plaintiff must demonstrate that 'an independent, noncommunicative, wrongful act was the gravamen of the action....' [Citation.]" *(Ramalingam, supra,* 151 Cal.App.4th at p. 503, 60 Cal.Rptr.3d 11.) Here, the gravamen of the action was Heck's completion of the DMV evaluation form on September 2, 2008. Although the complaint alleges that Heck negligently cared for Sarieh prior to September 2, 2008, the complaint is clear that the allegedly negligent act that caused the injury was allowing Sarieh to drive. Appellants have not demonstrated that there was any wrongful act independent of Heck's completion of the DMV evaluation form. Heck's noncommunicative conduct prior to completing the DMV evaluation form on September 2, 2008, was necessarily related to the form itself. Thus, the litigation privilege extends to her conduct in deciding to complete the form.

"Any doubt about whether the privilege applies is resolved in favor of applying it." *(Kashian v. Harriman* (2002) 98 Cal.App.4th 892, 913, 120 Cal.Rptr.2d 576.) Although "the litigation privilege has its costs, ' "[I]t is desirable to create an absolute privilege ... not because we desire to protect the shady practitioner, but because we do not want the honest one to have to be concerned with [subsequent derivative] actions...." ' [Citation.]" (*Gallegos, supra*, 158 Cal.App.4th at p. 963, 70 Cal.Rptr.3d 501.)

Because we conclude that all of the conduct relied upon by appellants in the complaint falls within the litigation privilege, we need not address appellants' arguments that they established a triable issue of material fact as to Heck's conduct prior to September 2, 2008. The trial court did not err in granting summary judgment in favor of respondents.

DISPOSITION

The judgment is affirmed. Respondents shall recover their costs on appeal.

We concur: EPSTEIN, P.J., and SUZUKAWA, J.

FN1. Appellants' complaint named other defendants who are not parties to this appeal.

FN2. For ease of reference, we will refer to the statute as section 47(b).

FN3. Appellants' first and third causes of action, negligence by Sarieh and government tort liability against the DMV, are not pertinent to this appeal.

FN4. *Gootee* addressed the litigation privilege as it applied to communications made in connection with divorce proceedings. The principles articulated in *Gootee* regarding the litigation privilege apply to the instant case.

Cal.App. 2 Dist.,2012.
Cang Wang v. Heck
--- Cal.Rptr.3d ----, 2012 WL 207034 (Cal.App. 2 Dist.)

END OF DOCUMENT

Courtesy of Robert W. Frank, Neil Dymott Frank McFall and Trexler APC

APPENDIX G

KAISER FOUNDATION HEALTH PLAN INC. v. RAHM

Court of Appeal, Second District, Division 7, California.
KAISER FOUNDATION HEALTH PLAN, INC., et al., Petitioners,
v.
The **SUPERIOR COURT** of **Los Angeles County**, Respondent.
Anna Rahm et al., Real Parties in Interest.

No. B233759.
Feb. 15, 2012.

Background: Insureds brought action against health care service plan for breach of the implied covenant of good faith and fair dealing and intentional infliction of emotional distress, and sought punitive damages. Plan moved to strike the punitive damages allegations. The Superior Court, Los Angeles County, No. BC441742,James R. Dunn, J., denied the motion to strike. Service plan petitioned for writ of mandate. The Court of Appeal summarily denied the petition. Plan petitioned for review. The Supreme Court granted review and remanded with directions.

Holdings: The Court of Appeal, Zelon, J., held that:
(1) statute requiring leave of court for punitive damages allegations does not apply to claims against health care service plans, and
(2) insureds' punitive damages allegations did not require leave of court.

Petition denied.

West Headnotes

[1] Appeal and Error 30 🔑893(1)

30 Appeal and Error
30XVI Review
30XVI(F) Trial De Novo
30k892 Trial De Novo
30k893 Cases Triable in Appellate Court
30k893(1) k. In General.

The standard of review for an order on a motion to strike punitive damages allegations is de novo. West's Ann.Cal.C.C.P. § 425.13.

[2] Pleading 302 ⚿365(3)

302 Pleading
302XVI Motions
302k361 Striking Out Matter from Pleading
302k365 Application and Proceedings Thereon
302k365(3) k. Hearing, Determination, and Order.

In passing on the correctness of a ruling on a motion to strike punitive damages allegations, judges read allegations of a pleading subject to a motion to strike as a whole, all parts in their context, and assume their truth. West's Ann.Cal.C.C.P. § 425.13.

[3] Pleading 302 ⚿234

302 Pleading
302VI Amended and Supplemental Pleadings and Repleader
302k233 Leave of Court to Amend
302k234 k. Necessity.

The statute requiring leave of court to make punitive damages allegations in an action for damages arising out of the professional negligence of a health care provider does not apply to claims against health care service plans. West's Ann.Cal.C.C.P. § 425.13; West's Ann.Cal.Civ. Code § 3428(c).

See Annot., Medical malpractice: who are "health care providers," or the like, whose actions fall within statutes specifically governing actions and damages for medical malpractice (1993) 12 A.L.R.5th 1; Cal. Jur. 3d, Healing Arts and Institutions, § 445; Cal. Civil Practice (Thomson Reuters 2011) Torts, § 32:55; Flahavan et al., Cal. Practice Guide: Personal Injury (The Rutter Group 2011) ¶ 3:255.4e (CAPI Ch. 3-E); 6 Witkin, Summary of Cal. Law (10th ed. 2005) Torts, §§ 936, 1601.

[4] Pleading 302 ⚿234

302 Pleading
302VI Amended and Supplemental Pleadings and Repleader

302k233 Leave of Court to Amend
302k234 k. Necessity.

The statute requiring leave of court to make punitive damages allegations in an action for damages arising out of the professional negligence of a health care provider did not apply to claims by insured and her family against health care service plan for breach of the implied covenant of good faith and fair dealing and intentional infliction of emotional distress, based on a compensation scheme that allegedly encouraged health care service providers to deny medically necessary services to insured, since the claims did not seek to hold the plan vicariously liable for professional services rendered by health care providers. West's Ann.Cal.C.C.P. § 425.13.

[5] Health 198H ⚷780

198H Health
198HV Malpractice, Negligence, or Breach of Duty
198HV(F) Persons Liable
198Hk780 k. In General.

The statute providing that a health care service plan, any entity contracting with a plan, and providers are not liable for the acts or omissions of others prohibits claims that seek to impose vicarious liability on health care service plans for the acts of their providers. West's Ann.Cal.Health & Safety Code § 1371.25.

[6] Pleading 302 ⚷234

302 Pleading
302VI Amended and Supplemental Pleadings and Repleader
302k233 Leave of Court to Amend
302k234 k. Necessity.

It is not the case that the statute requiring leave of court to make punitive damages allegations in an action for damages arising out of the professional negligence of a health care provider applies whenever a plaintiff asserts claims against a health care service plan that is part of a larger group of entities that includes medical care providers. West's Ann.Cal.C.C.P. § 425.13.

[7] Mandamus 250 ⚷172

250 Mandamus
250III Jurisdiction, Proceedings, and Relief
250k172 k. Scope of Inquiry and Powers of Court.

Court of Appeal would not review hospitals' contention that the statute requiring leave of court to make punitive damages allegations in an action for damages arising out of the professional negligence of a health care provider applied to patient's claims against hospitals, on hospitals' petition for writ of mandate, where patient dismissed her punitive damages claims against the hospitals after they filed the petition. West's Ann.Cal.C.C.P. § 425.13; West's Ann.Cal.Civ.Code § 3532.

APPEAL from an order of the Superior Court of Los Angeles County. James R. Dunn, Judge. Affirmed.Arnold & Porter, Lawrence A. Cox, Brian K. Condon; Taylor Blessey, N. Denise Taylor and Jennifer A. Scher for Petitioners.

Cole Pedroza, Curtis A. Cole and Cassidy E. Cole for California Medical Association, California Hospital Association and California Dental Association, as Amici Curiae on behalf of Petitioners.

No appearance for Respondent.

Schernoff Bidart Echeverria, Michael J. Bidart, Ricardo Echeverria, Steven Schuetze; The Ehrlich Law Firm and Jeffrey Isaac Ehrlich for Real Parties in Interest.

ZELON, J.

INTRODUCTION

***1** Anna Rahm and her parents, Lynnette and James Rahm, filed a complaint against Kaiser Foundation Health Plan and two Kaiser health care providers. The complaint alleged that the defendants had devised an insurance compensation scheme that induced Kaiser's physicians to deny costly medical services to plan members. Plaintiffs asserted that, as a result of the scheme, Kaiser's health care providers had improperly delayed an

MRI for Anna, resulting in significant injuries. The complaint included four causes of action against each defendant and sought punitive damages for breach of the implied covenant of good faith and fair dealing and intentional infliction of emotional distress.

Defendants filed a motion to strike the punitive damages allegations arguing that plaintiffs had failed to comply with the requirements of Code of Civil Procedure section 425.13, subdivision (a). The trial court ruled that statute did not apply to plaintiffs' punitive damages claims and denied the motion.

Defendants filed a petition for writ of mandate seeking an order directing the superior court to grant the motion to strike. We summarily denied the petition and defendants filed a petition for review in the California Supreme Court. While defendants' petition for review was pending, plaintiffs dismissed their punitive damages claims against the Kaiser health care providers. The Supreme Court granted review and directed this court to issue an order to show cause; this court issued that order on August 25, 2011.

We now conclude that plaintiffs were not required to comply with section 425.13 because: (1) the statute does not apply to plaintiffs' claims against Kaiser Foundation Health Plan, and (2) plaintiffs have dismissed their punitive damages claims against the health care provider defendants.

FACTUAL AND PROCEDURAL BACKGROUND

A. Summary of Facts Preceding Plaintiffs' Lawsuit FN1

Anna Rahm is a member of the Kaiser Permanente Traditional Plan (the plan), which provides its members medically necessary health care in exchange for monthly premiums. In August of 2008, Anna began experiencing back pain. Anna's parents, Lynnette and James Rahm, took Anna to a chiropractor. After the treatments failed to alleviate Anna's pain, the chiropractor recommended that Anna "consult with a medical doctor because she was in need of an MRI."

In March of 2009, Anna met with Charlene Huang, a primary care physician at Kaiser. Lynnette accompanied Anna to the appointment and requested that her daughter receive an MRI. Although Huang acknowledged that

Anna's chiropractor had determined that her back pain was " 'severe,' " Huang refused to order an MRI. Huang referred Anna "to the physical medicine department at [Kaiser] and also prescribed pain medications and steroids, a much less expensive treatment than an MRI...." Anna took the prescribed medications but her pain persisted.

Two weeks later, on March 24, 2009, Anna met with Ngan Vuong, a physical medicine doctor at Kaiser. Lynnette accompanied Anna to the appointment and again requested that Anna receive an MRI. Vuong, however, recommended that Anna receive an epidural and suggested that her pain could be remedied through changes to her nutrition and exercise habits. Lynnette told Vuong she did not want her daughter to receive an epidural and renewed her request for an MRI. Voung refused to authorize an MRI.

***2** In April of 2009, Anna sought acupuncture treatment for her pain. The treatments were unsuccessful and the acupuncturist recommended that Anna request an MRI from her doctor. Lynnette called Vuong and informed her that Anna's acupuncturist had recommended an MRI. Vuong again declined an MRI and referred Anna to Kaiser's physical therapy department.

In May and June of 2009, Anna continued her acupuncture treatments. Two different acupuncturists concluded that Anna was in need of an MRI. Anna also attended several physical therapy sessions at Kaiser, but was forced to discontinue the treatments because they were too painful. Kaiser's physical therapy department "recommended that [Anna] receive an MRI."

Lynette called Vuong again and explained that a chiropractor, two acupuncturists and Kaiser's physical therapy department had all recommended an MRI. Vuong rejected these recommendations because they were not made by medical doctors, but invited the Rahms to seek a second opinion.

Lynnette elected to schedule a meeting with another doctor. Prior to the appointment, Lynnette contacted Huang, Anna's primary care physician, "as a last ditch effort" to get an MRI. Lynnette summarized the treatments Anna had undergone since her initial visit with Huang. Huang finally agreed to authorize an MRI, which was performed on July 2, 2009.

Anna's MRI indicated that she had an "aggressive mass" in her pelvis. A biopsy revealed that Anna was suffering from a "high grade" osteosarcoma, which is "one of the fastest growing types of osteosarcoma, meaning that [Kaiser's] three month delay in ordering [Anna's] MRI allowed the cancer to spread and ultimately substantially contributed to [Anna's] poor prognosis." Anna underwent chemotherapy and had numerous surgeries that resulted in the loss of her right leg and portions of her pelvis and spine.

B. Plaintiffs' Complaint

On July 15, 2010, Anna and her parents filed a complaint against Kaiser Foundation Health Plan (Kaiser Health Plan or Health Plan), which administered Anna's health care plan. The complaint also named Kaiser Foundation Hospitals (Kaiser Hospitals) and Southern California Permanente Medical Group (SCPMG), which contract with Kaiser Health Plan to provide hospital and medical services to the Plan's insureds. The complaint asserted four causes of action against each defendant: (1) breach of the implied covenant of good faith and fair dealing; (2) breach of contract; (3) negligent infliction of emotional distress; and (4) intentional infliction of emotional distress.

Plaintiffs alleged that the defendants, who were collectively referred to as "KAISER," had devised "a system of withholding benefits from insureds which necessarily results in KAISER unreasonably depriving its insureds the benefits of their contacts with KAISER. This system is one where KAISER has bestowed upon its contracted physicians the responsibility of determining whether or not to give insureds benefits under their contracts. Underlying this system is a cost saving component: each determination a KAISER physician makes must be based, in part, upon the cost to KAISER of the treatment or care requested. [¶] ... [T]his system, with a heavy emphasis on cost saving to KAISER, results in pressures on KAISER's physicians that removes (*sic*) the physicians' abilities to give medical care which is in the patient's best interests. This system also results in little or no investigation by KAISER as to whether a patient is in need of certain medical care and/or treatment. This system is concealed from KAISER's insureds and ultimately causes them harm."

***3** The complaint further alleged that Kaiser's "physicians are rewarded for adhering to the cost saving system that KAISER has put into place.

Specifically, that the physicians receive bonuses which are dependent upon the cost savings realized by KAISER due to the physicians withholding of treatment and or care of the insureds."

In describing their individual causes of action, plaintiffs alleged that defendants had breached the implied covenant of good faith and fair dealing by: (1) "unreasonably denying and delaying care and treatment to Anna that was covered under [the plan]"; (2) "unreasonably avoiding incurring expenses for diagnostic testing ... for its own financial gain by ignoring the seriousness of Anna's medical condition and needs"; (3) "placing its own financial interests ahead of Anna's health care"; and (4) "unreasonably engaging in a pattern and practice of failing to conduct a thorough, fair and balanced investigation in evaluating requests for benefits and/or services for its members under [the plan]."

Plaintiffs' claim for intentional infliction of emotional distress alleged that the defendants "refus[ed] to grant [Anna's] requests for diagnostic testing, even though defendants knew, or should have known, that the medically necessary diagnostic testing was covered under the [plan]. Defendants knew, or should have known, that their refusal to approve diagnostic testing for [Anna] caused [Anna, Lynnette and James] to be fearful and extremely worried about [Anna's] condition." The complaint further asserted that defendants "intentionally ... and unfairly refused to provide [Anna] with the requested, medically necessary care," thereby causing Lynnette, James and Anna to "suffer [ ] fear, depression, humiliation, and severe mental anguish and emotional and physical distress."

Plaintiffs' claims for breach of the implied covenant and intentional infliction of emotional distress each included an allegation asserting that the defendants' misconduct "constitute[d] malice, oppression or fraud under California Civil Code section 3294, thereby entitling plaintiffs to punitive damages in an amount appropriate to punish or set an example of defendants."

C. Defendants' Motion to Strike

On January 7, 2010, defendants filed a motion to strike the punitive damages allegations. Defendants argued that plaintiffs had failed to comply with Code of Civil Procedure section 425.13. subdivision, (a) which states:

"In any action for damages arising out of the professional negligence of a health care provider, no claim for punitive damages shall be included in a complaint or other pleading unless the court enters an order allowing an amended pleading that includes a claim for punitive damages to be filed." The section further provides that the trial court may allow an amended pleading claiming punitive damages only if the plaintiff submits evidence establishing "that there is a substantial probability that the plaintiff will prevail on the claim pursuant to Section 3294 of the Civil Code."

***4** Defendants argued that plaintiffs were required to comply with section 425.13 because they were seeking "punitive damages 'for an injury that is directly related to the professional services provided by a health care provider acting in its capacity as such....' " FN2 Plaintiffs, however, argued that their claims did not arise out of defendants' professional medical services, but rather from defendants' "insurance decisions and practices." Plaintiffs contended that, in essence, their tort claims alleged that defendants had improperly withheld "insurance policy benefits" by denying necessary medical treatments and "creat[ing] a system whereby [their] financial interests were put ahead of Anna's life."

On April 14, 2001, the trial court heard oral argument on the motion to strike and ruled that section 425.13 was inapplicable to plaintiffs' claims, explaining: "this is an insurance bad faith case against an insurance company ... it's a different animal [from medical malpractice]." In a subsequent minute order, the trial court stated that section 425.13 did not apply because plaintiffs' suit was not "merely an action for professional negligence."

D. Petition for Writ of Mandate

On June 16, 2011, defendants filed a petition for writ of mandate seeking an order from this court directing the superior court "to vacate its order ... denying [p]etitioners' motion to strike [plaintiffs'] punitive damages claims and to enter a new order granting the [m]otion to strike the punitive damages claims." On June 23, 2011, we summarily denied defendants' petition. Defendants then filed a petition for review in the California Supreme Court.

While defendants' petition for review was pending in the Supreme Court, plaintiffs dismissed their punitive damages claims against Kaiser Hospitals and SCPMG without prejudice. In their opposition to defendants' petition for review, plaintiffs argued that, in light of the dismissals, the court need not reach "the merits of the denial of the motion to strike with respect to ... [Kaiser Hospitals and SCPMG]." Plaintiffs further argued that section 425.13 did not apply to their claims against Kaiser Health Plan because it was not a health care provider.

On August 10, 2011, the Supreme Court granted defendants' petition for review and entered an order directing this court to vacate our "order denying mandate and to issue an order directing respondent superior court to show cause why the relief sought in the petition should not be granted." In compliance with that order, we vacated our order dated June 23, 2011 and issued an order to show cause.

DISCUSSION

A. Standard of Review

[1][2] "The standard of review for an order on a motion to strike punitive damages allegations is de novo. [Citation.] 'In passing on the correctness of a ruling on a motion to strike, judges read allegations of a pleading subject to a motion to strike as a whole, all parts in their context, and assume their truth.' [Citation.]" (*Turman, supra,* 191 Cal.App.4th at p. 63, 119 Cal.Rptr.3d 166.)

B. Summary of Cases Interpreting the Scope of Section 425.13

***5** "Section 425.13(a) establishes a procedure for claiming punitive damages in certain cases. It provides, 'In any action for damages arising out of the professional negligence of a health care provider, no claim for punitive damages shall be included in a complaint or other pleading unless the court enters an order allowing an amended pleading that includes a claim for punitive damages to be filed. The court may allow the filing of an amended pleading claiming punitive damages on a motion by the party seeking the amended pleading and on the basis of the supporting and opposing affidavits presented that the plaintiff has established that there is a substantial probability that the plaintiff will prevail on the claim pursuant to Section 3294 of the Civil Code....' " (*Central Pathology Service Medical Clinic, Inc. v. Superior Court* (1992) 3 Cal.4th 181, 186, 10 Cal.Rptr.2d 208, 832 P.2d 924 (*Central Pathology*) [italics omitted].)

In *Central Pathology, supra,* 3 Cal.4th 181, 10 Cal.Rptr.2d 208, 832 P.2d 924, the California Supreme Court considered the scope of claims subject to section 425.13. The plaintiffs, Constance and Michael Hull, filed a complaint against a pathology clinic and a physician for negligence and loss of consortium. Two months before trial, plaintiffs moved to amend their complaint "to add causes of action for fraud and intentional infliction of emotional distress. The new causes of action alleged that [the physician] performed a pap smear on Constance, which was sent to [the pathology clinic] for analysis. It was further alleged that despite the presence of abnormal cells, defendants failed to notify Constance that she was developing cancer ... and that [the physician] denied using [the pathology clinic] in an effort to cover up her medical negligence. The cause of action for intentional infliction of emotional distress alleged that defendants acted in an outrageous manner with the intent to cause severe emotional distress. Plaintiffs sought punitive damages under the new causes of action." (*Id.* at p. 185, 10 Cal.Rptr.2d 208, 832 P.2d 924.)

The pathology clinic filed a motion arguing that the trial court was required to strike plaintiffs' punitive damages allegations because they had failed to comply with section 425.13. Plaintiffs, however, contended that section 425.13 was limited to claims "arising out of ... professional negligence" and therefore did not apply to their intentional tort claims. The trial court agreed with plaintiffs and denied the motion. The appellate court denied the defendants' petition for writ of mandate. The California Supreme Court granted review.

The Supreme Court began its analysis by considering the language of section 425.13. Concluding that it was unclear whether the phrase "action for damages arising out of the professional negligence of a health care provider" was intended to encompass claims for "intentional torts allegedly committed by health care providers" (*Central Pathology, supra,* 3 Cal.4th at p. 186, 10 Cal.Rptr.2d 208, 832 P.2d 924), the court reviewed the legislative history for further guidance.

***6** In summarizing the legislative history, the court noted that a comment from the Assembly Subcommittee on the Administration of Justice indicated that section 425.13 was intended to " 'provide protection to health practitioners *in their capacity as practitioners.*' " (*Central Pathology, supra,* 3 Cal.4th at p. 189, 10 Cal.Rptr.2d 208, 832 P.2d 924.) The comment emphasized that "lawsuits *unrelated* to a practitioner's conduct in providing health care related services were intended to be excluded from the ambit of section 425.13." (*Id.* at p. 190, 10 Cal.Rptr.2d 208, 832 P.2d 924.) The court concluded that these comments demonstrated that the statute was not meant to apply solely to medical malpractice claims asserted against health care providers. Rather, according to the court, the Legislature intended section 425.13 to apply "whenever an injured party seeks punitive damages for an injury that is directly related to the professional services provided by a health care provider acting in its capacity as such...." (*Central Pathology, supra,* 3 Cal.4th at p. 191, 10 Cal.Rptr.2d 208, 832 P.2d 924.) The court clarified that, in making this determination, "[t]he allegations that identify the nature and cause of a plaintiff's injury must be examined to determine whether each is directly related to the manner in which professional services were provided." (*Id.* at p. 192, 10 Cal.Rptr.2d 208, 832 P.2d 924.)

The court then applied its interpretation of section 425.13 to plaintiffs' tort claims and found that the statute applied: "Plaintiffs' cause of action for fraud in this case is directly related to the manner in which defendants provided professional services. The claim emanates from the manner in which defendants performed and communicated the results of medical tests, a matter that is an ordinary and usual part of medical professional services. It is therefore governed by section 425.13(a). Plaintiffs' cause of action for intentional infliction of emotional distress is predicated on the same alleged acts as the fraud claim. Therefore, it too is directly related to defendants' performance of professional services and is governed by section 425.13(a)." (*Id*. at pp. 192–193, 10 Cal.Rptr.2d 208, 832 P.2d 924.)

The holding in *Central Pathology* has been applied to numerous other types of tort claims brought against medical care providers. For example, in *Davis v. Superior Court* (1994) 27 Cal.App.4th 623, 33 Cal.Rptr.2d 6 (*Davis*), the plaintiff sued his employer's workers' compensation carrier and a physician who treated injuries the plaintiff sustained during the course of his employment. Plaintiff alleged that the carrier and the doctors it contracted with entered into a conspiracy whereby the doctors agreed to provide medical advice and treatment to patients below the standard of care. In exchange, the carrier agreed to continue sending patients to the doctors. Plaintiff further alleged that his treating physician had participated in this scheme by providing substandard care at the direction of the carrier.

Plaintiff asserted that the physician's "acts were designed to curtail expensive treatment needed by [p]laintiff," thereby "ensur[ing] that [the physician] would continue to get business from [the carrier]." (*Id.* at p. 626, 33 Cal.Rptr.2d 6.) The complaint included claims for fraud and conspiracy, and sought punitive damages against each defendant on both claims.

***7** The physician filed a motion arguing that the trial court should strike the punitive damages allegations asserted against him because the plaintiff had failed to comply with section 425.13, subdivision (a). In opposition, plaintiff argued that his claims were not subject to the statute because he sought "damages based on criminal conduct—conduct which cannot be considered to have arisen out of ... professional negligence." (*Davis, supra,* 27 Cal.App.4th at p. 627, 33 Cal.Rptr.2d 6.) The trial court agreed with the plaintiff and denied the motion.

The appellate court reversed, holding that the circumstances of the case were indistinguishable from *Central Pathology.* The court explained that "[the physician defendant] is accused of misrepresenting that he would properly treat [the plaintiff], and that he was qualified to perform certain medical procedures. It is also alleged he lied about [plaintiff's] medical condition and falsified his findings. Even if, as [plaintiff] alleges, [the carrier] directed [the physician] to conduct himself in this manner, the fact remains that [plaintiff] is seeking damages for an injury that is directly related to the professional services rendered by [the physician] acting in his capacity as a health care provider. The conduct of which [the physician] is accused, if true, is unethical, illegal and immoral. It is, however, no more outrageous than the conduct of the *Central Pathology* defendant physician. [Plaintiff] was, therefore, required to comply with the requirements of section 425.13(a)." (*Davis, supra,* 27 Cal.App.4th at p. 629, 33 Cal.Rptr.2d 6 .)

Similarly, in *Palmer v. Superior Court* (2002) 103 Cal.App.4th 953, 127 Cal.Rptr.2d 252 (*Palmer*), the court concluded that section 425.13 applied to claims arising from a health care provider's recommendation that certain health care services were not medically necessary. The plaintiff, William Palmer, filed a complaint against his medical insurer, PacifiCare, and his primary health care provider, Sharp Rees–Stealy Medical Group (SRS). SRS performed various medical services for PacifiCare's insureds, which included "'making decisions as to whether requested medical services equipment and supplies for PacifiCare members [we]re "medically necessary." ' " (Id. at p. 958, 127 Cal.Rptr.2d 252.)

Palmer, who had lost his right leg to a bacterial infection, alleged that his prosthetist recommended that SRS provide Palmer with a new type of prosthetic leg that was engineered from ultra-light components. SRS informed Palmer that its utilization review department had determined that the prosthetic leg was not medically necessary and referred him to the PacifiCare appeals process. Palmer alleged that an SRS employee later informed him that the costs of the prosthetic leg greatly exceeded the fixed amount that SRS received from PacifiCare to provide Palmer with care. Palmer pursued authorization for the prosthetic through PacifiCare's appeals process, but PacifiCare continued to deny the request.

*8 Palmer's complaint alleged that PacifiCare had breached "the implied covenant of good faith and fair dealing in the subscriber agreement ... [through its] denial of the requested medical services and equipment." (*Palmer, supra,* 103 Cal.App.4th at p. 960, 127 Cal.Rptr.2d 252.) The complaint also alleged intentional and negligent infliction of emotional distress against SRS "due to the manner in which plaintiff's request for the medical services and equipment was processed. Palmer claim[ed] that SRS intentionally and willfully found that the prostheses were not medically necessary when they were, in fact, medically necessary...." (*Ibid.*) SRS moved to strike the punitive damages allegations appearing in the intentional infliction of emotional distress claim, arguing that the plaintiff had failed to comply with section 425.13. The trial court granted the motion.

On appeal, Palmer argued that section 425.13 was inapplicable to his claim against SRS claim because "the services SRS was performing on behalf of PacifiCare, i.e., conducting utilization review services by evaluating Palmer's request for medical services ... to determine their medical necessity," did not qualify as "health care services." (*Id.* at p. 967, 968, 127 Cal.Rptr.2d 252.) Rather, according Palmer, "his injuries relate[d] to actions taken by SRS and PacifiCare in administering the HMO subscriber agreement, and those actions operated to prevent him from receiving the requested health care services." (*Id.* at p. 968, 127 Cal.Rptr.2d 252.)

The appellate court rejected the argument, explaining: "the allegedly injurious utilization review ... conducted by ... SRS ... amounted to a medical clinical judgment such as would arguably arise out of professional negligence. We disagree with Palmer that this was a purely administrative or economic role played by SRS. Rather, the ... utilization review[s][are] conducted by medical professionals ... [who] carry out these functions by exercising medical judgment and applying clinical standards. [Citations.] Recall, Palmer's chief complaint is with the substance and conduct of the PacifiCare appeals process, and he is pursuing that claim through his cause of action against PacifiCare for the breach of the implied covenant of good faith and fair dealing in the subscriber agreement. That is the proper forum for those claims. However, to the extent Palmer seeks to plead intentional infliction of emotional distress against SRS for its part in those decisions, he was required to comply with the pleadings procedure of section 425.13...." (*Palmer, supra,* 103 Cal.App.4th at p. 972, 127 Cal.Rptr.2d 252.)

C. Section 425.13 Does Not Apply to Any Claims Remaining in This Suit

As originally filed, plaintiffs' complaint included punitive damages allegations against two different types of entities. First, the complaint sought punitive damages from Kaiser Foundation Health Plan, which is a "licensed health care service plan" under California's Knox–Keene Health Care Service Plan Act of 1975 (Health & Saf.Code, § 1340 et seq.) The Knox–Keene Act defines a health care service plan as: "[a]ny person who undertakes to arrange for the provision of health care services to subscribers or enrollees, or to pay for or to reimburse any part of the cost for those services, in return for a prepaid or periodic charge paid by or on behalf of the subscribers or enrollees." (Health & Saf.Code, § 1345, subd. (f)(1).) In its role as a health care service plan, Kaiser Health Plan does not directly provide medical care to its subscribers. Instead, the Health Plan contracts with other Kaiser entities to deliver medical care to subscribers who enroll in its plans.

***9** The complaint also sought punitive damages from Kaiser Hospitals and SCPMG, which are health care providers that contract with Kaiser Health Plan to provide medical services to Plan members. The phrase "health care providers" generally applies to "licensed medical practitioners [and medical groups comprised of such practitioners] ... who provide direct medical services to patients." (*Palmer, supra,* 103 Cal.App.4th at p. 967, 127 Cal.Rptr.2d 252.) FN3

Defendants contend that section 425.13 applies to claims against both health care services plans and health care providers and, as a result, the trial court should have struck all of the punitive damages allegations in plaintiffs' complaint. We independently consider whether section 425.13 applies to claims against: (1) health care service plans, and (2) health care providers.

1. Section 425.13 does not apply to claims against health care service plans

[3] Plaintiffs argue that section 425.13 does not apply to their claims against Kaiser Health Plan because the statute is limited to claims against health care providers. Defendants, however, argue that section 425.13 applies to any claim against a health care service plan that seeks compensation for injuries that are directly related to the quality and nature of medical services rendered by a medical care provider. Defendants further contend that plaintiffs' claims against Kaiser Health Plan are predicated on injuries caused by Kaiser health care providers' refusal to administer proper care, thereby triggering section 425.13's requirements.

A superficial reading of section 425.13 suggests that it could be reasonably interpreted in the manner proposed by defendants. The text of the statute does not state that it is limited to claims against medical care providers. Rather, the statute says it applies to "any action for damages arising out of the professional negligence of a health care provider...." Based on this language, section 425.13 could be interpreted to apply to claims against any type of defendant—including health care service plans—if those claims "arise out" of the professional negligence of a medical care provider.

The California Supreme Court has repeatedly stated, however, that the intended scope of section 425.13 cannot be determined based solely on the language of the statute. (*College Hospital Inc. v. Superior Court* (1994) 8 Cal.4th 704, 709, 34 Cal.Rptr.2d 898, 882 P.2d 894 (*College Hospital*) ["the language of section 425.13(a) is uncertain ..."].) For example, in *Central Pathology,* the court ruled that the "words of the statute" did not "clarif[y]" whether "intentional tort causes of action can 'arise out' of professional negligence." (*Central Pathology, supra,* 3 Cal.4th at p. 188, 10 Cal.Rptr.2d 208, 832 P.2d 924.) Similarly, in *Covenant Care v. Superior Court* (2004) 32 Cal.4th 771, 11 Cal.Rptr.3d 222, 86 P.3d 290 (*Covenant Care*), the court concluded that the language of section 425.13 was inconclusive as to whether an "elder abuse claim is one 'arising out of the professional negligence of a health care provider'...." (*Id.* at p. 780, 11 Cal.Rptr.3d 222, 86 P.3d 290.) In both cases, the court consulted the legislative history to aid in determining whether the precise type of claim at issue was subject to the statute.

***10** Consistent with those decisions, we conclude that the text of the statute is unclear as to whether section 425.13 is intended to apply only to claims against health care providers, or whether it was intended to apply to claims against any type of defendant—including claims against health care service plans—that seek punitive damages for injuries that are directly related to professional services rendered by a health care provider. We therefore turn to the legislative history for guidance.

As originally drafted, section 425.13 left no ambiguity as to whether it was intended to extend to claims asserted against defendants other than medical care providers. The original version of the statute "provided, 'No claim for punitive damages *against a health care provider* shall be included in a complaint or other pleading unless the court enters an order allowing an amended pleading that includes a claim for punitive damages to be filed.' [Citation.]" (*Central Pathology, supra,* 3 Cal.4th at p. at 188, 10 Cal.Rptr.2d 208, 832 P.2d 924 [emphasis added].) However, the statute was later "amended ... by incorporating former section 425.13 into new subdivision (a) of that section and by altering the first sentence to read, 'In any action for damages arising out of the professional negligence of a health care provider, no claim for punitive damages shall be included....' [Citation.]" (*Id.* at p. 189, 10 Cal.Rptr.2d 208, 832 P.2d 924.) According to the Legislature, " 'this amendment was [intended to be] declaratory of existing law. [Citation.]'" (*Id.* at p. 189, 10 Cal.Rptr.2d 208, 832 P.2d 924.)

The purpose of the Legislature's amendment was to address concerns that "the original version of section 425.13 was overbroad ." (*Central Pathology, supra,* 3 Cal.4th at p. at 189, 10 Cal.Rptr.2d 208, 832 P.2d 924.) An assembly subcommittee comment regarding the amendment explained that " 'as [originally] written, Section 4215.13 [*sic*] could apply to any lawsuit against any health care provider ... Arguably, this could include lawsuits unrelated to the practitioner's practice, such as defamation, fraud, and intentional torts. [¶] The author [of the original version of section 425.13] asserts that the intention ... was to provide protection to health practitioners in their capacity as practitioners. Specifically, relief was sought from unsubstantiated claims of punitive damages in actions alleging professional negligence. There was no intent to protect practitioners in any other capacity. [The amendment] limits the application of Section [425.13(a)] to lawsuits involving allegations of a health practitioner's "professional negligence." '[Citation.]" (*Ibid.* [emphasis omitted].)

This legislative history clearly implies that, as originally drafted and as amended, section 425.13 was only intended to apply to medical care providers. The original version of section 425.13 specifically limited the statute to claims against medical care providers. Although this language was subsequently amended in a manner suggesting that the section might apply to a broader category of defendants, the Legislature's comments regarding that amendment demonstrate that was not its intent.

***11** First, the legislative comments noted that the amendment was "declaratory of existing law," thereby indicating that the amendment was not meant to broaden the scope of the statute beyond claims against medical care providers. (*Lone Star Security & Video, Inc. v. Bureau of Security and Investigatory Services* (2009) 176 Cal.App.4th 1249, 1256, 98 Cal.Rptr.3d 559 ["declaration by the Legislature that a statutory amendment is declaratory of existing law is .... a factor entitled to due consideration"].) Second, the legislative history demonstrates that the purpose of the amendment was to preserve the original intent of the statute, which was "'"to provide protection to health practitioners in their capacity as practitioners.' " (*Central Pathology, supra,* 3 Cal.4th at p. at 189, 10 Cal.Rptr.2d 208, 832 P.2d 924 [italics omitted].) More specifically, the amendment was intended to clarify that the statute did not apply to claims "'"unrelated to the practitioner's practice, such as defamation.'" (*Ibid.* [italics omitted].) Nothing in the history of the amendment suggests that the Legislature meant to broaden section 425 .13's applicability to claims against any type of defendant that arose from the professional negligence of a health care provider. Rather, the clear intent was to protect health care providers in their professional capacity as such.

Our conclusion that the Legislature intended section 425.13 to apply to claims against medical care providers, as opposed to other classes of defendants, finds substantial support in the case law. For example, in *Central*

Pathology, the Supreme Court concluded that that the legislative history of section 425.13 demonstrated that the statute was passed "because [the Legislature] was concerned that unsubstantiated claims for punitive damages were being included in complaints *against health care providers.*" (*Central Pathology, supra,* 3 Cal.4th at p. at p. 189, 10 Cal.Rptr.2d 208, 832 P.2d 924 [emphasis added].) The court emphasized that "the essential purpose" of the amendment to section 425.13 was "to restrict the application of section 425.13 to lawsuits brought *against health practitioners* 'in their capacity as practitioners.' " (*Id.* at p. 190, 10 Cal.Rptr.2d 208, 832 P.2d 924 [emphasis added]; see also *id.* at p. 192, 10 Cal.Rptr.2d 208, 832 P.2d 924 ["The clear intent of the Legislature is that any claim for punitive damages *in an action against a health care provider* be subject to the statute if the injury that is the basis for the claim was caused by conduct that was directly related to the rendition of professional services"] [emphasis added].)

In subsequent decisions, the Supreme Court has reiterated that the central purpose of the statute is to protect medical care providers. For example, in *College Hospital, supra,* 8 Cal.4th 704, 34 Cal.Rptr.2d 898, 882 P.2d 894, the court stated: "Although the language of section 425.13(a) is uncertain, its prophylactic purpose is clear—to protect health care providers from the onerous burden of defending against meritless punitive damage claims." (*Id.* at p. 709.) *College Hospital* also "emphasized that the primary purpose of section 425 .13(a) was to establish a pretrial mechanism that bars '"unsubstantiated" 'punitive damage claims brought against health care providers ' "in their [professional] capacity." ' [Citation.]" (*Id.* at p. 714, 34 Cal.Rptr.2d 898, 882 P.2d 894.) Similarly, in *Covenant Care, Inc. v. Superior Court, supra,* 32 Cal.4th 771, 11 Cal.Rptr.3d 222, 86 P.3d 290, the court explained that "the Legislature's intent in enacting the statute was to protect health care providers (or practitioners) ... *in their professional capacity as providers.*" (*Id.* at p. 785, 11 Cal.Rptr.3d 222, 86 P.3d 290.)

***12** Numerous appellate courts have made similar statements regarding the intended scope of section 425.13. For example, in *Little Co. of Mary Hospital v. Superior Court* (2008) 162 Cal.App.4th 261, 75 Cal.Rptr.3d 519, this division stated that the language of section 425.13 demonstrated that the statute's application was "limited both by the identity of the defendant [i.e., medical care providers] and the nature of the plaintiff's claim." (*Id.* at p. 269, 75 Cal.Rptr.3d 519.) In *Johnson v. Superior Court* (2002) 101 Cal.App.4th

869, 124 Cal.Rptr.2d 650, another division in this district concluded that the statute "was ... adopted to protect health care providers" by "provid[ing] health care practitioners with a procedural hurdle designed to weed out meritless punitive damage claims." (*Id.* at pp. 878–879, 124 Cal.Rptr.2d 650.) Numerous other appellate decisions include similar language. (See *Hung v. Wang* (1992) 8 Cal.App.4th 908, 920, 11 Cal.Rptr.2d 113 ["Code of Civil Procedure section 425.13 requires that a plaintiff seeking punitive damages against a health care provider obtain court permission before pleading that allegation"]; *Community Care and Rehabilitation Center v. Superior Court* (2000) 79 Cal.App.4th 787, 791, 94 Cal.Rptr.2d 343 [section 425.13 was "enacted [as] a protection for medical professionals"] [disapproved of on other grounds in *Covenant Care, supra,* 32 Cal.4th at p. 791, fn. 12]; *Palmer, supra,* 103 Cal.App.4th at p. 961, 127 Cal.Rptr.2d 252 ["the Legislature added section 425.13 ... due to related policy concerns ' "that unsubstantiated claims for punitive damages were being included in complaints against health care providers" ' [Citation.]"].)

Defendants' argument that section 425.13 may be applied to claims against health care services plans, rather than health care providers, is also in conflict with other sections of the California Code. Civil Code section 3428, subdivision (c) states that "[h]ealth care service plans ... are not health care providers under any provision of law, including, but not limited to ... section [ ] ... 425.13 ... of the Code of Civil Procedure." Likewise, Health and Safety Code section 1367.01, subdivision (m) clarifies that a health care service plan's role in determining the medical necessity of a requested procedure "shall [not] cause a health care service plan to be defined as a health care provider for purposes of any provision of law, including ... Section[ ] ... 425.13 of the Code of Civil Procedure." The language of these statutes demonstrates a clear intent to exclude health care service plans from the procedures required under section 425.13.

Defendants have not cited a single decision that has applied section 425.13 to claims pleaded against a health care service plan or any other type of entity that was not a medical care provider. They argue, however, that the facts of this case cannot be meaningfully distinguished from *Davis v. Superior Court, supra,* 27 Cal.App.4th 623, 33 Cal.Rptr.2d 6, or *Palmer v. Superior Court, supra,* 103 Cal.App.4th 953, 127 Cal.Rptr.2d 252. As discussed above, the plaintiff in *Davis* alleged that his physician had conspired with his workers' compensation carrier to provide substandard medical care to the carrier's members. In *Palmer*, the plaintiff sued his health care service plan and his primary care physician for falsely stating that certain services were not medically necessary, and therefore not covered by the plaintiff's health plan. In both cases, the court concluded that the plaintiffs' claims against the medical care providers were subject to section 425.13 because they were directly related to the nature and quality of the medical care provider's professional services.

***13** Although there are similarities between the Rahms' claims and those alleged in *Palmer* and *Davis*, defendants overlook a critical distinction: in both *Palmer* and *Davis* only the medical care providers moved to strike the punitive damages allegations pleaded against them; neither opinion considered or decided whether section 425.13 applied to the other defendants in the cases, who were not medical care providers. Therefore, neither decision has any relevance to the issue presented here: whether the statute applies to claims asserted against a health care service plan.

[4] Defendants next assert that, even if section 425.13 does not generally apply to health care service plans, we should apply the statute under the circumstances of this case because plaintiffs' claims against Kaiser Health Plan "derive[ ]" entirely from "decisions of Kaiser's [health care providers]." Stated more simply, defendants contend that section 425.13 applies to claims that seek to hold a health care service plan vicariously liable for the acts of a health care provider. There are several reasons why this argument fails.

First, as explained above, the legislative history of section 425 .13 and other statutes regulating the medical care industry demonstrate that section 425.13 was not intended to apply to health care service plans. Defendants have cited no authority indicating that the Legislature intended the statute to apply to such entities in instances where a plaintiff proceeds under a theory of vicarious liability. We decline to read such an exception into the statute.

[5] Second, extending section 425.13 in the manner suggested by defendants would serve no purpose because the California Code immunizes health care service plans from liability for acts committed by medical care providers. Health and Safety Code section 1371.25 states that "[a] plan, any entity contracting with a plan, and providers are each responsible for their own

acts or omissions, and are not liable for the acts or omissions of ... others." This statute has been interpreted as "prevent[ing] a health care service plan from being held vicariously liable for a medical provider's acts or omissions." (*Martin v. PacifiCare of California* (2011) 198 Cal.App.4th 1390, 1393, 130 Cal.Rptr.3d 714 (*Martin*); see also *Watanabe v. California Physicians' Service* (2008) 169 Cal.App.4th 56, 63–64, 86 Cal.Rptr.3d 374.) Extending section 425.13 to claims that seek to impose vicarious liability on health care services plans for the acts of their providers would therefore serve no purpose because the Legislature has expressly prohibited such claims.

Third, even if we were to accept defendants' contention that section 425.13 may apply to claims seeking to hold a health care plan vicariously liable for professional services rendered by a health care provider, that is not what plaintiffs have alleged here. "A claim is based on vicarious liability when a party free from fault is held liable for another party's acts or omissions. [Citation.] A claim is based on direct liability when a party is held liable for its own acts or omissions." (*Martin, supra,* 198 Cal.App.4th at p. 1407, 130 Cal.Rptr.3d 714.) According to defendants, plaintiffs' claims against Kaiser Health Plan allege that it "engaged in conduct with respect to [plaintiffs] that is derivative of, and not separate or independent from, the actions of Kaiser's physicians."

***14** We disagree with defendants' characterization of plaintiffs' claims. A fair reading of the complaint indicates that plaintiffs allege that Kaiser Health Plan devised a compensation scheme that encouraged Kaiser health care providers to withhold medically necessary services from plan members. This scheme allegedly required Kaiser's physicians to take into account "the cost ... of the [requested] treatment" when determining whether the care was medically necessary. The physicians, in turn, were paid "bonuses which [we]re dependent upon the cost savings realized .... due to the physicians withholding of treatment and/or care of the insureds." Thus, liberally construed,[FN4] the complaint does not merely assert that Kaiser Health Plan is liable for the improper medical decisions made by Kaiser's physicians (delaying authorization of an MRI of Anna's back.) Rather, the complaint asserts that Kaiser Health Plan induced such conduct by providing financial incentives to deny expensive medical treatments.

[6] Finally, defendants argue that section 425.13 applies to claims against Kaiser Health Plan because the Plan is part of "a fully integrated medical

services program" that includes medical care providers such as Kaiser Hospital and SCPMG. In support, defendants cite language from the health plan service agreement stating that "Kaiser Permanente provides Services directly to our members through an integrated medical care program [in which] Health Plan, Plan Hospitals, and the Medical Group work together to provide our Members with quality care." Defendants appear to contend that section 425.13 applies whenever a plaintiff asserts claims against a health care service plan that is part of a larger group of entities that includes medical care providers. FN5 We disagree.

The legislative history of section 425.13 and various provisions in the California Code demonstrate that the procedural requirements described in the statute do not apply to claims against health care service plans. Because defendants admit that Kaiser Health Plan is a health care services plan, rather than a health care provider, the trial court did not err in refusing to strike the punitive damages allegations asserted against the Health Plan.

2. Plaintiffs have dismissed their punitive damages allegations against Kaiser's health care providers

[7] The defendants' petition for writ of mandate also argues that the trial court erred in failing to strike plaintiffs' punitive damages allegations against Kaiser Hospitals and SCPMG, which are both health care providers. However, after defendants filed their petition, plaintiffs dismissed their punitive damages claims against Kaiser Hospitals and SCPMG without prejudice. Plaintiffs argue that, in light of those dismissals, "the merits of the denial of the motion to strike with respect to [Kaiser Hospitals and SCPMG] are no longer an issue in the case." The defendants' reply brief, which was filed after plaintiffs dismissed their punitive damages allegations, does not state any grounds for review of the portion of the trial court's ruling that pertains to the health care providers. Instead, defendants' reply brief argues only that section 425.13 applies to plaintiffs' claims against Kaiser Health Plan.

***15** Currently, there are no punitive damages allegations pending against Kaiser Hospitals or SCPMG. Therefore, ordering the trial court to strike such allegations would serve no purpose. We decline to review an issue that will have no effect on the parties. (See Civ.Code, § 3532 ["The law neither does nor requires idle acts"]; *Garibaldi v. Daly City* (1943) 61 Cal.App.2d 514, 517, 143 P.2d 397 ["An appellate court will not determine a question which will no effect upon the status of the parties"].)

DISPOSITION

The petition is denied. The parties shall bear their own costs on appeal.

We concur: PERLUSS, P.J., and WOODS, J.

FN1. This factual summary is based on allegations in plaintiffs' complaint, which we assume to be true for the purposes of reviewing the trial court's order denying defendants' motion to strike. (See *Turman v. Turning Point of Central California, Inc.* (2010) 191 Cal.App.4th 53, 63, 119 Cal.Rptr.3d 166 (*Turman*) ["'In passing on the correctness of a ruling on a motion to strike [punitive damages allegations], judges read allegations of a pleading subject to a motion to strike as a whole, all parts in their context, and assume their truth.' [Citation.]"].)

FN2. Defendants' motion to strike also argued that the facts pleaded in the complaint were insufficient to support punitive damages and that numerous other portions of the complaint should be stricken. None of these alternative arguments are relevant to defendants' petition for writ of mandate, which is predicated solely on the question of whether plaintiffs' claims are subject to section 425.13, subdivision (a).

FN3. The Knox–Keene Act defines "providers" as "any professional person, organization, health facility, or other person or institution licensed by the state to deliver or furnish health care services." (Health & Saf.Code, § 1345, subd. (i).) Section 425.13 subdivision (b) contains a similar definition: "For the purposes of this section, 'health care provider' means any person licensed or certified pursuant to Division 2 (commencing with Section 500) of the Business and Professions Code, or licensed pursuant to the Osteopathic Initiative Act, or the Chiropractic Initiative Act, or licensed pursuant to Chapter 2.5 (commencing with Section 1440) of Division 2 of the Health and Safety Code; and any clinic, health dispensary, or health facility, licensed pursuant to Division 2 (commencing with Section 1200) of the Health and Safety Code. 'Health care provider' includes the legal representatives of a health care provider."

FN4. Code of Civil Procedure section 452 requires that, when "determining [the] ... effect [of a pleading]," its "allegations must be liberally construed...."

FN5. The record contains no evidence concerning the relationship or corporate structure that exists between Kaiser Health Plan, Kaiser Hospitals and SCPMG. The only allegation regarding the nature of these entities is that Kaiser Health Plan contracts with Kaiser Hospital and SCPMG to provide medical services to Plan members.

Cal.App. 2 Dist.,2012.
Kaiser Foundation Health Plan, Inc. v. Superior Court
--- Cal.Rptr.3d ----, 2012 WL 473092 (Cal.App. 2 Dist.), 12 Cal. Daily Op. Serv. 1928

END OF DOCUMENT

Courtesy of Robert W. Frank, Neil Dymott Frank McFall and Trexler APC

ASPATORE